Only Paradoxes to Offer

Only Paradoxes to Offer

FRENCH FEMINISTS
AND THE
RIGHTS OF MAN

Joan Wallach Scott

HARVARD UNIVERSITY PRESS
CAMBRIDGE, MASSACHUSETTS
LONDON, ENGLAND
1996

Library of Congress Cataloging-in-Publication Data
Scott, Joan Wallach.
Only paradoxes to offer : French feminists and the rights of man / Joan Wallach Scott.
p. cm.
Includes bibliographical references and index.
ISBN 0-674-63930-8 (alk. paper)
1. Feminism—France—History. 2. Feminism—France—Case studies.
3. Feminists—France—History. 4. Feminists—France—Case studies.
5. Human rights—France—History. 6. Women—France—History.
I. Title.
HQ1616.S38 1996
305.42′0944—dc20
95-31953
CIP

For Lizzie, Tony, and Don

Contents

Preface

Political struggle is frequently most heated when the issues at stake cannot be grounded in nature or truth. Historically this has been the case for arguments about gender, whether they concerned the rights of women to education or to citizenship. Did biology determine the capacity for reason, moral reflection, or political action? Did reproduction conflict with intelligence? Precisely because these questions were undecidable, those offering opposing answers sought to pin down a solution, often in the form of laws or regulations. As a result, law substituted for truth as a guide for human action. But this substitution was not acknowledged as such; instead whatever law passed was said to be based upon nature or truth. The winners attributed their victory not to politics, but to the superiority of their scientific or moral understanding. In this way, the influence of law on perceptions of nature was obscured.

Debates about gender typically invoked "nature" to explain the differences between the sexes, but they sought to establish those differences definitively by legal means. By a kind of circular logic a presumed essence of men and women became the justification for laws and policies when, in fact, this "essence" (historically and contextually variable) was only the effect of those laws and policies.

This was the case with citizenship in France. From the Revolution of 1789 until 1944, citizens were men. The exclusion of women was attributed variously to the weaknesses of their bodies and minds, to physical divisions of labor which made women fit only for reproduction and domesticity, and to emotional susceptibilities that drove them either to sexual excess or to religious fanaticism. For each of these reasons, however, the ultimate authority invoked was "nature." And nature was a difficult authority to challenge.

Nonetheless feminists did challenge the practice of excluding women from citizenship. They argued that there was neither a logical nor an empirical connection between the sex of one's body and one's ability to engage in politics, that sexual difference was not an indicator of social, intellectual, or political capacity. Their arguments were powerful and compelling, as will become evident in the course of this book. But their arguments were also paradoxical: in order to protest women's exclusion, they had to act on behalf of women and so invoked the very difference they sought to deny.

The terms of women's exclusion from politics involved attempts to produce an authoritative definition for gender. These terms confronted feminists with an irresolvable dilemma. It has come to us in the form of debates about "equality" or "difference." Are women the same as men? And is this sameness the only basis upon which equality can be claimed? Or are they different and, because or in spite of their difference, entitled to equal treatment? Either position attributes fixed and opposing identities to women and men, implicitly endorsing the premise that there can be an authoritative definition for sexual difference. As a result, sexual difference is taken to be a natural phenomenon that must be reckoned with but that cannot itself be altered, when in fact it is one of those indeterminate phenomena (others are race and ethnicity) whose meaning is always in dispute.

The intensity of feminist politics—of feminist actions and antifeminist reactions—follows from the undecidability of sexual difference. So does the paradoxical quality of feminist claims for rights. Drawn into arguments about sameness or difference that they did not initiate, the French feminists I discuss in this book tried to reverse the terms used to discriminate against them. But, like Blacks or Jews or Muslims in other historical circumstances, they took on the group identity attributed to them even as they refused its negative characteristics. This affirmation of group identity made it impossible to declare it entirely irrelevant for political purposes.

These difficulties did not, however, hinder feminism; indeed I argue that they gave it some of its political force. The feminists' position was paradoxical—in the words of the French revolutionary Olympe de Gouges, they were women who had "only paradoxes to offer." On the one hand, they seemed to accept authoritative definitions of gender; on the other hand, they refused these definitions. This simultaneous avowal and refusal exposed the contradictions and omissions in the definitions of gender that were offered in the name of nature and imposed through law. Feminist claims revealed the limits of the principles of liberty, equality, and fraternity and raised doubts about their universal applicability. They offered a critique not only of the uses made of ideas of sexual difference, but also of the very attempt to ground sexual difference authoritatively in nature. For this reason their story has great relevance for us today, as politicians attempt to legislate the meanings of gender by appealing to the supposedly immutable natures of women and men. If we can understand the French feminists' struggles in terms of the politics of undecidability, we can also, perhaps, better understand, and so better address, the conflicts, dilemmas, and paradoxes of our own time.

———————■———————

This book took shape in contexts in which the operations of difference were theorized, debated, and examined. During 1987–88 a seminar on gender at the Institute for Advanced Study prompted me to present a paper on Olympe de Gouges as a way of thinking about feminist theory in concrete historical terms. (This concern to demonstrate the possibilities of a theoretically informed history was also a response to the fierce resistance my interest in poststructuralist theory had encountered among many historians.) I had already decided to write about de Gouges for a conference organized by Leslie Rabine and Sarah Melzer on women and the French Revolution, held at the University of California at Irvine during the bicentennial in 1989. Although my assignment had been "the effects of the Revolution on women in the nineteenth century," I found it impossible to consider those effects without first considering the Revolution itself; and de Gouges, as an important feminist figure, seemed a good point of entry into it. After I presented the paper Donna Haraway and I had one of those long talks that become formative only retrospectively. She encouraged me to pursue more cases through the nineteenth and twentieth centuries and to write a book about the history of French feminism, continuing the deconstruction of the "equality versus difference" opposition I had begun with de Gouges. Under the influence of the enthusiasm such conversations often generate, I began to think about which other feminists I would include in such a book.

In response to an invitation from Washington University in Saint Louis to deliver the Tobias and Hortense Cohen Lewin Lectures in April 1991, I did the research for and preliminary drafts of what became Chapters 2 through 5 of this book. The following fall I presented revised versions of what are now Chapters 3 through 5 as the Carl Becker Lectures at Cornell University. Later I presented yet another version of Chapters 1, 3, 5, and 6 at the Institute for Human Sciences in Vienna. These lecture opportunities not only allowed me to crystallize the project but also provided astute audiences of faculty and students.

The critical responses of audiences, the questions and suggestions of students, colleagues, and friends, all in the context of the ongoing enterprises of scholarly exchange generally and of feminist scholarship in particular, helped the ideas and arguments of this book take shape. That many of the most fruitful exchanges took place in feminist centers (the Pembroke Center for Teaching and Research on Women at Brown, the Women's Studies Program at the University of California at Santa Cruz, to name only two) is testimony to the vital importance these institutions have assumed.

Among my best critics have been students, many of whom are now scholars in their own right; their questions and direct challenges have helped me to clarify my arguments and to refine my interpretations. They have also directed me to sources I had overlooked or ignored, generously shared references and insights with me, and provided the friendship and critical engagement that make teaching an integral and indispensable part of my academic life.

For their suggestions and help with sources or with individual chapters in various drafts, I thank the following students, colleagues, and friends: Andrew Aisenberg, Leora Auslander, James Bono, Wendy Brown, Joshua Cole, Marianne Constable, Drucilla Cornell, Paul Friedland, Donna Haraway, Steven Hause, Carla Hesse, Jonathan Kahana, Lloyd Kramer, Ruth Leys, Harold Mah, Mary Louise Roberts, Sylvia

Schafer, Charles Sowerwine, and Hayden White. Debra Keates provided skillful translation, research assistance, and editorial advice. For extraordinarily careful and exacting readings of the entire manuscript I am grateful to Ian Burney, Judith Butler, Christina Crosby, Laura Engelstein, Donald Scott, and Elizabeth Weed. Denise Riley deserves special thanks for a close, critical reading of the manuscript during what was supposed to have been a summer vacation. Two anonymous readers for Harvard University Press pointed up inconsistencies of argument and design in helpful and supportive ways.

Scholars can't work without libraries, and I have worked in several while writing this book: in Paris, the Bibliothèque National, the Bibliothèque Marguerite Durand, and the Bibliothèque Historique de la Ville de Paris; in Princeton, the Firestone Library of Princeton University and the Historical Studies/Social Sciences Library at the Institute for Advanced Study. At the Institute Library, I owe special thanks to Elliott Shore, Faridah Kassim, Marsha Tucker, and Rebecca Bushby, who helped locate obscure sources, taught me how to use computers to access information, and did all these things with intelligence, patience, and good cheer.

The technical preparation of the manuscript in all its intricacies was done by Meg Gilbert, secretary extraordinaire both in her patience with my foibles and in her consistently excellent work.

I am particularly fortunate to have family who have become intellectual colleagues and good friends. They are at once my severest critics and my firmest supporters. They have helped me think through many of the issues I deal with in this book, sometimes directly, sometimes through conversations about ideas and books only tangentially related, sometimes through arguments about other things entirely. I am grateful for their enduring presence in my life and for all that they have given me. This book is for them.

Only Paradoxes to Offer

1

Rereading the History
of Feminism

Those who fail to reread are obliged to read
the same story everywhere.

—*Roland Barthes*

This book is an attempt to rethink the history of feminism by
looking at specific campaigns for women's political rights in France
from 1789 to 1944. Through an analysis of the writings and actions of
individual feminist political activists at different historical moments, I
have sought to provide an alternative to the typical approach to the
history of feminism, one inherited from nineteenth-century feminists.
Those feminists constructed a history to parallel the great evolutionary
histories of their day. They wrote a teleological story of cumulative
progress toward an ever-elusive goal; a story in which women inevitably
found the means within themselves to struggle against their exclusion
from democratic politics; a story in which the imaginative identification
of feminists with the disparate and discontinuous actions of women in
the past became an orderly and continuous historical tradition. Different generations have drawn from these stories additional moral lessons
related to their own theoretical debates. Our late twentieth-century
version is the insistence that all feminists in the past demanded either
equality or difference and that one of these was (and still is) a more
successful strategy than the other.[1]

This nineteenth-century approach prevents us from analyzing, even
from seeing, the downside of feminist experience: its intractable contradictions, the obsessive repetitions that seem to doom one generation
to relive the dilemmas of its predecessors, and its inability to secure

equal representation for women even when a long-sought goal such as the vote has been won. A feminist history that takes for granted the inevitability of progress, the autonomy of individual agents, and the need to choose between equality or difference reproduces without interrogation the terms of the ideological discourse within which feminism has operated. What is needed instead is analytic distance.

My sense of the need for a different approach to feminist history was brought home by a recent *New York Times* report from France.[2] Fed up with the minuscule number of women holding seats in the National Assembly (the proportion is smaller than in any other western European democracy and has remained virtually unchanged—ranging from 3 to 6 percent—since women were granted the vote in 1944), a group (composed mostly of women) insisted on gender parity in the Assembly. In demands they acknowledged as "a bit utopian," they sought passage of a law granting half of all seats in the parliament to women. "Exclusion of women has been part of France's political philosophy since the Revolution," said Claude Servan-Schreiber, whose book *Au pouvoir citoyennes!* (Take power, citizenesses!) is a manifesto for the group. "Women of my generation—I am 55—didn't have to fight for the vote," she adds, "but nothing has happened here since universal suffrage" passed nearly fifty years ago. I would add that the current parity movement is an attempt, in new form, to address a problem that antedates the suffrage, one that Servan-Schreiber accurately traces to the great democratic revolution of 1789.

That problem is the problem of how feminists could establish women's status as autonomous, self-representing individuals entitled to full political rights in a democratic republic.[3] Posed as a question, it is: why has it been so difficult for so long for women to realize the Revolution's (and every subsequent republic's) promise of universal liberty and equality, of political rights for all? The answer calls for something other than a chronicle of feminism's heroic struggles, undeserved betrayals, and strategic mistakes (although even this new account is not without its struggles and betrayals). It calls for something other than an internal history of the women's movement treated as tangential to the "larger" political scene, but also something other than an explanation that depends either on social or economic factors that precede or are external to politics, or on the reasons given for their actions by politicians themselves. Instead, the answer requires reading the repetitions and conflicts of feminism as symptoms of contradictions in the political discourses that produced feminism and that it appealed to and challenged at the same time. These were the discourses of individualism, individual rights, and social obligation as used by republicans (and by some socialists) to organize the institutions of democratic citizenship in France.

Even as they wrote their own progressive histories, feminists were conscious of the repetitious quality of their actions. Writing in 1913, the psychiatrist and socialist activist Madeleine Pelletier associated the emergence of feminist movements with the turbulent revolutionary moments of the nineteenth century. But like Claude Servan-Schreiber in 1993, she traced these back to the trauma of the first revolution. It was then, she said, that feminism "learned how to enunciate all its claims for rights."[4] The legitimacy of those claims and their satisfaction depended on the recognition that the Revolution's proclamation of the rights of all was inconsistent with its refusal of citizenship to women. But what for feminists was a self-evident contradiction was not obvious as such to the legislators who repeatedly denied them the vote on the grounds of their difference from men.

Thus the theme of repetition in feminist history has regularly had to do with inconsistency and incongruity, and with arguments about what was and was not contradictory. But the question extends beyond the conflict between universal principle and exclusionary practice (a conflict that can presumably be reconciled) to the more intractable problem of "sexual difference." When exclusion was legitimated by reference to the different biologies of women and men, "sexual difference" was established not only as a natural fact, but also as an ontological basis for social and political differentiation. In the age of democratic revolutions, "women" came into being as political outsiders through the discourse of sexual difference. Feminism was a protest against women's political exclusion; its goal was to eliminate "sexual difference" in politics, but it had to make its claims on behalf of "women" (who were discursively produced through "sexual difference"). To the extent that it acted for "women," feminism produced the "sexual difference" it sought to eliminate. This paradox—the need both to accept *and* to refuse "sexual difference"—was the constitutive condition of feminism as a political movement throughout its long history.

The difficulty of dealing in paradox was described in 1788 by Olympe de Gouges (who would later establish her place in feminist history as the author of the 1791 *Declaration of the Rights of Woman and Citizen*). In a long treatise written in emulation of Jean-Jacques Rousseau, she set forth her version of the story of the social contract along with a set of observations about philosophy, science, progress, and the current state of the theater, as well as a list of proposals for political reform. At one point, in an aside about the ill effects on society of the pursuit of science and learning by artisans and tradesmen (their ambition led them—dangerously for social order—to want to escape their customary place and calling), she halted her diatribe with this comment: "If I go any further in this matter, I will go too far and attract the enmity of the newly rich, who, without reflecting on my good ideas or appreciating my good intentions, will condemn me pitilessly as a woman who has only paradoxes to offer and not problems easy to resolve."[5] For me this final description—"a woman who has only paradoxes to offer and not problems easy to resolve"—sums up the situation of Olympe de Gouges and her feminist contemporaries and successors. What was paradoxical was not only that de Gouges's opinions about social ambition contested widely held assumptions about the benefits of education and scientific progress; it was also that de Gouges's position as a woman in revolutionary France was produced by means of paradoxes and that she knew herself to be so constituted.

In de Gouges's time as in our own, "paradox" is used most often in its nontechnical sense. Technically, logicians define it as an unresolvable proposition that is true and false at the same time. (Robert's dictionary offers as an example the liar's statement: "I am lying.") In rhetorical and aesthetic theory, paradox is a sign of the capacity to balance complexly contrary thoughts and feelings and, by extension, poetic creativity. Ordinary usage carries traces of these formal and aesthetic meanings, but it most often employs "paradox" to mean an opinion that challenges prevailing orthodoxy (literally, it goes against the *doxa*), that is contrary to received tradition. Paradox marks a position at odds with the dominant one by stressing its difference from it.[6] Those who put into circulation a set of truths that challenge but don't displace orthodox beliefs create a situation that loosely matches the technical definition of paradox.

But the history of feminism is not simply a history of contrary women uttering dissenting opinions. Nor can it be captured by the oxymoronic description of "women claiming the rights of Man." The paradoxes I refer to are not strategies of opposition, but the constitutive elements of feminism itself. The history of feminism is the history of women who have had only paradoxes to offer not because—as misogynist critics would have it—women's reasoning capacities are deficient or their natures fundamentally contrary, not because feminism somehow hasn't been able to get its theory and practice right, but because historically modern Western feminism is constituted by the discursive practices of democratic politics that have equated individuality with masculinity.

The word "individual" has ambiguous meanings that are present in its various usages. On the one hand, the individual is the abstract prototype for the human; on the other, the individual is a unique being, a distinct person, different from all others of its species. The first definition was often employed in political theory as the basis for the claim (made in France by Enlightenment philosophers and revolutionary politicians) that there were natural and universal human rights (to liberty, property, happiness) that gave men a common claim to the political rights of the citizen. The revolutionary philosophers made abstract individualism the rhetorical basis for their republic, even though historically republics had not rested on such inclusive notions.[7] The second definition was present when philosophers as different as Diderot and Rousseau articulated a notion of a unique self and specified its uniqueness by its differentiation from an other. This other provided the boundaries of the self's existence, its distinctive qualities and characteristics, as in the entry for "individual" in the *Encyclopédie*:

> Peter is a man, Paul is a man. They belong to the same species; but they are distinguished from one another by *numerable* differences. One is handsome, the other ugly; one learned, the other ignorant. Each is etymologically an *individual* because he cannot be divided into another subject who has an existence that is really separate from him. His assembled traits are such that, taken together, they cannot apply to anyone but him.[8]

These differences were not categorical; it was precisely their endless variety that distinguished individuals from one another. What the human species had in common, according to this definition, was its individuality, the fact that every person was different from every other. And it was precisely through a relationship of contrast that individuality was established. This notion of radically different individuals existed in tense relationship with the political idea of the abstract individual, which sought to articulate some more essential human commonality. Indeed it was the search for a common basis for political community that made the kind of difference articulated here intolerable.

For political theorists at the time of the French Revolution, the abstract individual expressed this essence of human commonality. Its rights were considered natural because (in the words of the Marquis de Condorcet) "they are derived from the nature of man," defined as "a sensitive being . . . capable of reasoning and of having moral ideas."[9] To conceive of all humans as the same in this regard required abstracting individuals from the differentiating social statuses attributed to birth, family, wealth, occupation, property ownership, and religion.[10] It also meant treating them as disembodied, apart from the distinguishing physical characteristics of physiognomy, skin color, and sex. This abstraction made it possible to posit a fundamental human sameness, a set of universal traits, and thus opened the way for thinking about political, social, and even economic equality. If humans were fundamentally the same, they could be figured as a single individual. The abstract individual was such a singular individual.[11]

But precisely because it was a singular type, and because it was described as possessing "a certain set of invariant psychological characteristics and tendencies,"[12] the abstract concept of the individual could also function to exclude those who were thought not to possess the requisite traits. In the late eighteenth and early nineteenth centuries, sensationalist psychologists emphasized the physiological basis for cognition, and so raised the issue of difference.[13] When the body's organs were taken to be the source of one's impressions and experiences, then the skin in some cases, the generative organs in others, became markers of human ability. Psychologists used these organic differences to distinguish between those (white men) who exemplified the human indi-

abstract yet singular

vidual through their reason and moral integrity and those (others—women, and initially blacks as well) whose so-called natural tendencies precluded their ability to live up to the individual prototype. Thus, while the medical doctor Pierre-Jean-Georges Cabanis argued that all humans had in common a visceral sensitivity to the sufferings of others and so the capacity for morality, he differentiated between the profound and desirable sensibility of men and the fleeting feelings of women. These differences followed from the differences in their internal organs and determined their social roles. Men were, by nature, fully moral (and thus the better representatives of the human); women were less so.[14] Here then was one of the useful, even necessary, contradictions in the concept of the abstract individual: articulated as the foundation of a system of universal inclusion (against the hierarchies and privileges of monarchical and aristocratic regimes), it could also be used as a standard of exclusion by defining as nonindividuals, or less than individuals, those who were different from the singular figure of the human.

When abstract individualism referred to a prototypical individual, it at once made a generalization about all humans and evoked a notion of individuality as unique. But to conceive of the uniqueness of an individual still required a relationship of difference. What was an individual, after all, if not a distinct unit? How distinguish its unitary nature, if not by bounding it, by setting it off from others? How else secure a sense of individuality except by a relation of contrast? To put it another way, individuality required the very difference that the idea of the prototypical human individual was meant to deny.

Addressed as it was to eliminating political privilege, the concept of the abstract individual both raised and disregarded questions about this process of establishing the boundaries of individuality. But to disregard it was not to resolve or erase it; the problem of difference remained. The abstract individual, a singular type with specified characteristics, did not allow either for the existence of varieties of individuals or for the role of an other in securing any individual's existence. Yet the notion of individuality also carried with it a sense of distinction and differentiation.

Some theorists of rights, among them Condorcet, argued that the usefulness of abstract individualism for defining *political* participation lay precisely in its deliberate disregard for difference: "It would be difficult to prove that women are incapable of exercising the rights of citizenship. Why should individuals exposed to pregnancies and other passing indispositions be unable to exercise rights which no one has dreamed of withholding from persons who have the gout all winter or catch cold quickly?"[15] Social characteristics and relations of difference existed, of course, but they were not meant to be taken into account for purposes of determining formal political participation. Condorcet recognized that political equality was itself a paradoxical concept, necessarily ignoring the differences it must also recognize (in order to declare them irrelevant).

But Condorcet espoused a decidedly minoritarian position in the history of French politics. The more typical way of dealing with individuality and difference in politics explained difference as a function of gender, idealized sometimes in terms of a functional division of reproductive labor, sometimes as the natural and therefore unquestionable expression of heterosexual desire.[16] In this approach, the infinite variety of the self/other difference was reduced to a matter of sexual difference; maleness was equated with individuality, and femaleness with otherness in a fixed, hierarchical, and immobile opposition (masculinity was not seen as femininity's other). The political individual was then taken to be both universal and male; the female was not an individual, both because she was nonidentical with the human prototype and because she was the other who confirmed the (male) individual's individuality.[17]

A vignette from the official record of the National Convention in 1794 illustrates the way in which difference—for purposes of defining the individuality that conferred political citizenship—was equated with sexual difference. In 1794 the revolutionaries (seeking to defeat the British in the Caribbean) abolished slavery and conferred citizenship on former slaves. (Free men of color had been enfranchised in 1792.) As emancipation was proclaimed, the two deputies of color in the assembly walked to the tribune and there embraced and received a presidential kiss. Then the deputy Pierre-Joseph Cambon (also a member of the Committee on Public Safety) took the floor: "A citizeness [*citoyenne*] of colour who regularly attends the sittings of the Convention has just felt so keen a joy at seeing us give liberty to all her brethren that she has fainted. (Applause) I demand that this fact be mentioned in the minutes, and that this citizeness be admitted to the sitting and receive at least this much recognition for her civic virtues." The woman was allowed to sit near the president for the rest of the session; as she took her place, brushing tears from her eyes, she was greeted with cheers and applause.[18] The woman's "civic virtue" consisted in her outpouring of gratitude to legislators, who had acted on her behalf by permitting the men of her race to represent her. It was no accident that Cambon seized on this moment of fraternal inclusion to make a black woman the sign of the entry of black men into the ranks of citizenship. The men's difference from women served to eradicate differences of skin color and race among men; the universality of the abstract individual was in this way and at this moment established as a common maleness.

As we shall see in the chapters that follow, the gendering of citizenship was a persistent theme in French political discourse. Rousseau offers an important example since his formulations were often employed by later French revolutionaries. It was men's consciousness of sexual difference, experienced as the desire to possess a beloved object, that distinguished them from "savages," he wrote. This desire was the basis not only for gentle love between man and woman, but for jealousy and discord—for politics—among men. Whereas men must pursue their desire, Rousseau held, women ought to contain or redirect theirs in the interest of social harmony.[19] Rousseau affords by no means the only example. More than a century later the sociologist Emile Durkheim, writing against what he considered the moral egoism of the Rousseauian individual, insisted that ties of friendship—of "solidarity"—had come to replace more primitive, calculated forms of human interchange. His model of friendship was "conjugal society" because it was based on an attraction of fundamental difference. If social relations depended on likeness, he argued, they would not work:

> When the union results from the resemblance of two images, it consists in an agglutination. The two representations become solidary because, being indistinct . . . they confound each other, and become no more than one . . . On the contrary, in the case of the division of labor, they are outside each other and are linked only because they are distinct. Neither the sentiments nor the social relations which derive from these sentiments are the same in the two cases.[20]

The kind of attraction for difference that Durkheim wanted to portray as "organic solidarity" was best exemplified, he thought, by heterosexuality, where there could be no problem of fundamental resemblance. "Precisely because man and woman are different, they seek each other passionately." Their attraction was based, moreover, on the fact that their differences "require each other for their mutual fruition."[21] This passionate attraction for difference made inconsequential (but did not disturb) legally sanctioned differentials of power. Women's "withdrawal from politics," which Durkheim took to be a sign of civilization, was part of the new system of the division of labor. To the extent that citizenship was still consonant with individuality, it was deemed a prerogative of men.

On the question of individuality, there could be no more stark contrast than the one offered by the Italian criminologist Cesare Lombroso, who was widely read in France during the Third Republic: "All women fall into the same category, whereas each man is an individual unto himself; the physiognomy of the former conforms to a generalized standard; that of the latter is in each case unique."[22]

The historical variations on these themes, discussed in the following chapters, are crucially important since they stem from specific and historically distinct epistemologies that changed the meanings of the term "individual." Originally defined in opposition to the social and legal privileges of feudalism, the concept of the individual was a way of declaring all men equal before the law in 1789. By the end of the nineteenth century, the individual was defined by some theorists not in opposition to the social or society, but as its product. Others posed the individual against the crowd, which had been created by mass democracy. Rationality, independence, and autonomy were seen by the critics of mass democracy as attributes of superior intelligence and education; they were neither the prerequisites for nor the products of citizenship. Still, in France until 1944 the common ground for individuality, as for citizenship, was masculinity.

There was, then, a persisting theme evident in attempts to reformulate ideas about individuality and citizenship: the universal individual who exercised the political rights of "man" was at once abstract and concrete; difference from a woman (whether a matter of desire or reproductive function) secured both his typicality *and* the boundaries of his individuality. Individuality was not only a masculine prerogative;

[margin handwritten note: individual as opposed to the social or sprung from the social]

it was also racially defined. The superiority of white Western men to their "savage" counterparts lay in an individuality achieved and expressed through the social and affective divisions of labor formalized by the institution of monogamous marriage.

[handwritten margin note: abstract indiv. not so abstract → white/male & defined by oppositional colored/female]

———■———

Where philosophers and politicians offered "sexual difference" as an explanation for the limits they placed on the universality of individual rights, feminism emerged to point up the inconsistencies. The word "lie" echoed from one end of the nineteenth century to the other as feminists denounced the Revolution and the First, Second, and Third Republics for betraying the universal principles of liberty, equality, and fraternity by refusing citizenship to women. Feminists not only pointed to inconsistency; they attempted to correct it by demonstrating that they, too, were individuals according to the standards of individuality of their day. The law had even recognized this, they pointed out, in various pieces of civil legislation. But they could not avoid (or resolve) the problem of their presumed sexual difference. Feminists argued in the same breath for the irrelevance and the relevance of their sex, for the identity of all individuals and the difference of women. They refused to be women in the terms their society dictated, and at the same time they spoke in the name of those women.[23] The ambiguities of the republican notion of the individual (its universal definition and masculine embodiment) were thus carried into and exposed by feminist arguments.

Indeed feminists' agency consisted exactly in this: they were women who had "only paradoxes to offer." The courage and inventiveness of individual feminists, the subversive power and historical significance of their collective voice, lay (still lie) in the disturbing spectacle presented by paradox. For the identification and display of inconsistency and ambiguity—of self-contradictoriness—within an orthodoxy that strenuously denies their existence is surely destabilizing and sometimes even transformative. Ideological/political systems such as French republicanism work by endorsing the notion that coherence is a requirement for social organization and then by presenting themselves as fulfilling the requirements for coherence. In order to do this they deny or repress internal contradiction, partiality, or incoherence.[24] Thus the production of "sexual difference" was a way of achieving the otherwise inconsistent exclusion of women from the categories of individual and citizen. The first revolutionaries and later republicans had, after all, premised their government on the idea that all human individuals (whatever their differences) were equally (and naturally) endowed with rights. Feminists accepted the republican insistence on the need for coherence. Precisely because they shared the commitment to coherence, they suggested that the system was not meeting its own test. By defiantly denouncing as hypocritical and incoherent a republicanism that enunciated universalist principles and excluded women from exercising full political rights, but also by themselves embodying the difficulty of resolving the inconsistencies, feminists flagrantly revealed the repressed fault-lines of their ideological/political system, and so opened questions about the system's original design and about the need for rethinking it. That was (and is) the power and the danger of feminism, the reason it provokes both fear and scorn.[25]

Feminist strategies exemplified an almost uncanny ability to sniff out and exploit ambiguities in the foundational concepts of philosophy, politics, and common sense. This ability was, of course, not at all uncanny, but the result of being discursively positioned in and as contradiction. Feminists engaged with the foundational assumptions of their respective ages in a most disquieting way—not in their guise as moral or scientific certainties, but as ambiguous and contested attempts to impose order on human social organization. They made the link between these concepts and their quest for political rights by seizing on contrary implications in ordinary usage and making disagreements about meaning work to support their own cause. Thus, feminists refused to accept "nature" as an explanation for women's disenfranchisement when there was doubt even among scientists about how the natural field could be read: was its meaning transparent, or always subject to imperfect human interpretation? And in science, where explanation was at best inconclusive, why assume that gender was the key to all physical differences?

In the late eighteenth century Olympe de Gouges took her contemporaries' uncertainty about the human faculty of imagination as a license to think outside the constraints of revolutionary politics and to argue—in terms of Enlightenment debates about the relationship between reason and imagination—that she had the capacity (required of citizens) to represent herself. In 1848 Jeanne Deroin found in the ambiguities of the Romantics' notion of the androgyne an argument for the complementarity and absolute autonomy of the sexes. Hubertine Auclert accepted the importance of "the social" as defined by Third Republic politicians and then made the case for women's rights in terms of the right of "the social" to be the subject rather than the object of government policy. Madeleine Pelletier embraced radical individualism at the turn of the century and took up its claim to transcend homogenizing categories of social representation. She included gender as one of the categories that denied the uniqueness of individuals and urged women to reject feminine representations in order to achieve equality. In none of these cases was the strategy entirely successful, not merely because it did not attain the vote, but also because it was not without its own internal inconsistencies. In each case, albeit in different ways, the need to invoke "women" produced "sexual difference," thus undermining the attempt to declare it irrelevant for political purposes.

As these examples indicate (and as the chapters that follow will elaborate in detail), feminists formulated their claims for rights in terms of very different epistemologies, and their arguments must be read that way—not as evidence of a transcendent or continuous Woman's consciousness or women's experience. Although the notion of a repeated pattern of paradox carries with it an aura of timelessness, the concepts feminists used were rooted in their times and can finally be understood only in their specificity. History accounts not only for the variety of positions one finds in feminist writing, but also for the different ways in which the social and individual identity of "woman" was conceived. Jeanne Deroin, drawing on romanticism and utopian socialism, wrote rapturously of a spiritually pure and loving mother who, like the Virgin Mary, bore within herself the redemption of the world. Hubertine Auclert, accepting the Third Republic's standards, aspired to the heights of scientific, secular rationalism. Madeleine Pelletier drew on new psychological teachings in the early twentieth century to refute the idea of natural sexual differences. She defined femininity as "psychological sex" and deemed it the cause of women's subordination. Emancipated women, she thought, were those who knew how to "virilize" themselves. The difference among these women lies not in what each emphasized

but, far more profoundly, in the very identity of each as a feminist and
of the women whose rights she defended. The subject of feminism was
not constant; the terms of her representation shifted, and in those shifts
we find not only women's history, but also histories of philosophy,
psychology, and politics.

———————◼———————

The history of feminism can be understood as an interplay between a
repetitious pattern of exclusion and a changing articulation of subjects.
The terms of exclusion repeatedly produce "sexual difference" as a
fixed, natural boundary between the political and the domestic, or the
self-representing and the represented, or the autonomous and the
dependent. But the terms of exclusion are also variable and contradictory, based in different epistemologies, and this variability and contradiction result in fundamentally different conceptions of the "women"
whose rights are being claimed.

The repeated exclusion of women from politics provided a sense of
commonality among feminists, even as their vision of who they were
and what women should be differed. Indeed, the common experience
of being excluded was sometimes mistaken for a shared vision of the
meaning of being female. As a result histories of feminism, while they
have attended to sharp disagreements on questions of strategy and
tactics, have often neglected differences in the concepts "women" and
"feminist," assuming a self-evident and unchanging meaning for those
terms.

Following the lead of Denise Riley, I want to interrogate the terms
"women" and "feminist" by looking closely at the different ways in
which they have historically been used.[26] To do this, I have focused on
four feminists who claimed political rights (specifically, the vote) for
women in different revolutionary and/or republican contexts. It was in
moments of revolution or constitutional transformation that the question of political rights was most open to discussion; and it was under
republican governments that the extent and universality of the suffrage
could be contested. Olympe de Gouges demanded during the French
Revolution that women be made citizens on the same basis as men;
Jeanne Deroin defied the Second Republic's constitution and ran for
legislative office on the democratic-socialist ticket in 1849; Hubertine

Auclert was the first to call upon the Third Republic to live up to its promise by enfranchising women; and Madeleine Pelletier made the vote the cornerstone of a plan for the republican emancipation of women that also included abortion as an "absolute" right of control over one's body.[27]

None of these women were philosophers by training; their levels of education varied. All were political activists and writers who spoke in popular language and who improvised strategies (sometimes alone, sometimes in association with other feminists) to advance their claims for rights. What is of interest is how these women formulated their claims and in whose name, the ways in which they were constructed as feminist subjects, and the differences among them. Also of interest is the way in which universalist discourses, specifically the discourses of abstract individualism and of social duty and social right, enabled them to conceive of themselves as political agents even as those same discourses denied women political agency. And of greatest interest is the historical specificity of feminist agency, the incomparability of feminist philosophies, beneath the formal similarity of paradox.

Pursuing these topics requires the kind of close and detailed reading that focuses on individuals, however idiosyncratic. Precisely because these four women were neither typical—some held a decidedly minority position in the spectrum of feminist politics—nor unique—their views often overlapped and intersected with those of other feminists of their day—it seems to me that investigating them in depth—their ideas, their rhetoric and invective, their irony, and the outrageousness of their actions—can provide insight into the different political and philosophical issues historically involved in feminist claims for political rights.

Those seeking a biographical narrative with causal links between personal experience and individual action will not find them in this book. The personal life experiences of these women—their relationships to parents or teachers or lovers or children—do not provide a sufficient explanation for feminist politics. Biography tends to focus too narrowly on the circumstances of individuals, reducing the thoughts and actions of women to their personal life stories, neglecting the complex determinations of language (the social/cultural means by which subjects come into being). The biographical approach, moreover, fortifies the notion that agency is an expression of autonomous individual will, rather than the effect of a historically defined process which forms subjects. The notion of agency as an expression of individual will is not a description of human nature (although it is often offered as one), but a historically specific conception, tied, in fact, to many of the same ideas that denied women individuality, autonomy, and political rights. Instead of assuming that agency follows from an innate human will, I want to understand feminism in terms of the discursive processes—the epistemologies, institutions, and practices—that produce political subjects, that make agency (in this case the agency of feminists) possible even when it is forbidden or denied.[28]

I do not think of these women as exemplary heroines. Instead I think of them as sites—historical locations or markers—where crucial political and cultural contests are enacted and can be examined in some detail. To figure a person—in this case, a woman—as a place or location is not to deny her humanity; it is rather to recognize the many factors that constitute her agency, the complex and multiple ways in which she is constructed as a historical actor.

One argument of this book is that feminist agency is paradoxical in its expression. It is constituted by universalist discourses of individualism (with their theories of rights and citizenship) that evoke "sexual difference" to naturalize the exclusion of women. A second argument is that feminist agency has a history; it is neither a fixed set of behaviors nor an essential attribute of women; rather it is an effect of ambiguities, inconsistencies, contradictions within particular epistemologies. In order to make these arguments, I must write the history of feminism by reading for the historically specific paradoxes that feminist subjects embody, enact, and expose.

———————————❙———————————

Reading for paradox requires a different kind of reading than historians are accustomed to. We are used to reading for the clash of opposing positions (feminists versus liberal politicians, for example), but not for the internal tensions and incompatibilities (within feminism, within liberal individualism, within concepts such as liberty or separate spheres or the individual) of which these clashes are both symptom and cause. Reading in this technically deconstructive way does not work comfortably with linear narrative or teleology; it tends to undercut those stories that establish the truth or inevitability of certain views of the world by eliminating accounts of conflict and power within them.

The result, however, is well worth the effort. For to ignore the unsettledness that paradox, contradiction, and ambiguity imply is to lose sight of the subversive potential of feminism and the agency of feminists. It is precisely because feminism embodies paradox that it has been trivialized or consigned to marginality by those seeking to protect the foundations of whatever status quo they represent.[29] Such protection involves denying contradiction by rendering it invisible and by displacing the source of the problem onto those who would point it out. Feminist paradoxes have thus usually been interpreted as the products of their own confusions, and this interpretation has then become the justification for their continued exclusion. Repeatedly, their calls for a coherent implementation of the principle of universal equality drew the reply that feminists were unreasonable and themselves dangerously incoherent (the charge that they were "male females" or "female males"—an impossible combination—regularly expressed the sense of incoherence as abnormality). Olympe de Gouges was guillotined by the Jacobins for her excesses of imagination; Jeanne Deroin was ridiculed for wanting to turn the world upside down. Hubertine Auclert was likened to the Medusa and deemed to be "afflicted with madness or hysteria; an illness which makes her look on men as her equals," the police reported in 1880.[30] Madeleine Pelletier was considered a source of moral disorganization by pro-natalists in the 1920s, and was confined to a mental asylum at the end of her life.

The paradoxes feminists offered were not wholly of their own making, and we do the history of feminism a disservice to ignore that fact. By writing the history of feminism as if it were simply a matter of choosing the right strategy—equality or difference—we imply that one or another of these options was actually available, that closure or resolution was and is ultimately attainable. But the history of feminism is not the history of available options or of the unconstrained choice of a winning plan. It is rather the history of women (and some men) grappling repeatedly with the radical difficulty of resolving the dilemmas they confronted (however successful they were in achieving specific reforms).

A history of feminism that takes these problems as its subject, that

attends to the sources and operations of paradox, not only establishes
the historical significance of feminism; it also disputes those histories
of democracy—whether in France or elsewhere—that attribute earlier
exclusions to temporary glitches in a perfectible, ever-expansive plural-
ist system and that take the extension of the vote, outside its necessarily
relativizing historical contexts, as a consistent indicator of the absence
of inequality in a society. The history of feminism offered in the
following chapters is enacted as a critique of this conventional approach to history and of the ideology it supports. I do not deny that
feminism—at least when it claimed rights for women—was produced
by the discourse of liberal individualism nor that it depended on
liberalism for its existence; there was (is still) no alternative. My point
is to emphasize the fundamentally unresolvable, though changing,
nature of an enduring conflictual relationship. Feminism was not a sign
of the benign and progressive operations of liberal individualism, but
rather a symptom of its constitutive contradictions. These contradictions may have been displaced onto other arenas by reforms such as
the vote, but they did not disappear, and for that reason neither did
feminism.

Feminism has been historically a complex critical practice; its history
should be no less so. Indeed, it is by engaging in such critical practice
that the history of feminism becomes part of the project it writes about;
it is itself feminist history.

2

The Uses of Imagination: Olympe de Gouges in the French Revolution

Even as they announced the principles of their revolution in a ringing Declaration of the Rights of Man and Citizen in the autumn of 1789, the architects of the French Revolution were aware of the danger of such a universalistic pronouncement: it was certain to conflict with the practical details of any constitution that was finally elaborated. Honoré Gabriel Mirabeau and Pierre Victor Malouet, both former nobles, both deputies of the Third Estate, said as much to the National Assembly. They cautioned against telling people about their rights before it had been decided what exactly these rights were, how they were to be implemented, and for whom.[1] But the concerns of the two deputies were overruled by the majority, who felt that a declaration of principle would teach the nation to love the liberty that was theirs by right and would serve to mobilize urgently needed support for the replacement of the Old Regime by a government based on the sovereignty of the people and "the natural order of things." The Declaration succeeded in rallying patriots to the Revolution. But, just as Mirabeau and Malouet predicted, it also made possible the discontent of those (women, slaves, and free men of color among them) who were excluded from citizenship by the terms of the constitution promulgated two years later.

The revolutionaries' awareness of an inherent conflict between principle and practice, between the rights of individuals abstracted from all social contexts and the need for a political policy that took social differences into account, provides an appropriate beginning for the history of feminism in France. But there is an additional complication to this story. The Revolution quickly granted women civil rights, especially in the realm of marriage. In 1791 marriage was defined as a civil contract, and in 1792 divorce was made a legal right of both partners. Male legislators thus passed laws with a contradictory effect on women, rendering them both objects of legislative concern and subjects with civil rights. Women's ambiguous status as objects and subjects, their recognition as civil agents and their exclusion from politics, engendered feminism.[2]

As the constitution was being debated in 1791, Olympe de Gouges published her *Declaration of the Rights of Woman and Citizen,* a document which insisted both that women, by nature, had all the rights men did (that they too were individuals) and that their specific needs as women made the exercise of those rights all the more urgent. De Gouges's *Declaration* was not the first or the only feminist statement in the Revolution, but it has for good reason become the exemplary one for feminists and historians alike.[3] It is arguably the most comprehensive call for women's rights in this period; it takes the Revolution's universalism at its word; and it exposes the incompleteness of that universalism in its own paradoxical attempts to represent women as abstract individuals by calling attention to the differences they embody.

———————— ▮ ————————

De Gouges's challenge—to represent women as citizens—engaged with a troubling and far-reaching discussion among revolutionaries about the political and philosophical meanings of representation. Did the elected representatives of the people constitute the nation or only an imperfect substitute for it? What was the relationship between the general will and those who presumed to express it? If citizenship was an attribute of abstract individuals, could it also represent people in their concrete existences; did the citizen, in fact, represent a man, or did the conferral of citizenship create the possibility of his being as a political individual? (If the latter, then citizenship was clearly the key to representation for women.) All these questions involved not only the wisdom and practicality of delegating authority for purposes of governing, but also the nature of the relationship between sign and referent. To what real entities, after all, could the patently abstract notions of "nation" or "people" or "rights-bearing individual" or "citizen" or "general will" actually refer?

The revolutionaries debated these questions endlessly. For some, the National Assembly was the nation; for others, it merely represented the nation. For some, elected representatives were delegates of the people; for others, they *were* the sovereign people. For some, the law was the general will; for others, it was an expression or reflection of that will; and so on. Epistemological problems *were* political problems. And the effort to settle them foundered on their ultimate unresolvability; whether representation accurately reflected a prior reality or created the very possibility of imagining such a reality could finally not be known, but the stakes in knowing were nonetheless high.[4]

One of de Gouges's strategies—a strategy characteristic of feminism—was to push the ambiguity of representation to its limit by toying with the relationship between sign and referent, using each interchangeably to establish reality. She did this not only in her many writings (in addition to the *Declaration* there is a rich lode of plays, pamphlets, and brochures) but in the very construction of her self. Indeed her efforts in this area have made the task of conventional biography difficult, as is evident in the struggle of one of her early biographers to sort out truth from fiction. Léopold Lacour spent many pages of his 1900 work trying to establish the facts of de Gouges's life: the accurate date of her birth in the town of Montauban (it is generally taken as 1748, though she changed it to appear younger as she grew older); all the sources of the name she took (she was born Marie Gouzes and changed her name after she was widowed in 1764); whether she left her husband, Louis Aubry, to go to Paris before or after his death; the exact occupation of this husband to whom she was very briefly married at age sixteen (cook? caterer? supplier of food for the intendant—provincial administrator—of Montauban?); the number of her children (there is a record of only one son, Pierre Aubry, but Lacour takes de Gouges's reference after she was arrested in 1793 to "two earlier pregnancies" to suggest the possibility of another living child); the names and number of her lovers (she lived as a courtesan in Paris in the years before the Revolution); and the identity of her father (the butcher Gouzes was listed in the birth records, but there were repeated rumors—which she denied—that she was the bastard child of Louis

XV, as well as stories—which she seems to have originated—that she was the illegitimate daughter of the Marquis le Franc de Pompignan).[5]

Lacour's painstaking speculations on these matters yield no conclusive proof, and they overlook the historical importance of the fact that de Gouges sought to control the representation of her self. By rejecting the names of her father(s) and her husband, she in effect declared her autonomy, her refusal of the secondary status that patriarchal law assigned to women. No name other than the one she had given herself could designate (and define) her existence. She was unique; her self originated with herself. There was no preexisting subject, no malleable matter on which to stamp an impression; rather, through representation, de Gouges produced a self that had no antecedent to her enactment of it. She was thus, in the terms of her epoch, an active citizen, equivalent to, even identical with, the "new man" of the Revolution. Moreover, whatever their accuracy, her attributions of familial origins worked to produce the figure she wanted to be. By suggesting that Le Franc de Pompignan was her father she established a lineage for her elevated social aspirations and (since the Marquis had won a reputation as a man of letters) for her literary activities as a playwright and, from 1788 on, a political pamphleteer. (The final report on her trial and execution in 1793 lists de Gouges as "une femme de lettres," testimony to her success in controlling at least some of the terms of her self-definition.)[6] Lacour's struggle to establish the truth about Olympe de Gouges betrays a belief in the transparent relationship between a name and a person, a sign and its referent—a belief that she, along with philosophers of her own epoch, questioned. While the nature of this relationship plagued Rousseau and the revolutionaries influenced by him, de Gouges was willing to accept and even exploit his recognition that all signs might be arbitrary, particularly, perhaps, the sign of the self.[7]

De Gouges understood her ability to represent her self as an attribute of her imagination. It was by means of imagination that she portrayed herself as the possessor of the rights of "Man and Citizen" and explained her interventions in politics at a time when the political rights of women were highly contested. Sometimes she appealed to imagination directly, as when she explained the audacity of her attempt to describe the origins of human society—a subject about which so many great minds had already ventured opinions—as a dream. Dreams and imagination were often synonymous for de Gouges and her contemporaries, or, if not synonymous, closely related. "I was, perhaps, lost in my dreams . . ."[8] In this she claimed she was no different from Rousseau or Voltaire, who had also imagined their accounts and whose genius did not protect them from criticism or error. "I want, ignorant as I am, to try to lose myself like the others."[9] At other times de Gouges simply acted imaginatively in the terms of her time, taking on the role to which she aspired, improbably recombining elements of her world, inserting herself into stories from which she might otherwise have been excluded. She was a second Cassandra, a wise man, Rousseau's imitator and his better, a lawyer defending the king at his trial. She compared herself to Homer and Joan of Arc.[10] In a pamphlet denouncing the crimes of Robespierre she signed herself with the anagram Polyme, described as "an amphibious animal." "I am a unique animal; I am neither man nor woman. I have all the courage of the one and, sometimes, the weaknesses of the other."[11] She was neither a woman nor a man, but also both a woman and a man. "I am a woman and I have served my country as a great man."[12] The achievement of citizenship was, in her terms, the result of her creative imagination.

For a woman to claim the powers of creative imagination at the end of the eighteenth century was to posit something that was at once plausible and inconceivable in the terms of existing debates. For imagination was an increasingly troubling concept as philosophers grappled with, but did not resolve, its ambiguities. In the dictionaries of the early eighteenth century, imagination referred primarily to the facility of the mind to represent things external to itself in the form of images or thoughts; secondary definitions involved inventiveness (the ability of the mind to make things up), but often this was taken as a degenerate form of reflexive imagination (as in the case of the hypochondriac, the "malade imaginaire," "the man whose imagination is so seriously compromised that he believes himself sick even though he is well").[13] It was in this sense that dreams were connected to imagination: "All objects of dreams are clearly tricks of the imagination," asserted an article in Diderot's *Encyclopédie*.[14] As the century wore on, the question of fantasy and invention seems to have gained ascendancy and, with it, what one dictionary called the "nobler and more precise" definition, the ability of the mind to produce poetry and art, "to create by imitation."[15]

At the same time, as inventiveness and creativity were increasingly stressed, their relation to both reason and reality came into question. "The real world has its limits," Rousseau wrote in *Emile;* "the imaginary world is infinite. Unable to enlarge the one, let us restrict the other, for it is from the difference between the two alone that are born all the pains which make us truly unhappy."[16] He might have added that the difference between the two established the meaning of each term: without something designated as fiction to set its limits, the boundaries of the real were not always immediately apparent; without the imagination, how could the operations of reason be distinguished? In pursuit of impossible answers to this vexing question, Enlightenment philosophers came up with sharp (but necessarily ambivalent) distinctions.

Writing in the *Encyclopédie,* Voltaire attempted to reconcile these two aspects of imagination by positing two kinds: the passive and the active. The passive imagination was mimetic, simply mirroring to the mind things outside it. Imposed from the outside, these images possessed and inhabited an individual. As with a dream one had while sleeping, there was no control to be exercised over them. The passive imagination took one over, as did passion; it was associated with error and led to subjugation. Voltaire offered the example of uneducated people whose passive imagination became the instrument of their domination by others.[17] His colleague Diderot spoke of imagination in terms of imitation and equated such passivity with women. "Think of women," he wrote in *Le paradox sur le comédien.* "They are miles beyond us in sensibility; there is no sort of comparison between their passion and ours. But as much as we are below them in action, so much are they below us in imitation." Commenting on this passage, Philippe Lacoue-Labarthe writes, "This does not mean that women do not imitate . . . But if they imitate . . . it happens only in passion and passivity, in the state of being possessed or being inhabited. Consequently, only when they are *subject.*"[18] Imagination imprints itself on an unresisting woman: she has no role in shaping it; rather she is (in Lacoue-Labarthe's words) "the matrix or the malleable matter on which the imprint is stamped." When they have genius, Diderot commented in his essay *Sur les femmes,* "I think the imprint is more original on them than on us."[19] Originality here means likeness to the original as imagined by others; it is the imprint that displays originality, not the medium on which it is stamped. Absent is the autonomy of self-creation exhibited by the possessor of an active imagination.[20]

The active imagination, in contrast, assumed a sovereign subject. Voltaire described it as the source of the triumphs of creative genius in poetry, mathematics, and scientific invention. The active imagination involved considered thought, the recombining of existing images and ideas "because," as the philosopher pointed out, "it is not given to man to create ideas himself; he can only modify them."[21] But the modification meant also improvement: the surpassing of what was given in nature by the art of man. And, through this production that was not mere reproduction, man became the source of his own articulation.[22]

The most difficult ambiguity for Voltaire lay not in the passive/active contrast, but in the active imagination itself. At its best, the active imagination could be directed to useful and enlightening ends. But there was always the danger of excess, for although the imaginative faculty might be susceptible to reason's regulation it was not inherently reasonable. In fact, to the extent that imagination (of whatever kind) involved imitation or re-presentation, what Lacoue-Labarthe calls a "logic of semblance," it was "articulated around the division between appearance and reality, presence and absence, the same and the other, or identity and difference . . . This is the division that grounds (and that constantly unsteadies) mimesis. At whatever level one takes it . . . the rule is always the same: the more it resembles, the more it differs. The same, in its sameness is the other itself, which in turn cannot be called 'itself,' and so on infinitely."[23] An active imagination became active precisely through a positive form of alienation, in which one literally created oneself (there being no prior subject on which to act). At the same time, there lurked the possibility of another kind of alienation: what could operate successfully as art might also lead, destructively, to madness. Writers, for example, might merge with the characters they so skillfully fashioned, and such identification, Voltaire warned, "can degenerate into madness." This kind of imagining took one literally beyond oneself, into an ecstatic or exalted state that constituted a misidentification, a confusion of self and other. There were, moreover, two aspects to this confusion. The imitator lost a proper sense of self and failed to appreciate the distinctive features that made the other different from him or her self; both the imitator and the object of imitation were thus called into question by the blurring of the boundaries of difference. Thus Rousseau warned in the preface to *La nouvelle Héloise:* "Wanting to be what we are not, we come to believe ourselves something other than what we are, and this is how we become mad."[24]

Voltaire, seeing the danger of excess implicit in the active imagination, expressed it in terms of the loss of reason's power to regulate—the identifying mark of the self.[25] While fiction and poetry were acceptable products of the creative mind, the "fantastic" imaginings of fairy tales went too far. "Always bereft of order and good sense, they cannot be esteemed; one reads them from weakness, and one condemns them by reason."[26] From a different perspective Condillac shared this concern about the dangers posed to understanding by the active imagination: it had the power to recombine sensory impressions in a manner "contrary to truth."[27]

The correction to the potential dangers of active imagination lay in the ever-vigilant, regulatory powers of reason. The line between fiction and reality, error and truth, madness and sanity, disorder and order needed constant policing by internal mechanisms of self-government. Indeed, the active imagination was a characteristic only of self-regulating, self-governing individuals; and they often became the external agents of regulation for those who could not control themselves. The entry for "songe" (dream) in the *Encyclopédie* seems to carry this double implication of external and internal regulation: "The waking imagination is a policed republic, where the voice of the magistrate restores everything to order; the imagination of dreams is the same republic in a state of anarchy, where the passions make frequent assaults against the authority of the legislator even while his law is in force."[28]

The voice of reason is the voice of the (male) magistrate, the voice of the Law whose prohibitions regulate waking imagination. Order— both political and personal, the metaphor suggests—depends on internalization of this law. The anarchy of dreams is figured as an attack by passion and desire on "the authority of the legislator" (a male figure, to be sure). The difference between day and night is the difference between order and chaos, reason and passion, discipline and desire, active and passive. Waking dreams are coherent, the author suggests, unlike the dreams of sleep, in which "all is unravelled, without order, without truth."[29] As long as subversive dreams are confined to sleep they are only potentially disruptive; their existence is nonetheless troubling. The difference, for Diderot, was also the difference between men and women. In his essay *Sur les femmes,* Diderot described the phantoms, the delirium, the "extraordinary ideas" produced in women by the uterus, "the organ specific to her sex," an organ susceptible to "terrible spasms." He went on to describe cases of what seemed incurable hysteria, cured nonetheless by the intervention of doctors or magistrates. For "this fiery imagination, this spirit that seemed irrepressible, one word sufficed to beat it down."[30] "One word," the word of the Law, laid these eruptions of fevered imagination to rest.

Still, for Voltaire the dilemma persisted, evidence for us of the futility of trying to fix the necessarily unstable logic of imagination; the source of creativity and the autonomous self, it was ever prone to excess and to alienation. For him the distinction between men and women offered by the Abbé Féraud ("an exalted imagination leads men to heroism and precipitates women into terrible disorders")[31] did not offer sufficient reassurance. The line between dreams and waking thoughts was difficult to establish, he wrote, because apparently coherent ideas could appear in dreams. But then were they to be trusted? And "if it is incontestable that coherent ideas form in us, despite ourselves, during sleep, what assurance do we have that they are not produced the same way while we are awake?"[32]

Rousseau's conception of imagination added yet another dimension to these discussions by explicitly raising the question of desire in terms of the self/other, male/female relationship. For Rousseau imagination was both a consoling and perverse faculty. It could lead to the pleasurable abandon of reverie, when a man was transported beyond himself, without diversions or obstacles.[33] In this state he was somehow closer to nature, free of the restraining discipline imposed by directed thought, open to sensations otherwise unknown to the reasonable mind. But this romantic conception was checked by a sense of danger. Imagination was a projection of desire and, as such, both a cause and a product of civilization. While men in nature acted only to satisfy physical wants and formed no permanent emotional attachments, he wrote in the Second Discourse *(On the Origin of Inequality)*, with society came the human faculties of memory, imagination, egoism, and reason. "The imagination, which causes such ravages among us, never speaks to the heart of savages." As men began to live in closer proximity, imagination not only expressed desire, but fixed it on a single object: "[Men] acquired imperceptibly ideas of beauty and merit, which soon gave rise to feelings of preference." From this followed the twin passions of love ("a tender and pleasant feeling") and jealousy ("impetuous fury"). Without imagination there would be no love, no commerce, no creativity, but also no competition, no murderous passion, no war. Imagination was at once the foundation of social organization and politics and the seed of their destruction.[34]

In Rousseau's conception, imagination and desire were one. Man's imagination, he warned in *Emile*, "scandalizes the eye in revealing to it what it sees not only as naked but as something that ought to be clothed. There is no garment so modest that a glance inflamed by imagination does not penetrate with its desires."[35] Women, too, were driven by desire; indeed it was their desire that stimulated men's. For Rousseau the way finally to manage, if not to eliminate, the dangers of erotic excess in both sexes was to restrain it in women. Thus Sophie's education aims at making her a modest, selfless creature whose only goal is to serve her husband; her job is to confirm Emile in his vision of himself, not to seek through him a self of her own. The key to her education lies in the control if not the repression of her imagination.

Or perhaps it is better to say that the point of her training is to serve as the screen upon which Emile can project his imagination. In this sense, she exercises only a passive imagination in eighteenth-century terms, one that bears the imprint of what others offer it rather than producing images of its own. Sophie is the object of Emile's imagination, not the subject of her own. To the extent that imagination expresses desire, it confirms (really creates) a self through its quest for an other; the restriction of imagination to the passive reflection of another's desire then denies (women) the possibility of articulating an independent sense of self. Rousseau's solution acknowledged its own socially contrived nature and hence was open to criticism and revision.

One could grant the connection between desire and imagination abstractly, without making it an exclusively male activity. Taking advantage of the ambiguities, not only in Rousseau but in all these attempts to address the issue of imagination, was exactly what Olympe de Gouges did.

The ambiguity of imagination made it both appealing and risky as a way of justifying one's behavior. On the one hand, Olympe de Gouges claimed imagination to align herself with great creative minds. Her strongest identification was, in fact, with Rousseau, whom she described as her "spiritual father."[36] It also gave her the license (when she ignored Diderot's insistence that women's imagination was only of the passive sort and took literally the ungendered discussions of Voltaire) to demonstrate her abilities, to challenge the limits placed on women by a society increasingly unwilling to appreciate the diversity of their talents. If by exercising active imagination one became autonomous and self-governing, de Gouges would construct herself accordingly. She would win recognition of her capacity for self-representation (and hence of her right to political representation) on the strength of her imagination. On the other hand, the appeal to imagination could be seen as transgressive or, worse, mad. Diderot, after all, ruled out the possibility that women could exercise active imagination; their efforts resulted only in inauthenticity, in the imitation of something they were not. Such imitation constituted a misrepresentation, a betrayal of both referent and sign, as when de Gouges declared that she had made herself a man for the country.[37]

The danger of this kind of misidentification lay in its blurring of the lines of sexual difference, of those boundaries of nature the revolutionaries deemed increasingly important for social organization. If, by the exercise of creative imagination, women could convincingly enact men's characteristics, social roles, or both, then how was one to distinguish between the real or natural and its imitation, how justify the restriction of citizenship to men? The only way was to establish some authority endowed with the ability to recognize and enforce the distinctions that were said to constitute sexual difference. But, as the Jacobins' reign of terror and their punishment of de Gouges demonstrated, rigid enforcement of such distinctions belied the transparency of the differences between public and private, virtue and treason, male and female. For what was natural about woman's passivity, after all, if the only way to prevent her from exercising an active imagination was to declare her mad and an outlaw and put her to death? Feminists lived and died by exposing such paradox.

———————■———————

Long before the tumultuous days of revolution, Olympe de Gouges was known in Parisian literary circles for her plays, some of which were performed by the Comédie Française. A flamboyant and outspoken critic of the machinations of the world of the theater, she often attributed her lack of greater success to prejudices held by the *comédiens* against women playwrights. De Gouges rejected (and probably also exemplified) Rousseau's objections to theatrical representation as an artifice associated with the behavior of women. She insisted that the theater was a place where moral teachings and aesthetic pleasure could be combined.[38] In this she continued a tradition of women's criticism of established theatrical productions associated with *Le journal des dames* and its editors, especially Louis-Sébastien Mercier (who helped her publish many of her plays and pamphlets).[39] Many of her plays took up current political themes: one, *Zamore et Mizrah, ou l'esclavage des nègres* (which demonstrates the shared humanity of blacks and whites), was closed after a few performances by the authorities in Paris in 1789 to satisfy an organization of slaveholders who feared it would encourage rebellion in the colonies.[40] In an early suggestion to the National Assembly, she called for the creation of a second national theater, this one for women. She assured those who doubted its potential for success that women had the talent to produce the many plays required to maintain a regular audience. "It is not up to me to reply on behalf of all my sex, but if I am to be the basis for judgment, I can offer thirty plays for consideration."[41]

In 1788 she entered politics with a pamphlet, *Lettre au Peuple, ou projet d'une caisse patriotique,* proposing that the Estates General (which had been summoned but had not yet met) could solve the financial crisis of the kingdom by establishing a patriotic fund consisting of voluntary contributions from all citizens. De Gouges said that she wrote as "a member of the Public"[42] to this same Public, that body of literate opinion which had emerged during the eighteenth century as an institutional counter to absolute royal authority.[43]

There was nothing unusual about identifying herself as a member of the Public. During the Old Regime, women were very much a part of the opposition to absolutism, and their activity took more and less overtly political forms. The salons, run by elite women, sponsored the discussions that contributed to what became a critical and dissenting "public opinion." This Public included women, but only those of wealth, education, and social grace.[44] De Gouges was not a *salonière*, and she did not participate in these polite, learned centers of sociability, although they provided one arena for a public role for women. Rather, she was associated with the more activist and reformist circles of journalists whose newspapers appealed to a wider and more disaffected constituency. Nina Gelbart sees this oppositional journalism—exemplified by *Le journal des dames* in its twenty-year history (1759–1778)— as the well-spring not only for de Gouges's demands that women participate in politics, but also for much of the republican feminism of the Revolution.[45]

As she appealed to her membership in the Public, de Gouges was nonetheless conscious of the limited credibility women had to speak about political matters. Their position was, in the later years of the Old Regime and in the early years of the Revolution, at best a matter for debate.[46] De Gouges argued persistently for full emancipation, against those who refused it and those who preferred to delay consideration. "This sex, too weak and too long oppressed, is ready to throw off the yoke of a shameful slavery." And she added, "I have placed myself at its head."[47] She reminded her readers that women were not taken seriously enough, even though, as her own wise suggestions demonstrated, they could be the source of clever and praiseworthy political ideas. Her writing was meant to dispute directly and by contrary example the notion that women were too vague and flighty for the serious business of government. It was true, she acknowledged, that some women were excessively devoted to "luxe," but even beautiful women would reduce the number of their purchases once the patriotic fund opened, "because beauty does not exclude reason and love of country."[48] Here she drew on ideas associated most in this period with the Girondin faction of republicans and especially with Condorcet, who wrote, "the rights of men result simply from the fact that they are sentient beings, capable of acquiring moral ideas and of reasoning concerning these ideas. Women, having these same qualities, must necessarily possess equal rights."[49] Functional and biological differences between the sexes were irrelevant, he argued, for they did not constitute "a natural difference between men and women which may legitimately serve as a foundation for the deprivation of a right."[50] For Condorcet, politics was an activity engaged in by people with varying identities; one became political, but politics did not define the whole person (man or woman). The political person was, in this sense, an abstract individual.

Condorcet's argument was itself located in what Keith Baker calls "a rationalist discourse of the social," originating with the physiocrats, and "grounded on notions of the rights of man, the division of labor, and the apolitical rule of reason."[51] But the case for the abstract individual contained a paradox: even a fully self-sufficient individual existed as such only in the eyes of an other. In the revolutionaries' rhetoric, the sexual division of labor solved the problem by ruling women out of the public sphere and denying to them the individuality required of citizens. But gender, of course, denied the abstractness (and the self-sufficiency) of the abstract individual.

When de Gouges argued for women's inclusion in politics on the grounds of their individuality, she ran up against the self/other problem. In the political discourse of her time, the independent individual was being constituted as the antithesis of the dependent female. Condorcet's notion of the abstract individual did not provide a full enough answer for de Gouges.[52] How in the end would de Gouges secure the individuality of woman? Was symmetry possible in the self/other, man/woman opposition, or would the equality of women somehow deprive men of the individuality conferred by an other by making everyone the same? Could others simply be other selves (male or female), with gender making no difference, or would the absence of gender confuse the boundaries in a self-regarding narcissism? These were the nagging questions that Condorcet's call for an equality based on shared human reason did not address. His writing nonetheless fueled de Gouges's arguments and her actions.

De Gouges crafted an identity as a member of the Public from available ideas about women, reason, and public opinion (all of which were matters of controversy). In the heated atmosphere of the Revolution, with many definitions of appropriate behavior open to reinterpretation, she imagined herself—and became—a political figure of some visibility. She did this not by reproducing the role of politically active men, but by appropriating political action for women. For every designation of herself as "a man of state," for every invocation of her "beneficent genius," there is a reference to her femininity.[53] "It is a woman who dares to show herself so strong and courageous for her King and her country."[54] "Oh people, unhappy citizens, listen to the voice of a just and feeling woman."[55] One of her pamphlets was titled *Le cri d'un sage: Par une femme.* When she put herself forward to defend Louis XVI during his trial she suggested both that sex ought not to be a consideration ("leave aside my sex") and that it should be ("Heroism and generosity are also women's portion, and the Revolution offers more than one example of it").[56] The point was not to establish women's likeness to men in order to qualify for citizenship, but to refute the prevailing equation of active citizenship with masculinity, to make sexual difference irrelevant for politics *and,* at the same time, to associate women—explicitly as women—with the notion of the "active" subject. But when the active citizen was already defined as a male individual, how could she make the case for women?

The apparent contradiction—between the irrelevance and relevance of sexual difference, between equality and difference—was at the heart of the feminist project of making women political subjects. The attempt to achieve this project involved an act of self-creation, in which a woman defining herself as a woman enacted the public/political role usually performed by men. "She made herself a man for the country."[57] But this led de Gouges, inevitably, to the paradoxical "logic of semblance." To the extent that her imitation was successful, it pointed up the difference she sought to overcome, a difference she constantly remarked on with a kind of wonder and joy (look, her references to herself proclaim, here is a woman making herself a Man!). To the extent that the difference of Woman then evoked the active/passive distinction, the resemblance she had achieved established not autonomy, but its antithesis. De Gouges assumed the role reserved for men instrumentally, in order to make it available to women. This enactment challenged received understandings of feminine and masculine qualities by exposing the necessarily contradictory nature of the exclusive association of "Man" and active "Citizen," but it also could be read (as it was in 1793) as inauthentic because it was a misidentification, and thus as confirmation of the grounds for exclusion.

For de Gouges the active imagination led to, literally produced, active citizenship. Indeed, in her use of the one to attain the other, de Gouges reveals something of the connection between them. In both terms, "active" connotes independence and productivity, the workings of reason in the exercise of individual initiative. Those who had an active imagination, in Voltaire's definition of it, were self-governing. They had the ability to produce the ideas, images, and, by extension, institutions and laws that ordered and changed societies. Theirs was the work of art and science, but also of law and politics. Thus the Abbé de Sièyes described active citizens in 1789 as those with sufficient education and reason to participate in the creative work of the nation.[58] Only autonomous, self-creating men were qualified, he argued, to represent themselves in the exercise of the vote. (This representation was reliable because sign and referent were one.) De Gouges's insistence on the imaginative basis for her own thought and action was meant to establish her autonomy, her ability to produce an authentic self (not a copy of anything else)—to be what she claimed to be—and so her eligibility for the franchise.

By taking the stance of an active citizen, de Gouges challenged the Revolution's continuing definition of women as passive citizens, expanding a debate that focused almost entirely on men's rights, to include those of women. The distinction between active and passive citizens rested on contrasting theories of natural rights that were developed long before 1789. Those who enjoyed active rights were considered individual agents, capable of making moral choices, exercising liberty, and speaking on their own behalf (literally, representing themselves). It was they whose common interest as propertyholders enabled them to realize the social interest—the basis on which a unified nation could rest. Those who enjoyed passive rights were, in a functional division of labor, protected or taken care of by others; they had "the right to be given or allowed something by someone else."[59] (This definition echoes Diderot's equation of women and passivity: they were taken over, inhabited by passion, molded by the impressions of others.)

Historians of natural rights theories usually describe active and passive rights as antithetical systems of law that cannot prevail at the same time. But this does not reckon with the ingenuity of the French revolutionaries, who, in their first effort at constitution-making in 1791, reconciled their fear of democracy and their commitment to liberty by establishing two categories of citizen—the active and the passive. Nor does it take account of how gender operates within the universal languages of political theory.

In the Assembly's debate on the constitution of 1791, the minority position (one de Gouges supported) was articulated by deputy Camille Desmoulins: "The active citizens," he told his colleagues, "are those who took the Bastille."[60] The majority that prevailed, however, refused the notion that political action established citizenship and defined instead two categories of citizenship. Active citizens were men over twenty-five who were independent (they could not be domestic servants) and who possessed measurable wealth (they had to pay a direct tax equivalent to three days of labor). The prerequisite was property in the forms of land, money, and the self. After the fall of the monarchy in 1792, a more inclusive interpretation of citizenship prevailed: all men over twenty-one and self-supporting were granted the vote, and women were explicitly denied it. But the active/passive distinction did not entirely disappear, even if it was no longer mentioned in official political documents. The theory of representation on which it was based—one that derived unity from a social division of labor and a shared social interest—endured. It differentiated between those entitled to select representatives (literally, to be represented in and as the nation) and those denied that right, those capable of self-representation and those who could only be represented, those with and without autonomy.[61] These latter were largely, though not exclusively, women.

Unlike distinctions of wealth, those of gender were deemed natural and so outside the legislative arena. Since constitutions and legal decrees dealt, for the most part, with the rules of (active) political participation, references to passive rights were dropped. But invisibility did not mean absence. The terms *citoyen* and *citoyenne* carried the active/passive contrast, and from time to time it was clearly invoked—

by the exasperated Chaumette, for example, who, as he denounced Olympe de Gouges to a group of women protesting the closing of their political clubs in 1793, shouted (I imagine), "Impudent women who want to become men, aren't you well enough provided for? What else do you need?"[62]

De Gouges took up Desmoulins's definition of active citizenship and jumped into the fray. She moved with "public opinion" into print, the streets, and the forum of the National Assembly. She rented lodgings adjacent to the Assembly to facilitate her attendance at its sessions. She spoke from the podium at meetings of various clubs and at least once rushed to the rostrum in the Assembly; her proclamations on everything from the abolition of slavery and the rights of illegitimate children to the royal veto and maternity hospitals often covered the walls of the city of Paris. She conceived plans for a huge funeral cortège for a hero of the nation in 1792 in order to demonstrate women's support for and importance to the Revolution, and she agitated among officials until it was carried out. In 1791, acting as a self-appointed legislator, she wrote a *Declaration of the Rights of Woman and Citizen* that she urged be adopted as a supplement to the constitution. Even when, as in this instance, her projects were ignored, she behaved as a person charged with shaping the future of France.

Although de Gouges's spoken eloquence was admired by her contemporaries, for herself it was writing that constituted the most important form of political action. This writing is the more striking because she apparently accomplished it with great difficulty, dictating her texts to a secretary. She felt it was worth the expense and the effort, however, since writing, unlike speech, was a way of communicating her ideas in lasting form, of maintaining what was otherwise a transient relationship between herself and her auditors. Whereas speech required a physical audience, the written word could be transmitted to a vast public, the variety and number of whose members was limited only by her imagination.[63]

De Gouges enacted Rousseau's anxiety that writing was a less authentic means of expression than speech, that its marks imperfectly stood in for an absent speaker. She used writing to establish her identity, just as Rousseau had. She exploited the paradox in the philosopher's position: writing may have been merely a supplement to speech, but it was the means he regularly chose to present his ideas, to demonstrate the consciousness identified by the signature "J.-J. Rousseau." And that signature, although it only substituted for the real man, also established his existence. This surely was the implication of de Gouges's repeated comparisons of herself with Rousseau and of her insistence on recognition of her standing as an author. Her emulation of him in both respects exposed the fact that, in his case as in hers, the existence of the man was the effect, rather than the origin, of his signature.[64]

For de Gouges, writing, signing, and publishing demonstrated, for her contemporaries and for posterity, what the law erased: the fact that women could be, already were, authors. Under revolutionary legislation women did not have the rights of authors, of individuals who possessed their intellectual property, because they did not have the rights of active citizens. To be recognized as an author, then, meant for de Gouges recognition as an individual and a citizen. Referring to her plays, which she argued proved that gender was no bar to talent, she called them her "property," the results of productive, creative labor. "Isn't it my asset? isn't it my property?" she asked rhetorically.[65] She considered the loss of the possibility of writing equivalent to the loss of life, as this oath to the veracity of her opinions in the 1788 *Lettre au Peuple* makes clear: "Oh, sublime truth, you who have always guided me, who uphold my opinions, take away the means of writing if ever I betray my conscience, which is illuminated by your light."[66] She described herself as irresistibly driven to write, as compelled by her "itch [*démangeaison*] to write."[67] "I had a craze to write, a craze to have myself published."[68] To have herself published ("de me faire imprimer") meant not only to see her work in print, but literally to have herself imprinted, to be the source of her own representation, to be established as an author, and so to secure her very identity.

Writing required, depended upon, the imagination of the author. And so de Gouges attributed her abilities, such as they were, to her imagination. She likened herself to the great thinkers of the age, not in her command of philosophy and political theory, but in her ability to "dream": "But don't expect to see me discuss these matters in political and philosophical discourses; only in dreams have I been able to pursue them."[69] By appealing to the imagination, de Gouges evoked notions of direct inspiration and disinterestedness that did not require education to be effective. In fact, education could be an obstacle to clear vision, she maintained, using Rousseau against himself to claim that her version of the story of man's social origins was more plausible than his. The philosopher was probably too brilliant, she argued, to imagine the true character of early man. ("Jean-Jacques was too enlightened for his genius to carry too far . . .") Whereas, she, de Gouges, "who feel the effects of this first ignorance, and who am placed and displaced at the same time in this enlightened century, my opinions may be taken to be more correct than his."[70] Here a similar innocence gives de Gouges the ability to make an imaginary identification with early humans, or at least makes her invented story more realistic. Imagination is a thinking process unmediated by erudition; it thus transmits images that are closer to nature and to truth. "I am, in my writings, a student of nature; I should be, like her, irregular, even bizarre, but also always true, always simple."[71]

This Romantic (Rousseauian) conception of imagination comes perilously close to rejecting the discipline of reason entirely. It is described as almost purely reflective, the passive imagination's reproduction of nature itself. In de Gouges's account nature has nothing of the hierarchy men create; it is characterized instead by anarchic but harmonious confusion: "Look, search, and then distinguish if you can, the sexes in the administration of nature. Everywhere you will find them mixed up [confondus], everywhere they cooperate harmoniously in this immortal masterpiece."[72] Similarly, on the question of color, de Gouges argued that nature provided no model for the distinctions that men invent: "Man's color is nuanced, like all the animals that nature has produced, as well as the plants and minerals. Why doesn't the night rival the day, the sun the moon, and the stars the firmament? All is varied, and that is the beauty of nature. Why then destroy her work?"[73] But while de Gouges claimed that nature proved her points, she also insisted that her readings were more than simple reflections. Her projects might take their lead from nature, but they were productive arrangements, extensions to human society of what she had seen. In this sense, her imagination was active, not passive: considered thought acting on transparent truth.

When it came to imagination, de Gouges refused to accept the limits of gender. Like Condorcet, she argued that reason and the capacity to imagine knew no boundaries of sex. She offered evidence of her own self-regulating abilities when she attributed a mistaken judgment she had made (about the King's good intentions toward the National Assembly) to the temporary loss of bearings of her imagination (my imagination "wandered," she explained). The acknowledgment of this loss was itself a correction, an exemplary instance of her capacity for self-control.[74]

For de Gouges imagination offered a good way of escaping the restrictive boundaries of gender and of demonstrating new and contrary kinds of relevance for it. In *Séance royale,* subtitled *Les songes patriotiques,* dedicated to the Duc d'Orléans in 1789, de Gouges envisioned a royal session in which first the Duke and then the King spoke, reasserting the need for the royal veto (which the Assembly wanted to abolish). De Gouges spoke in several voices to make her point. First, in her own, she dedicated the pamphlet to the Duke, and reminded him of the need for recognition for women authors as well as of his promise to help secure a commission for her son. She linked her particular situation to the needs of her sex: "it is dreadful that women don't have the same advantages as men for the advancement of their children." Then she spoke as the Duke, proposing her plan to the king. "Well, Sir, a woman, an ignorant being, a visionary spirit . . . has the courage to alert her King to the sole means that can save France." Then she took the voice of the King, insisting on the royal prerogative in the name of his paternal duties to his people, the Nation. Then Orléans spoke again, proposing as articles for the constitution, along with the veto, divorce and the rights of illegitimate children to equal standing in society.[75] (De Gouges was particularly adept at inserting feminist demands into other political agendas. When she wrote the *Declaration of the Rights of Woman,* she dedicated it to Marie Antoinette, holding out the promise that if the Queen supported it, she would regain the adulation of her subjects.)

In one reading, *Les songes patriotiques* is like a play with three long monologues; it is undeniable that de Gouges used the form with which she was familiar to advance her political ideas. But, in another reading, the pamphlet is an example of the political potential of dreamwork; dreaming (which was synonymous with imagining) permitted an extraordinary mobility both for de Gouges, who assumed at least three

identities (two of them male), and for the characters she invented. The
Duc d'Orléans became an ardent supporter of feminist claims as he
defended monarchical power; a dream perhaps, but its appearance in
print might influence the real Duke's thinking, de Gouges suggested
coyly, and so "will, perhaps, come close to reality."[76]

As dreams called into question, and even renegotiated, the boundary
between fiction and reality, so they also tampered with established lines
of sexual difference. De Gouges's repeated descriptions of herself as a
"man" might be taken by some readers today as an example of a
transgressive sexuality.[77] But I do not think that was the issue for her.
If anything, she sought to eliminate the question of sexual identity from
discussions of politics, all the while assuming the importance of heterosexual attraction in human social relationships. She did not advocate that women become men physically or psychically, and she thought
that desire for the opposite sex played a role in the construction of the
self. She wanted to produce a political identity for women that at once
appropriated those (supposedly masculine) qualities required to assert
individuality and incorporated them into a definably female subject. It
was emulation—the drive to acquire for oneself the moral virtues of
an idealized figure—that was at stake.[78] Emulation was not the acquisition of the fixed traits of masculinity; rather it was the enactment of
the continuing process of self-construction then reserved for men. But
where was the affirmation of the self to come from? In the economy
of heterosexual attraction it had to come from woman's other: man.

De Gouges seems to have taken heterosexuality for granted in her
own life and as a social force, much as Rousseau did in his visions of
politics. But there was a twist to her imaginings. Although she often
described her dreams as realizable because of women's ability to inspire
desire in men, she also explained her actions as the result of her own
desire. "Only the well-being of my country and the love and respect I
have for my King, only these have excited my verve." She sought to
inspire similar imagination in others, "to inflame them with the love
of country that I feel penetrates me."[79] The statement has a familiar
hyperbolic ring, but it does assume female agency.

De Gouges accepted Rousseau's notion that woman was somehow
responsible for provoking man's desire, but this was only half the story.
Love and marriage were based on the "reciprocal leanings" of the

couple. In *Le bonheur primitif de l'homme,* she attributed to adultery
the transition from a harmonious large family to a more complex
society: bored with his own wife and with the uniformity of life around
him, one of the sons of the first father coveted his neighbor's wife and
eventually seduced her. De Gouges described the woman as "weak and
more guilty than her lover," presumably because she failed to control
his desire, but also because she failed to control her own: "The same
vice, the same tendency, subjugated her reason and her virtue."[80]

For Rousseau, the gentle feeling of love meant its contradiction:
man's desire for the unique possession of the love object led to the
discord and jealousy that animated society and politics. For de Gouges,
in contrast, love and desire could be disruptive, but this disruption was
not inevitable. Social institutions rendered desire good or bad, and
these were changeable human constructions. To secure change she
campaigned for the rights of illegitimate children and drew up a prototype for a new kind of marriage contract in which each parent
recognized offspring as legitimate "from whatever bed they come."[81]
She insisted, in the *Declaration of the Rights of Woman,* that the right
of free speech entailed the right of women to reveal the identity of the
fathers of their children ("without being forced by barbarous prejudice
to hide the truth"). These proposals all accepted the inevitability of
men's and women's desire and sought to render its social and personal
outcomes innocuous. In effect, de Gouges denied that male possessive-
ness was a necessary accompaniment of love, instead suggesting greater
fluidity for the imaginative projections that constituted this emotion.
If she believed that women could stir men to action (she boasted once
that "nothing can resist our seductive organ"),[82] she had none of
Rousseau's misogynist fantasies that this was a power that could totally
engulf any man. Rather female sexual desire was an equal component
in the construction of the heterosexual couple and of the selfhood of
each partner. It was the result not of men's objectification of women,
but of women's own desire for another, the expression of a woman's
willing self.

De Gouges actively sought alternatives to women's political subordination. When she claimed the rights of Man for women, she sought to
realize woman's individuality, not by rejecting sexual difference, but by
equalizing its operations. For her, the imaginative identification of

Woman with Man involved not the restructuring of sexual identity itself, but the enlargement of its social and political possibility.

The *Declaration of the Rights of Woman and Citizen* was a step in that direction. In it, she sought to provide the grounds on which active citizenship for women could be granted. Her *Declaration*'s seventeen articles exactly paralleled those of the Declaration of the Rights of Man, most often replacing the singular "Man" with the phrase "Woman and Man," but also making a particularly strong case for the recognition of women's right to speech as the key to their freedom. The document is both compensatory—adding women where they have been left out— and a critical challenge to the universality of the term "Man." Simply by pluralizing the reference, de Gouges indicates that "Man" alone does not represent humanity. If Woman is not specified, she is excluded; her inclusion requires that her difference from Man be acknowledged in order to be rendered irrelevant from the point of view of political rights.[83] That surely is the meaning of the stunning assertion that concludes the preamble to the *Declaration of the Rights of Woman:* "the sex superior in beauty as in courage during childbirth recognizes and declares, in the presence and under the auspices of the Supreme Being, the following rights of woman and citizen."

In articles X and XI, de Gouges restated the Revolution's guarantees of freedom of opinion and of the free expression of ideas, but she added explicit reasons for acknowledging that these rights also belonged to women. "Woman has the right to mount to the scaffold; she ought equally to have the right to mount to the tribune."[84] "Monter à la tribune" meant not only to speak in public, but specifically to address the assembled delegates of the nation. If women were subject to the coercive power of the law, de Gouges argued here, they ought also to be subjects of the law, that is, active participants in its formulation.

Article XI called speech women's most precious right and then specified the reason: "The free communication of ideas and opinions is one of the most precious rights of woman, since this liberty guarantees that fathers will recognize their children. Any citizen [*citoyenne*] can thus say freely: I am the mother of your child, without being forced by barbarous prejudice to hide the truth . . ." In this formulation, freedom of speech not only leads to shared responsibility for children by both parents; it also undercuts the image of men as purely rational, by calling attention to them as sexual beings. It gives voice to the oppressed to expose the transgressions of the powerful, to demand enforcement of the obligations on which social cohesion and individual liberty were said to rest. De Gouges's article XI assumes, as Rousseau did not, that women will tell the truth, even about such matters as pregnancy—usually unverifiable by any but themselves. It makes pregnancy an epistemological rather than a natural problem, and it insists *maternity* that maternity is a social, not a natural function. The article moves between the registers of universality and particularity; it names a specific interest women have in the exercise of the right of speech and a specific interest men have in denying them that right. It thereby vitiates the very idea of universality, showing it to be a cover for a particular (male) interest. The specificity of the article also exposes and refutes the implicit ground for excluding women from the ranks of active citizens: their reproductive role. In de Gouges's *Declaration* women *and* men are agents of reproduction; as such both are entitled to a public voice. De Gouges refused the oppositions—between public and private, productive and reproductive, reasonable and sexual, political and do- *opposition* mestic—by which the revolutionaries tried to justify the consignment of women to the ranks of passive citizens. Appealing to the possibility that gender was not a difference that mattered for politics—a possibility still alive in the proposals of Condorcet and some members of the Gironde—she wrote, "The principle of all sovereignty resides in the Nation. It is nothing but the coming together [*la réunion*] of Woman and Man." *"social contract"*

She went on, in a postscript to the *Declaration,* to reconceive that joining of Woman and Man in a new form of "social contract." The revolutionaries had included in the constitution of 1791 the statement that marriage was a civil contract, primarily to detach it from control by the church. But the move to laicize marriage in these terms opened the way for the divorce laws of September 1792 (which allowed either partner to dissolve an unsatisfactory or unhappy marriage) and for proposals like de Gouges's, aimed at restating the terms of the contract itself.[85] Designed to replace marriage, "the tomb of love and trust," de Gouges's marital contract declared the complete equality of the spouses. There were, of course, differences between them; otherwise the notion of union would be unnecessary. But these differences implied neither hierarchy nor the social and political exclusion of women. The couple was "united, but equal in force and virtue"; union neither subordinated one to the other, nor erased the visibility and function of the woman. Instead the partners had individual discretion with regard to transmission of property; children could be given either a father's or a mother's name; and all children were legitimate, whether they were the offspring of the union or of other alliances. Families became units of love and affection that transcended the particular desires of marital partners, which were taken to be inconstant. Above all, de Gouges's "social contract" ended the subordination of women by denying husbands discretionary authority over property and children; patriarchal power was swept away with the elimination of the father's name as the legal signifier of the family.[86]

De Gouges considered her proposals for a reform of marriage to be within the boundaries of the universal law upon which societies were based. In her view they offered a new arrangement of relationships between women and men similar to other new arrangements created by the Revolution. If the hierarchy of estates could be replaced by a National Assembly, if sovereignty could be granted to the people, then why not entertain plans to end slavery and alter the legal bonds of marriage? These plans would not only make French laws conform to the principles of universal law, she argued; they would also improve morals and make women more virtuous.[87]

Although she appealed to law in a straightforward way, however, her notion of it was contradictory. De Gouges accepted the premise that law was a key to coherence in society; but her conception of universal law incorporated a symbolic (masculine) representation that ultimately subverted her plans for reform. This conception was set forth in the story de Gouges told about the origin of society. It began with a family gathered around the bed of its dying father, whose last words pronounced the law that would guide his children in his absence. Although he recognized their tendency to "disobedience and revolt," he knew his children also wanted "to be subordinated" to his law. After recounting the history of his emergence from a savage state (in which observation of a bird's nest gave him ideas about how to shelter himself and his family from the elements), he offered his law. The key to happiness, he said, lay in cooperation, care for the earth, equality, and especially in the golden rule: "respect absolutely the rights of your brothers, neighbors, and friends." Violators should be driven from the family, excluded from all benefits of society.[88]

This father's law is designed to control the impulses that run counter to equality and happiness. It is through this law that the father creates his family and society; his is not a biological, but a regulatory role. Moreover, there is no first mother in de Gouges's account. Aside from one reference by the father to his "compagne," the mother who presumably gave birth to these children is invisible, absent, irrelevant. Symbolically, the elimination of the mother in this origin story establishes the autonomy of the father (and subsequently of his sons) in social and political matters. Women are one of the things that men ("brothers, neighbors, friends") have individual rights to; even though de Gouges describes marriage as a union of equals based on mutual inclination, women are never associated with the articulation of law or the creation of society. The lawgiver is male. "Brothers, neighbors, and friends" who subject themselves to the law do so by identifying themselves with the father; they in turn become subjects—lawmakers. The "brothers', neighbors', friends'" identification with the father depends on a shared maleness that consists both in the right of uncontested sexual access to a woman and in the exclusion of women from the realms of politics and law. The symbolism of the male lawgiver, in other words, establishes the terms of heterosexual monogamy and the restriction of citizenship to men. This symbolism enacts sexual difference as an asymmetrical relationship in which woman guarantees the individuality of man.[89] It provides some of the meanings that associate women with "natural" functions of childbearing and sex and men with social reproduction and rationality. As such it sits paradoxically with de Gouges's goal to end the subordination of women in political life. It seems that her acceptance of her culture's symbolic construction of sexual difference was fundamentally at odds with de Gouges's practical suggestions for reform of the institution of marriage.

Her symbolic association of law with masculinity led de Gouges to endorse monarchy as the most coherent form of government. (She adjusted her ideas to the behavior of Louis XVI in the course of the Revolution, condemning his flight and treasonable actions in June 1791, but then supporting him after his arrest. In the circumstances of the

pro monarchy?

Terror she announced that she was "born with a republican character and would die with it," but in her general discussions of government she seems to have preferred monarchy.)[90] De Gouges often referred to the king as "the father of his people," but she considered him more than an ordinary father, and she did not think that male predominance in families followed from a nation's need for a king. For her the king was a wise lawgiver, the embodiment of the law itself. Like the magistrate evoked in the *Encyclopédie*'s entry on "dreams," the king was the external figure responsible for order and rational administration. The presence of the king guaranteed flexibility in the personal relations of his subjects because it established limits for those relations. The extent of these limits depended on the magistrate, the expert charged with maintaining boundaries in the name of reason. According to de Gouges, kings were best suited for the job because they had the most developed capacity for disinterested and benevolent leadership. One of the problems with a republic was that there was no obvious figure to stand above the fray as lawgiver; there were only lawmakers, imperfect, unreliable and conflicting siblings contending for the first father's role. Another problem with the republic was that it was already in the hands of sons, who would not readily share power with their sisters. A king, she felt, would have no stake in establishing a monopoly for his sons; his benevolence would allow him to see the merits of a case made by the likes of de Gouges for the recognition of the political rights of women.[91] De Gouges's endorsement of monarchy thus served as both a critique of and a correction to the exclusionary practices of the republic.

De Gouges did not think that male monopolies of political power followed from monarchy. Her writings therefore had the contradictory effect of both reproducing and seeming to undermine the idea of law as the Law of the Father. She conceived of her proposals for marriage reform as a way of challenging women's exclusion from politics, but she did not think them subversive of the very order of her society. Others, however, did. Her early endorsement of kingship was taken as a sign of her disloyalty to the Revolution in the same way as her campaign to extend the rights of Man to women. While support for the monarchy was, in de Gouges's terms, support for the law, others saw her campaign to reform marriage and make women active citizens as a threat to erase the lines of sexual difference that established the authority of the law. (That they were treated as aspects of the same crime suggests more of a connection between them than de Gouges herself understood.) De Gouges did keep in place a notion of sexual difference, understanding it to be established through mutually experienced heterosexual attraction, but this was ultimately not enough to keep her within the boundaries of the law.

———————■———————

In the early days of the Revolution there was no limit placed on the imagination. Ordinary citizens were free to invent political schemes and to dream of new futures for France, as long as they did not have the power to put them into practice. In this context de Gouges's activity was tolerated; her proposals might be dismissed as wild and improbable, but they seemed to pose no great threat. The consolidation of Jacobin rule from late 1792 on, however, brought with it a tightening of the connection between law, order, masculine virtue, and sexual difference and so an attempt by the state to control the expression, if not the experience, of imagination. Jacobin politics were based on an epistemological view that attributed singular and transparent meaning to physical objects, language, thought, and visual representation.

From this perspective de Gouges's challenges became dangerous. Her calls to imagination implied a wanton disregard for reality, for the established correspondence between ideas and things. In her writings and actions she seemed willfully to obscure clear issues by trafficking in signs whose referents were ambiguous.

Although the issue of women's rights had come up many times in the course of the Revolution, it was repeatedly and directly addressed in 1793. That year, during discussion of a new constitution (which was never implemented), the deputy for Ile-et-Vilaine, Jean Denis Lanjuinais, reported to the Convention that despite several pleas to the contrary, his committee would uphold the denial of the vote to women. Even in the future, he argued, "it is difficult to believe that women will be called to exercise political rights. It is beyond me to think that, taking all into account, men or women would gain anything good from it."[92]

After the execution of Marie Antoinette on October 16, attacks on women's political role became more vehement. Using the occasion of a street disturbance between market women and members of the Society of Revolutionary Republican Women, the Convention outlawed all women's clubs and popular societies, invoking Rousseauian themes to justify its actions. "Should women exercise political rights and meddle in the affairs of government?" asked André Amar, the representative of the Committee on General Security. "In general, we can answer, no." Because they would be obliged to sacrifice the more important cares to which nature calls them. The private functions for which women are destined by their very nature are related to the general order of society; this social order results from the differences between man and woman. Each sex is called to the kind of occupation which is fitting for it; its action is circumscribed within this circle which it cannot break through, because nature, which has imposed these limits on man, commands imperiously and receives no law.[93]

An even more explicit articulation of these so-called natural facts came from Chaumette. On behalf of the Commune of Paris he indignantly rejected an appeal for support from female petitioners protesting the Convention's decree: "Since when is it permitted to give up one's sex? Since when is it decent to see women abandoning the pious cares of their households, the cribs of their children, to come to public places, to harangues in the galleries, at the bar of the Senate? Is it to men that nature confided domestic cares? Has she given us breasts to feed our children?"[94]

Like many of his fellow politicians, Chaumette appealed to the rules of nature to justify his vision of social organization. In his understanding, nature was the source of both liberty and sexual difference. Nature and the body were synonymous; in the body one could discern the truths upon which social and political order must rest. Whereas Condorcet (and de Gouges with him) had insisted on a separation between biology and political identity, the Jacobins offered a totalizing vision. Constantin Volney, who had represented the Third Estate of Anjou at the meetings of the Estates General in 1788–89, argued in his catechism of 1793 that virtue and vice "are always ultimately referable to . . . the destruction or preservation of the body." For Volney, questions of health were questions of state; "civic responsibility is health-seeking behavior."[95] Individual illness signified social deterioration; the failure of a mother to breastfeed her infant constituted a refusal of nature's corporeal design, hence a profoundly antisocial act. The misuse of the body incurred not only individual costs but also social consequences, since the body politic was, for Volney, not a metaphor but a literal description.

The body, of course, was not considered a singular object; sexual difference was taken as a founding principle of the natural, hence the social and political, order. For establishing social and political distinctions between men and women, genital difference made all the difference: masculinity or femininity constituted the entire identity of biological males or females. Dr. Pierre Roussel had earlier articulated the view the Jacobins adopted: "The essence of sex is not confined to a single organ but extends, through more or less perceptible nuances, into every part."[96] And women, in this scheme, were more thoroughly defined by sex than men. The anatomist Dr. Jacques-Louis Moreau offered as his own Rousseau's comment that the location of the genital organs, inside in women, outside in men, determined the extent of their influence: "the internal influence continually recalls women to their sex . . . the male is male only at certain moments, but the female is female throughout her life."[97]

For the Jacobins, women's entire social function could be read literally from her body's reproductive organs, and especially from her breasts (an external organ!). The breast was the synecdoche for woman; it appeared with great frequency in Jacobin speeches and iconography (as Madelyn Gutwirth has so amply demonstrated).[98] The breast had many resonances, since the word *sein* in French means chest, breast, and uterus, but the fixation on the physical breast itself seems significant. It served as a fetish in the Freudian sense, drawing attention away from that which was most troubling to something seemingly more benign. The frenetic preoccupation with the breast, of course, called attention to the entire female body, but it also served to distract from that body's more problematic birth-giving function. Birth could, after all, be understood to be not only natural (and therefore prior to society), but also an act of social creation, part of—because indispensable to—the social contract. Indeed, the depiction in a royalist caricature of a revolutionary giving birth to a constitution (which has issued forth from between his legs) is a commentary on the revolutionaries' self-conscious usurpation of women's social role. This usurpation was not accomplished, however, by banishing women's bodies. Quite the contrary. The concealment of women's social body was achieved through the proliferation of images of her physical body. As women were definitively excluded from politics, their bodies were represented with obsessive frequency, most typically as nursing mothers.[99] In August 1793, at the fête of Unity and Indivisibility staged by Jacques-Louis David to honor the Republic, this iconography was writ large. The deputies came forward to pledge their loyalty to the nation and then sealed their vows by drinking (water) that was spouting from the breast of a statue of an oversized maternal figure. Underscoring the difference between male and female was a contrast between West and East: the statue was a fertile Egyptian goddess.[100]

Woman as breast—nurturer, but not creator. Man as citizen—the conqueror of nature. The differences between women and men were taken to be irreducible and fundamental; they existed in nature and therefore could not be corrected by law. The functional complementarity of male and female was considered to be asymmetrical: the association of masculinity with virtue, reason, and politics depended for its realization on a contrast with femininity, defined as devious, sensual, vain, given to artifice and the whims of fashion, and for those reasons necessarily restricted to modest, domestic functions. In fact it can be argued that the opposition between men and women, reason and passion, was a way of displacing the disorderly impulses of sex onto women, impulses that Rousseau had recognized could not be uprooted from the male imagination. His Jacobin followers, however, entertained no sense of irony or ambiguity. As they attributed all political opposition to enemies of the Republic, so they attributed to women the qualities they considered the antithesis of virtue—that virtue, according to Robespierre, which was the fundamental principle of democratic government and which, in time of revolution, drew its potency from terror, "justice prompt, severe and inflexible . . . an emanation of virtue."[101]

Terror was the repression of all that was contrary to virtue; it was the implementation of truth in the face of error. It was driven by those whose virtue enabled them to know the difference between truth and error, nature and its misrepresentations. Truth was transparent to the virtuous; its meaning was literal and unambiguous. There was no room here for Voltaire's active imagination, that creative recombination that might produce new ideas, but that also might confuse fiction and reality. Instead, ideas must be direct readings of nature; imagination was ruled out of order lest it misrepresent the truth.

In this context de Gouges began to deny that her ideas had anything to do with an active imagination. Earlier, in 1791, she had attributed to the temporary wandering of her imagination a misplaced enthusiasm for the monarchy. In that instance she was eager to demonstrate her ability to distinguish the good and bad workings of her imagination, to put brakes on its disorderly tendencies. In 1793, however, she entirely discounted the influence of imagination. When she predicted a dismal future for the Revolution, she insisted that her thoughts were a reflection of the reality of "the depraved morals" of France's leaders and not the product of her own "exalted imagination."[102] With biting sarcasm she wrote to Robespierre that his discourses on morality had brought her to her senses, making her aware of the need "to repress in myself those stirrings of exaltation that a sensible soul ought always to mistrust, and which the seditious know so well how to exploit."[103] This broadside went on to attack his lack of virtue and his self-interested behavior, and it condemned the excesses of his "misguided patriotism" ("patriotisme égaré") in the name of "truth." At the same time, de Gouges identified herself as "plus homme que femme," unable entirely to dissociate her active imagination from her quest for individuality, even as she claimed only to see and speak the truth.[104]

In any case, her attack on Robespierre only confirmed her fate as a woman whose private fantasies had intruded unacceptably on public life. She was arrested in July 1793, and subsequently sentenced to death, for having placarded the walls of Paris with a poster advertising her brochure, *Les trois urnes, ou Le salut de la patrie,* which advocated federalism (a position associated with the Girondists and their theories of representation).[105] She appealed her sentence by pointing to her patriotism (her philosophical writings, she insisted, had helped to prepare the Revolution) and by claiming first that she was ill and then that she was pregnant. The public prosecutor, Fouquier-Tinville, investigated and reported to the Revolutionary Tribunal that de Gouges had had no opportunity to become pregnant and that the midwife and doctor called in to verify her condition had been unable to do so. Given these facts, he suggested that de Gouges had "only imagined" an occasion for contact with a man and a subsequent pregnancy in order to postpone or avoid execution.[106] There was a terrible irony in Fouquier-Tinville's reference to de Gouges's imagination at this moment. It was as if her mental disorder had gone so far that even her own attempt to recall the most fundamental aspect of her nature—her womanhood (defined as her ability to reproduce)—must be derided as a figment of her imagination. The sign of woman could have no referent in the monstrous Olympe de Gouges.

It was as a traitor to Jacobin centralism (equated with preservation of the integrity of the Republic) that de Gouges was finally put to death in November. In July, when she was arrested, the danger of national dismemberment threatened, in the form not only of civil war and imminent invasion, but also of gender transgression and personal dissolution. The Jacobin response was to tighten the reins of control and, since political and personal control were equated, to evaluate the one in terms of the other.[107] It is in this light that we can read the report of de Gouges's death carried by *La feuille du salut public:* "Olympe de Gouges, born with an exalted imagination, mistook her delirium for an inspiration of nature. She wanted to be a man of state. She took up the projects of the perfidious people who want to divide France. It seems the law has punished this conspirator for having forgotten the virtues that belong to her sex."[108]

This was a particularly fitting epitaph for the woman who, as she spitefully denounced Robespierre, told him that she was "plus homme que femme" and who sought to exonerate herself by pointing out that she was "un grand homme," while he was a vile slave.[109] But it spoke as well to the perception that de Gouges had deliberately deserted reality, imaginatively departing from the existing social and political conditions of women's lives. In her desire to emulate Man, she had "forgotten the virtues of her sex," literally losing her way. The notion of forgetfulness recalls the loss of bearings of the dreamer, so longingly evoked by Rousseau and echoed by de Gouges ("I want . . . to try to lose myself like the others").[110] This loss was depicted here, however, not as a benign transcendence, but as pathology. The loss of de Gouges's coherent self (her "exalted imagination" overcame reason's internal regulation; she mistook her delusions for reality) and the adoption of perfidious projects aimed at "dividing France" are connected; indeed they are one and the same. The natural integrity of the self guarantees the natural integrity of the nation; both are compromised by unregulated desire, by the excesses of imagination. The discourse on federalism was produced by an imagination gone astray; and it was figured as a transgression of both geographic and gender boundaries. Only an "imagination exaltée," the product of a divided, incoherent self, could entertain the divisive idea of federalism, an onslaught on what was insistently referred to as the "Republic, one and indivisible."[111] Only such an imagination could have simultaneously generated the threats of political, social, and physical dismemberment—of castration.

In 1793, de Gouges was read as an embodiment of the danger of chaos and unlawfulness that "une imagination exaltée" or "l'imagination des songes" posed for rational social order and for the meanings of masculinity and femininity on which it had come to depend—a danger that for Rousseau, as for his Jacobin interpreters, was synonymous with women.

As with the eighteenth-century attempt to codify "imagination," so with de Gouges's use of it, sharp distinctions were impossible to maintain. Its ambiguity was both the source of her empowerment as an active citizen, even though women were given no such rights in the constitution of 1791, and the sign, for her opponents, of her inability to reason within the terms of the law. As with the notion of imagination itself, it was legal authority, acting in the name of reason, that decided whether and when she had crossed the line.

———————◼———————

Some months after de Gouges was sent to the guillotine, her son asked for and was granted a correction of the record. The name of his mother was to be changed in the minutes of the Revolutionary Tribunal from "Marie-Olympe de Gouges, veuve [widow] d'Aubry," to "Marie Gouze, veuve de Louis-Yves Aubry."[112] Pierre Aubry thus sought to restore his mother's identity as a daughter and wife, to set the record straight on her (and his own) genealogy. In fact this gesture changed little, and posterity remembered her by the name Olympe de Gouges had given herself. Historically, the reality of Olympe de Gouges was, in the best sense, the product of her imagination. And historians do her an injustice to ignore the importance of the performative in the establishment of her self. Whether reviled or revered, she was treated as an independent "woman of letters" whose writings and actions established her reputation.

That reputation had at least two sides, which played off the possibilities seen by Voltaire for the active imagination and spoke to the nineteenth century's increasing emphasis on the inventive definition of imagination.[113] E. Lairtullier, writing in 1840 in *Les femmes célèbres de 1789 à 1795*, referred to her as the fiery or ardent ("la fougueuse") Olympe de Gouges. She was one of the "furies" in his catalogue of types of revolutionary women. And he stressed the double aspect of the "brilliance" of her imagination: "More than once she surprised the most eloquent men of the day by the richness of her imagination and the fecundity of her ideas; and it was, to tell the truth, the brilliant side of celebrity that she did not hesitate to conquer."[114] Imagination for Lairtullier connoted a certain benign inventiveness, but it had another side, expressed through de Gouges's explosive nature, her emotional excesses, her inability to distinguish crude from informed ideas, and her provocative style. Her brilliant imagination seemed inevitably to have emanated from an eccentric and dangerous character.

Subsequent writers were clearer than Lairtullier in their diagnoses of mental disorder. De Gouges had crossed the boundary between reason and fantasy; taking on the role of a man, she had lost her bearings and her sanity. For Michelet, any intrusion by women into politics was dangerous: "all sides are destroyed by women."[115] In his account, de Gouges was "an unfortunate woman, full of generous ideas" who became "the martyr, the plaything of her unstable sensibility [*sa mobile sensibilité*]." Her true feminine nature was revealed, he wrote, when, "softened and wet with tears, she became a woman again [*elle se remit à être femme*], weak, trembling, she was afraid of death." At the guillotine, however, she was courageous (swinging back, he implies, to a more masculine position).[116] "Children of the fatherland," she cried, "you will avenge my death." And the spectators replied (with no irony, it seems), "Vive la République!"[117]

Michelet's characterization of de Gouges as unstable, oscillating between weakness and strength, feminine and masculine, recurs in the writings of the Goncourt brothers, who in their 1864 history of the Revolution labeled her "a heroic madman," using the masculine *fou* instead of the feminine *folle* to designate her malady.[118] The Goncourts' emphasis accorded with an increasing interest in psychiatric questions as defined by medical experts. This interest developed more fully by the end of the century and focused on collective as well as individual pathologies. Writing in 1904, a Dr. Guillois analyzed the records produced during de Gouges's arrest and diagnosed her as a case of revolutionary hysteria. Her abnormal sexuality (caused by excessive menstrual flow), her narcissism (evinced by a predilection for daily baths), and her entire lack of moral sense (proven by her repeated refusal to remarry) constituted the definitive signs of her mental pathology. De Gouges was an example of what happened when women tried to imitate men; driven by abnormal desires, they became courageous, but also more savage and cruel than any man.[119] For Guillois and his contemporaries an imagination gone astray was but a symptom of a defective or abnormal femininity. The problem lay not in the misuse of the mind's ability to imagine, but in a deviant sexuality, a fundamentally abnormal personality.

For nineteenth- and twentieth-century feminists, writing against these accumulating diagnoses of pathology, de Gouges was an entirely different figure, realizing the best of what the active imagination could produce.[120] She was remembered most for articulating the claim that became a motto of the nineteenth-century French feminist movement: "Woman has the right to mount the scaffold; she ought equally to have the right to mount to the tribune." This daring assertion had been made by a woman whose life and death exemplified its relevance. It was preeminently reasonable, taken to be a political adage rather than a fantastic invention. De Gouges's experience, moreover, seemed to figure the recurring fate of feminism: born of the republic, it was repeatedly sentenced to death by that same republic. It was in these terms that Jeanne Deroin (then in exile) reminded her readers of the price she and other feminists had paid for their actions in 1848: "Many, following the example of Olympe de Gouges, have had to pay with their lives for this devotion to Justice and Truth."[121] De Gouges was a martyr, and feminists believed she had died for their cause, the victim not of her own misdoings or disorders, but of the contradictions inherent in the republicans' definition of citizenship, and of their misapplications of the universal principles of liberty, equality and fraternity.

The concept of imagination was a condition of agency for Olympe de Gouges; it established her ability to act as a public, political figure. The agency of subsequent generations of feminists was shaped by other concepts, more central to the discursive configurations of their own times. But de Gouges was also incorporated into what might be called the feminist imaginary or the imagined (but for that no less real) feminist tradition. She was read out of her specific context and writ large as an example of courageous action; her words were used to inspire women of very different outlooks and beliefs from her own to take up the feminist cause. She was, in this way, both emulated and appropriated in much the way that she had taken on the role of the (male) active citizen in order to claim active citizenship for women. If the preoccupation with imagination in its relation to reason was specific to de Gouges's time, the process of creative recombination it involved was not. Her exercise of imagination drew on its ambiguities and exposed the contradictions it supported and contained. That this creative engagement was marked by paradox seems to be one of the characteristics of feminism, its way of testing the limits of the possible in the struggle to achieve women's political rights.

The Duties of the Citizen:
Jeanne Deroin in the
Revolution of 1848

During the Revolution of 1848, Jeanne Deroin thought of herself as an heir to Olympe de Gouges's campaign for women's rights. Although her own political formation in the utopian socialist movements of the 1830s and 1840s could not have been more different from the social and political influences on de Gouges, and although the politics of the 1848 revolution provided a different context for feminist struggle, Deroin was inspired by the sheer audacity of de Gouges's actions. To risk one's life for the cause of women's emancipation was an achievement that transcended the details of political engagement.

But details did matter, and they marked the differences between the two women. Deroin emerged, at age forty-three, as a political activist in the context of a new revolution. If de Gouges was a model for her action, the St. Simonians and Fourierists were her doctrinal mentors. Deroin's strategies addressed the rapidly unfolding events of the February revolution; in their content and their philosophical presuppositions they were necessarily different from those of 1792. In 1848 the right to work and the right to vote were inextricably intertwined; accordingly, Deroin organized associations of women workers to deal with their economic plight and to mobilize for the vote. In the outburst of journalistic freedom that followed the revolution, she wrote pamphlets and articles analyzing the relationships between social and economic reform and women's rights. She collaborated on *La voix des femmes* (The voice of women), the first feminist newspaper of the new republic, and then launched her own paper, *La politique des femmes*.

When women were forbidden to engage in politics in the summer of 1848, she changed the name of the paper to *L'opinion des femmes,* but without any intention of relinquishing her political engagement. Women's voice, opinion, and politics were undeniable, she thought, whether or not they were authorized by the government. In 1849, despite the fact that it was considered unconstitutional, Deroin stood for a seat in the Legislative Assembly.[1]

Unlike Olympe de Gouges, who often seemed caught between the needs simultaneously to avow and to disavow the position of women in order to argue for the equality of political rights, Deroin was clear in her endorsement of the special place held by women in the organization of social and spiritual life. She turned Romantic paeans to femininity and the feminine into arguments for feminism, and she used arguments about women's equality to challenge the limits of her socialist colleagues' visions of economic reform. (That these efforts were not without their contradictions is one of the themes of the following pages.) Usually offered by historians as an exemplar of the "difference" school of feminism, she is in fact a far more complicated figure. Jeanne Deroin's insistence on women's difference must be read as a feminist articulation of the utopian socialist critique of individualism. For such socialists, individualism was the ideological underpinning of the rapacious and destructive capitalism they hoped to replace with a more humane and cooperative society. Deroin's feminism offered an alternative to individualism by insisting on "sexual difference" as the basic unit of humanity. The couple, man and woman, she wrote, echoing the St. Simonians, was the "social individual." Deroin turned sexual difference into an argument for equality when for most of her contemporaries it was an argument against it. In this she both exposed the contradictions of the Second Republic's definitions of citizenship and revealed how difficult it was to depict the difference between the sexes as a symmetrical (rather than hierarchical) relationship.

———————■———————

The "right to work" was the rallying cry of the women and men who took to the barricades in February 1848 to bring down the constitutional monarchy of the Orleanist king Louis Philippe. More than a revelation about economic influences on the revolution (though certainly a comment on short- and long-term crises of wages and employment), the demand for the right to work posed a serious challenge to republican plans for electoral reform.[2] For it introduced what had come to be known as "the social question" into discussions of political rights; indeed it insisted that solutions to poverty and economic inequality must come from democratic governments not as philanthropic or expedient measures, but in recognition of a natural and inalienable human right. The right to work, as formulated by democratic-socialists (the left flank of this revolution), meant a guarantee of access, not just to a job, but to a livelihood, to the ability to earn a living wage. It refused political economy's vision of a market that functioned according to its own laws, and instead proposed government regulation in the name of the individual rights of the sovereign people. "The right to work has its origin and its legitimacy in the fundamental and absolute clauses of the social compact, and its justification in the natural need to work," wrote the jurist Louis Marie de Cormenin in his comments on the constitution.[3]

In the first days of the revolution, as crowds surged and politicians sought to contain them, the right to work was recognized cautiously by the Provisional Government: "The right to work is that of each man to live by working. Society ought, with the productive and general means at its disposal now and in the future, to provide work to able-bodied men who cannot find it themselves."[4] Even though that pronouncement would soon be qualified and later retracted, the fact that the right to work was proclaimed at the same time, and often in the same breath, as universal suffrage, introduced ambiguity into discussions of political rights. This ambiguity was apparent in the proclamation of March 16, in which the Provisional Government announced its plans for elections. First the right to vote was described as the "supreme right of man," the great equalizing force on the field of politics. "There will not be a citizen who can say to another, 'you are more sovereign than I.'" Then the significance of the vote was extended beyond the choice of government representatives to a larger realm: it was also "an exercise of social power" in the interests not only of individuals, but of specific social groups. From the fact that "the election belongs to all without exception" followed a remarkable conclusion: "From the day of this law, there will no longer be proletarians in France."[5]

On the one hand, the disappearance of the proletariat could mean simply the end of the *political* subordination or exclusion of a particular social group (in accord with liberal republican ideas about formal equality). On the other hand, it could mean the end of the social group itself, its dissolution in the great equalizing project of social reconciliation and justice. The ambiguity introduced when the right to work was linked to the right to vote made it impossible to determine which of these readings was intended and so kept the question of social distinction central in all considerations of rights. In the blurring of the line between formal and positive rights the abstract individual lost ground to the socially differentiated individual, and this individual was perforce located in a collective identity—in this period usually "the working classes," or "the proletarians," or "the poor." But the possibility for adding to the list was open, a possibility soon seized by feminists in the name of women.

The right to work forced consideration of social differences; it made politics a substantive matter of eliminating inequality. Universal (manhood) suffrage, from this perspective, was a commitment to the enactment and enforcement of positive rights. As such it contradicted the theory of formal political equality, articulated in terms of the rights of abstract individuals. In that theory, social differences were deemed irrelevant for purposes of determining political participation and were not to be the object of action or attention. Alexis de Tocqueville, defending the idea of formal rights, noted, "The Revolution required that politically there be no classes."[6] All men were on an equal footing as voters and as subjects of the law; this was the only kind of equality a democratic government could guarantee.[7]

But if the vote was the instrument for a social transformation and was every individual's right, then all those seeking social change must have the right to vote. On these grounds alone, women could make a claim. In addition, since women workers were included by those implementing the right to work in government employment centers and through government subvention of producer cooperatives, there seemed every reason to believe that women would also be considered citizens. If the right to work both preceded and followed from the right to vote, and if women's right to work had already been acknowledged in concrete acts of the government, how was it possible to deny them the vote? Not by direct exclusion, since only those serving criminal sentences were explicitly denied the franchise in the decrees of March 5 and 8 (all previous exclusions, including those of domestic servants, were abrogated). But by indirection. In the decree of March 16, which extolled the virtues of the suffrage ("the provisional electoral law which we have passed is the broadest that, for any people on the earth, has ever summoned the people to the exercise of the supreme right of man, his proper sovereignty"), citizens were defined as "all Frenchmen of virile age [*tout français en l'âge viril*]." [8]

Ostensibly seeking to clarify the ambiguity of the term "tout français"—*tout* in French, though masculine, was often used with no gender connotation and indeed had been used to include women when all were promised the right to work—a delegation of women from the newly formed Committee on the Rights of Woman (Comité des Droits de la Femme) met with Armand Marrast, mayor of Paris and member of the Provisional Government, on March 22. In the space opened by the February revolution's dreams of unlimited social regeneration and by its contradictory implementation of them, feminism emerged to insist on women's rights. [9]

The delegation was led by Jeanne Deroin, who articulated the women's concern thus: "We have come to ask you if women are included in the large generality in the same way that they are in the law concerning workers; we are even more justified in asking since you have not listed them in the categories to be excluded." [10] Deroin sought to force an acknowledgment of what was only implicit at this moment, but which would expose a contradiction if made explicit. Suffrage was pronounced to be universal, and women were not listed among those specifically excluded; yet this fact did not mean that they were included.

Marrast pointed to history. The Provisional Government, he said, was able only to restore lost rights (those recognized in the last republican constitution of 1793), not to create new ones, so the women's answer would have to await a constitution written by a soon-to-be-elected assembly (consisting entirely of men). [11] Although legislators sometimes were bound by precedent, this response was at best an evasion of the question, since the inclusion of women as citizens was never seriously contemplated. Indeed, I will argue that their exclusion was critical to attempts at reconciling the contradiction between formal and positive rights raised by the furor over the right to work.[12] A shared masculinity was the key to securing the universal status of citizens as abstract individuals; the right to work was translated as the right to property and family, and these were unequivocally the rights of men.

The issue of the right to work, important for the Provisional Government, became pressing for the elected legislators, who were in the process of writing the constitution of the Second Republic when civil war broke out in June. The June Days began as a protest against the dissolution of the National Workshops (which had been set up to provide jobs for the unemployed) in the name of "the right to work," and quickly escalated into a social uprising.[13] For the legislators the uprising demonstrated what could happen if workers considered substantive rights to be their due; their mood was far more determinedly conservative after June than before.

As they debated the "right to work" the legislators considered whether the government owed its citizens (as a fulfillment of some right) jobs and sufficient wages to support themselves and their families. Some argued that such "communism" was antithetical to a free society and that it would actually depress the incentive to work; others insisted that offering work was preferable to offering charity, since charity demeaned its recipients while work elevated and "ennobled" them.[14] Running through the debates, and ultimately resolving them, was the notion that the right to work was intimately linked to the right to property. Insisting on the need to grant the right to work, the republican Antoine Philippe Mathieu (who was referred to as Mathieu de la Drôme) maintained that "from the point of view of justice, the right to work is parallel to the right of property. The man who possesses nothing is the slave of owners. The right to work is the only answer to communism, since work permits men to become propertyholders."[15] Arguing against him and against the more radical proposals of the Fourierist Victor Considérant, the conservative Gustave de Beaumont did not dispute the association of work and property. "The constitution ought to guarantee the means of acquiring property" through labor; but this means, he suggested, was "la liberté du travail," the unfettered freedom to seek and take on employment. (It was this formulation that finally prevailed in the constitution adopted in November 1848.)[16] Cormenin summed up the equation between work and property this way: "The right to work implies the right of property in the person of the worker, who wants to 'arrive' as we did and in the same way; because without our own work or that of our fathers, how would we have 'arrived?'"[17] This property "in the person of the worker" could be a form of property or a means of acquiring it. The ambiguity of the association between labor and property rights opened the space for conceiving political equality among men. Alexandre Ledru-Rollin put it this way: "Whether a man works for himself or for you, you consider him still a man like yourself . . . politically, you recognize him to be a man, your equal, a citizen."[18]

The notion of labor as property "in the person of the worker" allowed legislators to turn the social question back into a question of formal political representation by supplying a common ground regardless of social condition. That common ground was a shared masculinity, represented by possession of property. "Property," the republican Alphonse de Lamartine proclaimed, "is not a law but an instinct, a condition inherent in human nature itself." It was the heart of life and the lifeblood of society.[19] Property was an expression of self; labor in this sense was a form of property. What men had in common was not only this property, but its objectification in the family, in the wife and child who carried a husband's and father's name and served as the instruments of the transmission of his property—the tangible emblem of his person.

Family was listed in section IV of the preamble along with labor and property as the basis for liberty, equality, and fraternity in the constitution of the Second Republic. "[The Republic] has as its principles Liberty, Equality, and Fraternity. It has as its foundation Family, Work, Property, and Public Order."[20] The family had been referred to, along with property, as a "sacred right" in discussions of public order on July 25, 1848. In these discussions maternity was not mentioned because it was assumed to be a natural function, something automatic, evident, owed, and given. Paternity was discussed as a right. It was taken as a political relationship secured through institutions such as marriage and the social contract and through symbolic practices such as the naming of children. Paternity was understood to be a mastery of nature, a more abstract concept (since, unlike maternity, it could not be established by direct evidence of the senses) and therefore a higher, more important form of human relation. Paternity was the way in which nature (equated with maternity and sexuality) was transformed into social organization; in the process all visibility for the mother's role and any sense of its independent importance was lost.[21] The rights to family and property were quite literally men's right to women; these rights enabled men of different means and social classes to recognize one another as equals and as citizens.

That family meant men's possession of women and children became clear when the protection of those "sacred rights" was linked to the exclusion of women from all political activity. The occasion was a debate in the Assembly in July. In the wake of the June Days, the debate was about the legality of political clubs, those centers of discussion and mobilization that had driven the revolution leftward from its inception. Over the objections of a handful of socialist deputies, the Constituent Assembly agreed that women must be barred from political activity. The report on clubs to the Assembly recommended that all meetings be open and public and that "women and minors not be allowed to be members of clubs or to attend their meetings." When the socialist deputy Ferdinand Flocon moved to delete "women" from this recommendation, commenting that they were not, after all, minors, a representative replied, to considerable laughter, "They are much more annoying when treated as adults."[22] A more definitive rejection cited "private life" as women's legitimate place and referred ominously to history without supplying details: "Historical memories of the presence of women in political assemblies give sufficient reason to exclude them."[23]

The sense of a need to control women by physically sequestering them was a way of ensuring "public order." "In the thinking of the committee," said its rapporteur, the Protestant pastor Anathase Coquerel, "the sacred rights of the family and of property are included in the words 'public order.' Public order cannot be understood without the family and without property."[24] But then why banish women from the public when, in a sense, they were already there in the family, already responsible for its order? This was the question of Flocon, who claimed that "the presence of women in [club] meetings . . . is a guarantee of order, moderation, and harmony."[25] Feminists posed the issue more strongly when they insisted that only the presence of women, unselfish by definition of their interest in the family, could guarantee the "public order" legislators sought.[26]

But the majority of legislators felt that the "sacred rights" of family and property could best be protected by men. Women's realm was understood to be both the physical location of the home and a set of intimate relationships among individuals; the doctrine of separate spheres for women and men, taken to be a reflection of the natural biological order, was ultimately relied on to justify the exclusion of women from citizenship. But it is also clear that arguments from biology served to protect the individual father's "sacred rights" to family and property, rights that boiled down to a single right to wife and child. Access to the child in a patriarchal regime came through the mother, whose relationship to it was tangible and visible. It was she whose body and whose labor produced the children, and hence the generational continuity that constituted families, protected their property, and guaranteed immortality. By insisting that the "rights" of family and property belonged to fathers, the legislators relegated the contribution of mothers to a biological imperative and a social obligation: women were said to "owe" children to their husbands and to society, and to "owe" maternal care to their children. These were duties performed in exchange for the care and protection women received as dependent beings, as possessions of their husbands.

The fact that women were also workers and were recognized as such in the decrees promising the right to work introduced a problem. For if labor conferred individuality and if women worked, how could citizenship be denied to women? Even as the legislature clarified its understanding of the right to work, making it compatible with theories of formal political rights and male citizenship, feminists brought back the social question as a demand for the consideration of the interests, and thus the rights, of women. For Jeanne Deroin the vote was a way of representing a definably different social interest: "A legislative assembly composed entirely of men is as incompetent to make laws that regulate a society composed of men and women as would be an assembly composed entirely of the privileged for discussing the interests of workers, or an assembly of capitalists for upholding the honor of the country."[27]

Rights were the instrument by which interests could be represented and satisfied, Deroin maintained; it was this substantive purpose and not an empty formality that universal suffrage was meant to achieve. An exclusively masculine suffrage allowed a particular interest to be enshrined in the name of liberty and equality. Formal equality, in other words, was but a mask for the perpetuation of social inequality. For Deroin, the gendered nature of the suffrage exposed a contradiction (between the substantive right to work and the formal right to vote) that the doctrine of labor as property was intended to resolve.[28]

The issue of the right to work produced the kind of crisis for republican theories of representation in 1848 that imagination had during the first revolution. In 1848 the question was about the relationship between the individual as a political abstraction and as a socially differentiated being. To which of these individuals did rights attach? The answer to that question had profound implications for government policy: did law exist simply to protect the individual in the exercise of his rights or to fulfill some set of needs common to all (the right to live by one's labor, for example) by correcting inequities that arose from social differentiation? The idea that law must protect the right to property (but not its substance or extent) was offered to shore up the abstract individual as the bearer of rights.

At the same time, in the conservative mood following the June uprising, the question of rights was made secondary to the issue of the duties ("les devoirs") of the citizen. The Constitution of 1848 had as its preamble a statement not of the rights of man and citizen, but of the reciprocal rights and duties of the republic and its citizens.[29] No rights, however, were enumerated in the preamble; these were saved for the second chapter of the constitution itself. Instead the bulk of the preamble was concerned with duties:

> Citizens ought to love the Fatherland, serve the Republic, defend it with their lives, and contribute to the expenses of the State in proportion to their wealth; they ought to secure, by their labor, the means of existence and, by savings, resources for the future; they ought to unite for the common good and fraternally help one another and public order by observing the moral and written laws that regulate society, the family, and the individual.[30]

In return, the republic owed the citizen protection of his person, family, religion, property, work, and poor relief for the impoverished unemployed.

Despite the fact that duties and rights were referred to as parallel and as existing "prior and superior to positive laws," they were antithetical concepts. Duties were by definition social; they established limits on individual rights, they subsumed selfish to collective interest, and they were governed by substantive moral precepts. The onus for social justice was placed on the moral behavior of individuals, not on the actions of the government. Whereas individuals possessed rights, they performed duties. And they performed them in specific contexts in relation to specific others. Rights could be conceived abstractly as attributes of "the individual"; duties were concrete practices of individuals. The result of this conceptualization was that, as Giovanna Procacci has put it, "observed through a network of duties, the individual appears to be fragmented in a series of experiences, instead of as the unified juridical subject of rights."[31]

Procacci points out that the notion of the duties of citizens, theorized most fully in this period by Auguste Comte (and restated as political doctrine in the constitution of the new republic), was part of an effort to articulate "the social" as an object of scientific study and government regulation, rather than as a repository of rights.[32] She neglects to add, however, that the notions of duty and the social both carried feminine connotations in this period. Indeed, one reason frequently given for the exclusion of women from the ranks of individuals and citizens had precisely to do with their (inter)dependent status: their duties to children, husbands, and society. Moreover, attention to the social as an object of inquiry and regulation was formulated in terms of the need to protect dependent populations: the poor as dependents became identified with (or as) women and children. That was why Comte thought that the idea of moral government contained in the concept of duty would appeal particularly to women who needed protection "against the oppressive action of the temporal power" and who anyway had so little influence in politics. "It is from the feminine aspect only that human life, whether individually or collectively considered, can really be comprehended as a *whole*."[33] By introducing the issue of social duty as a brake on the question of social rights and by making duty a prerequisite for citizenship, legislators undercut the singularity of the figure of the abstract individual—the man whose property (in himself) made him the equal of all men and thus a citizen—and thereby opened the way for pluralizing, even feminizing him.

There was a tension, then, in these various attempts to remove the social question from politics. On the one hand, legislators defined labor as a property right in an attempt to keep the abstract individual undifferentiated, the subject of formal rights only. On the other hand, they sought to remove the social question entirely from the domain of rights by moralizing it. But this involved emphasizing the duty of individuals, thus bringing the facts of social differentiation and interdependence back in to the issue of citizenship. Both moves opened the way for feminist claims. Not only did women work, thus qualifying at least for consideration as holders of property in the self, but they already exemplified the idea of moral duty. "The morality of a nation rests above all on the morality of women . . . There is no public devotion without private virtues, no private virtues without respect for the family, that temple where the mother devotes herself with such complete selflessness."[34]

According to the terms of the discourse of rights and duties, then, women were undeniably citizens. So Jeanne Deroin concluded when she decided to run for office in 1849: "By posing my candidacy for the Legislative Assembly, I fulfill my duty; it is in the name of public morality and in the name of justice that I demand that the dogma of equality no longer be a lie."[35] Taking literally the description of the citizen as one from whom duties were expected in return for the recognition and protection of rights, Deroin pronounced herself a citizen and sought to exercise her rights. Even before it was ruled illegal, her action exposed the contradictory premises of the constitution of 1848. Did she run as an individual—one of those workers/property-holders whose individuality established her commonality with other men? But on what terms could women claim to possess property as individuals? Surely not through the possession of a husband who carried their name. But what about the possession of a child? In 1834 the feminist St. Simonian Egérie Casaubon, in a brochure titled *Woman Is the Family*, had suggested exactly this: "The fruit ought to bear the name of the tree that gave it life, not that of the gardener who grafted its bud."[36] Deroin argued similarly for recognition of the fact that children belonged only to their mothers. Such a procedure might well establish the individual identities of women, but what would it do to the status of men as individuals? In the zero-sum calculations of the patriarchal economy, the achievement of individuality for woman necessarily compromised that of man.

When Deroin insisted that she ran for office to achieve representation for women, a social group with needs and interests of its own, she posed the social question in a particularly difficult way. It might be possible to imagine that universal suffrage would produce a new social order such that there were "no longer any proletarians in France," but could the same promise be made for women? Would the representation of women end not only oppression, but the distinctiveness of their identity? If women were allowed to plead their own case in the public/political realm, would they, could they still, be women? Many thought not, agreeing with the vehement warning from a writer to *Le Peuple,* the newspaper edited by the socialist Pierre-Joseph Proudhon, that "the emancipation of women will produce nothing but hermaphrodites."[37]

But despite the evocation here of monstrosity as the specific outcome of gender equality, the claim for the substantive equality of women was not exceptional; it was simply the most extreme case of the notion of positive political rights. As such, like all other demands for social equality, it threatened the hierarchy on which social order rested and which must be protected (in the double sense of "preserved" and "shielded from view") by the granting of formal political rights. But formal political rights could not be extended to women, because universality among men was secured by making women (under the sign of property and family) a right of man. Women's claims for rights, then, necessarily linked the substantive and the formal, exposing the relationship between the two and refusing any distinction between them.

When Deroin claimed rights based on the performance of duties, she further confounded constitutional reasoning. If rights and duties indeed predated positive laws, if each was the prerequisite for the other, then how could one invoke the duties of women (to family, children, society) as a bar to the exercise of their rights?—unless the emphasis on duty was a ploy to deny men their rights even while granting them the vote. Deroin insisted that by running for office "we have fulfilled a duty by claiming a right."[38] But when her action was ruled illegal, rights and duties were shown to be not above law, but the products of it. Many years later Deroin commented wryly on the nature of the relationship between rights and duties: "Duty and right are correlative. But to exercise one's right and to fulfill one's duty it is necessary to have power."[39] The experience of feminism during the Second Republic attested forcefully to the validity of this conclusion.

----■----

When the subject of rights was inserted into a network of duties, as it was in 1848, feminists had no trouble finding a woman who met the definition of citizen. They based their claims for citizenship on that exemplary figure of duty and devotion, the being worshipped in Catholic teaching and deified in Romantic eulogies: the mother. Here was an identity achieved through the performance of socially attributed duties, the very model for the meaning of reciprocity and obligation. In the logic of the constitution, duties were the correlatives of rights. It followed for feminists that rights must be granted to all those who performed duties; indeed the successful fulfillment of their obligations required that they be allowed to exercise rights: "It is especially the holy function of motherhood, said to be incompatible with the exercise of the rights of the citizen, that imposes on the woman the duty to watch over the future of her children and gives her the right to intervene, not only in all acts of civil life, but also in all acts of political life."[40] Deroin's Mother was an idealized figure, offered as an individual in full possession of herself and of the children produced through her labor. This idealized figure did not distill the experiences of ordinary women as an organizational strategy for feminists. It is not an example of symbolic expression reflecting previously existing lived reality. It did not require that women be good mothers, or indeed be mothers at all— Deroin, for one, turned the care of her three children over to others in the heat of the political struggles of 1848–1850. Nor did it mean restricting women's political action to the problems of family and children—although women's producer cooperatives took account of problems of childcare when they set hours and working conditions for their members.[41] Rather Deroin turned the trait that constructed the symbolic and distinctive meaning of womanhood in her time into a justification for political rights: she argued that childbearers were rights-bearers according to prevailing moral and political criteria.[42]

The holy function of motherhood brought children into the world; as such it was valuable social labor. "Women are the mothers of humanity," Deroin argued; "the most important of all work is the production of the human being."[43] This work, moreover, was presented as a fully female achievement. The Virgin Mary was the perfect representative of autonomous female productivity, since Christ was conceived without the help of any human male; she also mediated the realms of spirituality and corporeality. Her physical body was the means of moral and spiritual regeneration, the crucible from which a new order would emerge.[44] There was, moreover, no selfish motive in maternity; rather it captured the very essence of "duty": a "mission of sacrifice and devotion" to others. "She acts because she loves. Love of humanity is eternal love."[45]

To deny the social value of a woman's reproductive labor, to claim that children born to her were not hers, was an expropriation every bit as violent as capitalism or slavery. That the symbolic expropriation was achieved by the imposition of the husband's/father's name on his wife and children made it no less odious. Deroin called it "the branding iron that imprints the initials of the master on the forehead of the slave."[46] The custom of a family's bearing its father's name was not an innocent practice, she insisted, nor did it reflect an established reality. The equation of the family with the father's name was rather an appropriation of power disguised as the exercise of a right.[47] Its effect was to obliterate the social worth of motherhood and the identity of woman as an independent actor, to rob her of her individuality and of her children—the fruits of her labor, the demonstration of her sovereign status, of her property in her self.

The corrective for feminists like Deroin (as it had been for de Gouges) was to give children their mothers' names. Deroin believed in monogamy and fidelity in heterosexual relationships, but not in private property secured through marriage and signified by the husband's/father's name. In the early 1830s she had been among a group of St. Simonian women who replaced their patronym with an *X* when signing articles in their journal. When she married her fellow St. Simonian, an engineer referred to in my sources only by his surname Desroches, in a civil ceremony in 1832, their exchange of vows eliminated the husband's promise to protect and the wife's to obey. She did not take his name, but continued to use her birth (father's) name, Deroin.[48] The difficulty of establishing an independent status with a surname that was not her own led her to prefer to be called simply Jeanne: "Of all the names that designate a woman, whether of father or husband, I like only the Christian name that is hers."[49] When she was convicted of subversion in 1850 (for her part in organizing an Association of Associations designed to coordinate socialist attempts to establish an alternative to capitalism), the judges asked her why she had not taken Desroches's name. She replied that she did not want him to be held responsible for her misdeeds, but also that she wanted to "protest against marriage." Deroin's assertion of autonomy, her critique of current arrangements, and her attempt to alter them became, in the circumstances of the courtroom, further proof of her status as an outlaw.[50]

Deroin's portrayal of maternity as productive work emphasized its self-constituting quality as well as its social aspect. In her account, bearing children was not simply a biological reflex. Neither was it the by-product of an instinctual desire for sexual pleasure. Like all work, maternity was driven by the necessity of the species to survive and reproduce; it was social, not natural, labor. The association of maternity with sexual desire was thus in Deroin's view the mark of its corruption. Eve was the first mother, not the temptress responsible for the Fall. Her vilification was part of an attempt to devalue motherhood, part of a long process by which women's labor was exploited—sexually and socially—in the interests of patriarchal domination. Under those conditions, she suggested, "It ought not to be surprising that a woman takes refuge in Christian sentiment and that, since her human dignity is violated, she casts off human nature and reclothes herself as an angel, in order to be free of men's brutal domination and of humiliating servitude."[51]

By implication, sexual relations would be acceptable when women were treated as men's equals. But Deroin also suggested that celibacy might be the best guarantee of equality in marriage. She strongly rejected the idea that women could gain independence through the practice of "free love," having watched the St. Simonian leader Prosper Enfantin and his followers in the 1830s engage in promiscuous relations without taking responsibility for the progeny that resulted. (Many women in the movement were abandoned to raise illegitimate children on their own.)[52] The alternative to both celibacy and free love was asexual maternity. In the end Mary was the representation Deroin preferred. It allowed her to defer the question of sexual relations and the role of men in producing children. She argued instead that the state must provide financial support (a "social dowry") for all mothers so that they might be free from economic dependency on men—indeed from any relationship to men at all.[53] Like the proletariat, whose emancipation would be secured by unalienated labor, women would find reproductive labor fulfilling when maternity was granted the social recognition and compensation it deserved.[54] The spiritual, devoted mother attained her force as a laboring body; neither the instrument of another's desire nor someone else's property, she was fully in control of the conditions and product of her work. This work was both self-defining and the fulfillment of a social duty; as such it qualified women (as comparable work did men) for the vote.

By arguing that childbearing was socially necessary labor, Deroin refused the differentiation between men as productive workers (transforming raw materials into something of value) and women as forces of nature. This leveling of function was taken by her critics to be a denial of all gender difference, revealing the extent to which the nature of the work associated with them (and not nature itself) constructed the differences between women and men. Ironically, Deroin's insistence that a labor unique to women qualified them as citizens was taken as an assertion that men and women were the same. Proudhon railed against Deroin thus: "The political equality of the two sexes, that is to say the admission of woman to man's public functions, is a sophism that is refuted not only by logic but by the human conscience and the nature of things. Man, in measure as his reason develops, may see woman as his equal, but he will never see her as the same."[55] The illogic of this insistence on logic, the substitution of furious refusal for serious argument, demonstrates the overriding importance to Proudhon of keeping men and women separate and the crucial role of the idea of separate spheres in maintaining that separation.

Deroin's reply exposed the nature of his investment in separate spheres and denied his charge: "It is because woman is the equal of man and not the same as him that she must take part in the work of social reform."[56] For Proudhon "public functions" actually secured gender boundaries—there was finally no other way to establish the differences between men and women; for Deroin, it was the existence of these boundaries that created the definably different "interests" of women and hence the need for political representation. Deroin's own reasoning about these issues, though, reveals the difficulty of articulating women's equality in terms of their difference. On the question of maternity, she effaced the role of men as partners in the production of children in an effort to establish the autonomous individuality of women as producers. In other realms, however, she offered the heterosexual couple as a model for thinking about the social and political equality of irreducibly different beings.

Deroin took up the St. Simonian formula for equality in which "the couple, man and woman," was the social individual without whose union "nothing is complete, moral, durable, or possible."[57] Offered as a critique of the divisiveness of selfish individualism, this idea of the social individual stressed the complementarity of opposites, the necessary interrelatedness of qualities thought to be antithetical to one another, and the complexity of concepts presented as singular. The individual was a couple, and so Deroin's vocabulary insisted on its duality: she referred to it as "un et une" in the singular, "tous et toutes" in the plural. Humanity was man *and* woman: an androgyne in some of her representations, in others the copulating couple whose union merged two into one to form a child, in still others the two aspects of God. The marriage that would regenerate the world was that of two equals, "whom God has thus joined, no man can separate."[58] (Her thinking on this followed that of Pierre Leroux, who had written that God was "in effect . . . two principles, but He is neither he nor she: He is the two united by a third . . . love, which is His third face.")[59] Sometimes she endorsed a notion of androgyny, as when she urged that George Sand represent women's interests in the legislature in 1848 so that the writing of the constitution would not be left entirely in the hands of men. (Sand refused this nomination and bitterly ridiculed those who proposed it, insisting in this moment at least that women had no place in politics.)[60] According to Deroin, Sand's dual qualities would make her less threatening to the male legislators: "She is the type *un et une,* male because of her virility, female because of her divine intuition and poetry. She has made herself a man by her genius; she remains a woman because of her maternal side, her infinite tenderness."[61]

Deroin's thinking drew on a rich vein of Romantic and utopian socialist writings about androgyny. In some versions the androgyne expressed a longing for masculine wholeness achieved by the incorporation of the feminine. (That this involved not just the subordination but even the exclusion of women had been demonstrated in 1832 by the St. Simonian community at Menilmontant, an entirely male venture devoted to the cultivation of the feminine dimensions of men's psyches.)[62] In other versions, it offered a more egalitarian vision of the complementarity of masculine and feminine in terms of a partnership of man and woman. For Leroux, who left the St. Simonians in disagreement over Enfantin's promiscuous practices of "free love," androgyny was the original human state. With the Fall came "la séparation des deux sexes,"[63] which was also the separation between *le moi* et *le non-moi,* the realization of the uniquely human consciousness of the self. Redemption would come not with the restoration of the prelapsarian androgyne, Leroux thought, but with the political and social equality of man and woman, husband and wife. Their relationship must be entirely reciprocal, so that each self understood its dependence on the other. This was the premise of Deroin's argument for rights: man and woman complemented one another; neither was complete without the other. "God has created the human being in his image. He created it male and female; he brought it to life with divine breath, and with the two halves of the same being he formed the social individual—man and woman, to bring one another to life, to complete one another, and to walk together toward the same goal. He founded human society."[64]

Deroin's notion of completion understood the two sexes as so fully interdependent that one could not exist without the other. Complementarity was a relationship meant to complete or fill up, to compensate for lack or insufficiency in its constituent parts. But the equality of the relationship, in her view, required a perfect symmetry on a shared terrain between the nonidentical partners. "Our political aim is the same as theirs," Deroin explained in the first issue of *La politique des femmes,* "but our point of view is different. We are each entitled to our uniqueness under the vast banner of socialism; women's politics can march abreast of men's politics."[65] To make the case for parity or equivalence, Deroin emphasized the autonomous individuality and irreducible difference of each partner (if this were not the case, their union would result in the incorporation of one side by the other and the denial of representation to one side). If each partner were whole unto him or her self, then would the differences that made them necessary for each other's completion disappear? How could interdependence (or lack in each partner) presuppose independence (or self-sufficiency)? The difficulty of answering these questions is apparent in the clash between the two figures Deroin employed to argue for equality. On the one hand the individual was figured as a fully entwined heterosexual couple; on the other, the individuality of woman was figured as an autonomous mother, the sole agent of the generation of her child. The paradox of Deroin's attempt to argue for equality in terms of complementarity followed from her engagement with a political discourse that defined man's individuality in terms of a contrast with woman as nonindividual (her "otherness" established the individuality of his self). Any effort to establish woman's individuality threatened man's and yet had to be established in relation to his. In this context, Deroin's appeals to complementarity could not be sustained; rather than completing man, woman became his replacement, standing with him but in his place, playing his role—the lines between them were indifferent and so effectively erased. Or, to put it in literary critic Barbara Johnson's terms, "As long as there is symmetry, one is not dealing with difference but rather with versions of the same."[66]

The difficulty of maintaining complementarity was apparent in Deroin's efforts. She forcefully invoked the parity of men and women in the inaugural issue of *L'opinion des femmes:* "To work, men of the future! republicans, socialists of all schools, to work! Call woman to you, openly at last, this half of your soul, your heart, your intelligence too long unrecognized and abandoned; work together to usher in the new era, the law of the future, of solidarity, forbearance, and love."[67] In this joint enterprise women had their own interests to represent, as mothers and workers, but they also represented the social interest, the general health, prosperity, and moral well-being of France. "It is not only in the name of women" that women must act in the political realm, Deroin insisted, "but in the interest of all of society."[68] Only female expertise could bring order to "this large, badly administered household called the State," she warned, metaphorically transforming the public realm into a place where women presided.[69] And although she offered women's influence as a corrective to men's, it was not hard to hear in her choice of words an argument for replacement. Women stood for peace, love, and the principle of association (all stated goals of the revolutionaries); while men were selfish, cruel, and displayed a penchant for mutual destruction (all characteristics the revolutionaries condemned): "In politics the opinion of women, whether their inclinations are republican or aristocratic, can be summarized as thought of love and peace . . . They all agree in wishing that a politics of peace and work will replace the selfish and cruel politics that incite men to destroy one another . . . In all social theories, that which women best understand is the principle of association."[70]

In order to argue for complementarity, Deroin went beyond claims for simple parity because she had to conceptualize (against prevailing views) the possibility of an independent woman who lacked nothing, who (in order to be man's equivalent) was sufficient unto herself. This woman then was equated with the general interest and the social good, displacing man, whose exclusion of her demonstrated his selfish pursuit of special interest, his willingness to impose laws based not on justice but on the antiquated "law of the strongest."[71] In effect, Deroin's woman did not so much complete man as replace him. And she did this both by equating her own interest with the social good and by establishing her independence, thus undermining the ideal upon which complementarity rested: the interdependent union of the heterosexual couple.

By claiming politics as the domain of women, by equating the household and the state, Deroin distinguished her notion of complementarity from that of many of her contemporaries, who expressed the differences between the sexes in terms of their physical locations in "separate spheres." The justification offered for the law of July 28, 1848, which excluded women from all participation in clubs, whether as observers or as members, put it bluntly: "Only private life suits woman; she is not made for public life."[72] Later Proudhon echoed these ideas in the pages of *Le Peuple*: "Woman has a completely different nature from man. Man is apprentice, producer, and magistrate; woman is pupil, housekeeper, and mother. Woman must therefore have totally different social conditions."[73]

By "social conditions" Proudhon meant separate spheres. In December 1848 he lashed out at a "fraternal banquet" held by socialist women to demand reform and endorse political candidates. Women who initiated such events and, worse, who spoke at them violated the role that was given to them in the division of humanity:

> The role of woman is not the exterior life, the life of activity and agitation, but the intimate life, that of sentiment and of the tranquility of the domestic hearth. Socialism did not come only to restore work, but also to rehabilitate the household, sanctuary of the family, symbol of matrimonial union . . . we invite our sisters to think about what we have said and to penetrate to this truth, that purity and morality gain more in the patriarchal celebrations of the family than in the noisy manifestations of politics.[74]

Proudhon's invective was a reminder of women's duty and an insistence that it had nothing to do with political rights: if women's attendance at electoral banquets was outrageous, their candidacy for office was ludicrous. Aiming directly at Jeanne Deroin's campaign for a seat in the legislature in April–May 1849, Proudhon quipped that a female legislator made as much sense as a male wet nurse. Deroin's reply (which Proudhon refused to print in his paper, forcing her to publish it elsewhere) pointed to the absurdity of the argument from nature. She asked Proudhon to specify which were the organs necessary for the functions of the legislator: "If nature is as positive on this score as you seem to believe, I will concede the debate."[75]

This exchange pinpoints the radical impact of Deroin's arguments and actions, which reversed the usual explanation for differences between the sexes, making them less an effect of biology than of social organization. Deroin did not dispute the attribution of different characteristics and obligations to women and men; in fact she sought to intensify the differences in order both to consolidate a political identity for women and to make the case for equal rights. Women were by

nature more delicate, weaker, their natures more affectionate and compassionate than men's, she conceded, but these differences had nothing
to do with their ability to exercise their rights.[76] Deroin went further,
arguing that historically woman's mistake had been to try to deny
difference; she had tried to escape the yoke of oppression "by making
herself like man [*en se faisant semblable à l'homme*]."[77] In doing so,
women became mere imitations, and necessarily inferior versions because they were not actively representing themselves. Deroin's alternative was to emphasize the differences, and especially the unique responsibility of maternity, in order to win separate and independent
recognition.

But if sexual difference was a matter of character and interest, it did
not, for Deroin, correlate with separate spatial locations or spheres of
activity. For one thing, the distinction did not correspond to what men
and women actually did or were required to do. Women worked; men
were involved in domestic affairs; duty and morality (long associated
with women and the private) were now prerequisites for citizenship;
the state both administered the social and depended on it for order.
That was the meaning of her reference to the state as a "large, badly
administered household"; it was also at the heart of her redescription
of marriage, not as a private arrangement but as a social institution
"with a triple aspect: material, intellectual, and moral through labor."[78]
Life itself was so complex and multifaceted that it could not underwrite
a purely individualistic notion of rights: "Life is triple in its unity:
individual life, family life, and social life constitute a complete life," she
wrote.[79] The constitution's insistence on rights and duties had blurred
the boundaries not only between the individual and the social, but also
between the political and the familial, the public and the private. The
continued exclusion of women did not make sense in the newly drawn
order of things; Deroin felt it was her duty to point this out and correct it.

The heated reaction to her efforts, not only by Proudhon but also by
politicians and political caricaturists, reveals how much the rights of
man depended on denying similar rights to women, how dependent
her contemporaries were on separate spheres for establishing the physical boundaries of masculine and feminine bodies. Crossing the threshold from the hearth to the forum led to hermaphrodism, they charged,

the loss of distinguishing features of male and female.[80] The danger of androgyny was a sexually indecipherable, hence monstrous, body. Sharing political space meant sharing political rights, the creation of a leveling sameness depicted—and understood—as a natural abomination. "Women are not made to be men of state," opined Ernest Legouvé, whose lectures at the Collège de France in April 1848 had attracted scores of enthusiastic feminists. A supporter of improvements in women's status through education and changes in the Civil Code, Legouvé nonetheless disapproved of giving women the vote because it transgressed the spatial boundaries that established sexual difference. Emancipation for women could take place only within the family; political women were absurdities.[81]

The critics and caricaturists of the feminist campaign illustrated Legouvé's point again and again. Daumier and others played upon the theme of role inversion, depicting political women as ugly, comical, funny-looking, masculine imitators. There were manly wives rejecting marital authority on the advice of Mme. Deroin; children left in the arms of despairing fathers while their mothers played at politics; women with monocles, cigars, and beards; and men in skirts. One series of cartoons included a man pleading with the woman barring the door of the Women's Club to take his pants to his wife so she could sew a button on them. Another showed a man backing off from the door of the Women's Club as a female security guard advanced toward him, holding a huge pair of scissors pointed threateningly at his crotch.

The Paris police joined the fray, recruiting prostitutes to a bogus feminist society called the Vésuviennes. They even published a constitution for the group which was so successful in its parody that generations of historians have treated it as a genuine feminist document.[82] It included a section that threatened men who refused to perform their share of household tasks with service in an all-female civic guard. And it depicted the crossing of gender boundaries as transvestism. Women were enjoined to "work imperceptibly to efface the differences between masculine and feminine dress, without thereby exceeding the limits of modesty and ridicule, nor distancing themselves from gracious form and good taste. The result will be a change about which men, given their undertaker's getup, can hardly complain."[83] Jeanne Deroin cited the Vésuviennes as an example of official harassment of feminists: they "burlesqued everything we said and did in order to cast ridicule and contempt on our meetings and our acts."[84] Violent attacks on feminist meetings were also condoned. Meetings of the Club des Femmes were disrupted repeatedly beginning in April 1848. The organizers were taunted and chased through the streets; some were caught and threatened with beatings. At one point the club's meeting hall had to be cleared completely, so threatening and disorderly had the hostile crowds become.[85]

Ridicule, hostility, and violence were mobilized to prevent the transgression of social space and so of gender boundaries. In a variety of ways, this transgression was depicted as castration—as a threat to the sign of man's difference and the symbol of his power, now equated with his political rights.[86] The implication that castration would follow from the merging of spheres suggests that in the discourse of separate spheres the integrity of differently sexed bodies rested finally not on spirituality or biology nor on specialized activities, but on the segregated spaces within which these activities were performed. It was not nature but social organization that produced sexual difference. This was the point that separate spheres both acknowledged and denied; this was the contradiction that the feminist refusal of separate spheres revealed.

———————■———————

During the Revolution of 1848, feminists dramatized their conviction that their place was in the public sphere by entering it. In this they challenged directly the justification that their exclusion followed from biology or nature. Their protest aimed at exposing, by actions which made self-evident women's capacity as citizens), the "lie" of a regime that denied them the vote.[87] Law did not reflect some prior reality, they maintained; rather it constituted that reality, in this case the reality of women's inequality. Here a paradox for feminists was that, having been ruled outside the law, their attempts to reform it, to fulfill their duty by bringing it into conformity with the universal principles to which it was dedicated, were deemed illegal.

Feminists appealed to duty as they set about breaking the law; their sense of duty came, they said, from an inner conviction prior to any law, a deep consciousness of what was morally right. "Everywhere women are conscious of their rights," proclaimed an article in the feminist newspaper Deroin founded with Eugénie Niboyet, *La voix des femmes*.[88] The article then recounted the action of Deroin's friend Pauline Roland who arrived at the city hall of Boussac in March 1848 in order to cast her ballot for Pierre Leroux, the democratic-socialist candidate for mayor. When refused a ballot by outraged officials, she demanded that they file formal charges against her. Roland's action had wonderfully parodic elements about it. When the police arrived and arrested her, she gave her name as "Marie-Antoinette Rolland," invoking the recognized power and discredited status of the former queen. She had chosen the commune of Boussac because Leroux was an outspoken advocate of women's political rights. Being forbidden to vote for Leroux heightened the sense she wanted to convey of contradiction and injustice, as did her insistence that she be formally charged with committing an illegal act.

Deroin took Roland's protest further, standing for a seat in the legislature in the election of May 1849. Since the constitution (adopted in November 1848) did not explicitly forbid such action, Deroin felt it her "duty" to realize the as-yet-unrealized principle of equality for which the revolution had been fought. By invoking her "duty," Deroin sought to assuage fears that women's rights would lead to the nonperformance of their (maternal and familial) obligations, and, of course, she appealed to the "Declaration of Rights and Duties" that served as a preamble to the constitution of the Second Republic: "Inspired and guided by the feelings of right and justice, we have fulfilled a duty by claiming the right to take part in the work of the Legislative Assembly."[89]

Deroin's account of her electoral campaign describes an energetic attempt to assert her rights and so enact citizenship. It appeals to an inner conviction so powerful that it alone serves to establish that sense of self synonymous with citizenship.

Deroin's strategy in her campaign was to attain access to the tribune, the public forum forbidden to women by law. She campaigned by attending electoral meetings held by democratic-socialists in Paris and asking for the floor to explain her purposes. Deroin was given the podium at one electoral gathering on condition that she ask questions of the delegates (rather than appeal directly for endorsement as a

candidate). When she came to the rostrum, "a violent tumult erupted
. . . near the entrance to the room, and soon it spread to the whole
assemblage." The organizers suggested that she step down so that calm
could be restored. She stood her ground: "Fortified by the innermost
sentiment of the grandeur of our mission, of the holiness of our
apostolate, and profoundly convinced of the importance and the time-
liness of our work—so eminently, so radically revolutionary and social—we accomplished our duty by refusing to quit the tribune."[90]
Intimate sentiment, consciousness, inspiration, interior knowledge—
these were given as irresistible motives for actions that would make the
law recognize the fact that women already had rights. Subjective cer-
tainty was understood as a reflection of a self already in possession of
political rights. It enabled Deroin to put "principles into practice," to
"take active part" in struggles for justice, to raise her "voice with the
defenders of the rights of people, the friends of humanity."[91] And it
provided consolation when action failed to achieve its end: "You have
closed the highways of the world to me, you have declared me subaltern
and minor; but there remains in my consciousness a sanctuary where
the force of your arm and the despotism of your thought are brought
to a halt. There, no sign of inferiority blights my existence, no enslave-
ment binds my will and prevents it from reaching for wisdom."[92]

At the electoral meeting Deroin showed her conviction by holding
her ground. When the crowd was finally stilled, she spoke. Like an
outraged mother shaming her children, she scolded them for their
unjust pretensions. She expressed her "astonishment" at the behavior
of these socialists, "these men who call themselves men of the future,"
who sought the abolition of all privileges but those of men to dominate
women, who did not realize that inequality between men and women
promoted all other social inequalities, and that their own happiness
would be attained only when they practiced justice toward their mothers, sisters, and wives. In effect, she corrected the misapprehensions of
their vision of the future, providing the right script for those who would
make history.

Deroin sought to demonstrate that she was equal to the task of public
speaking, that a woman was indeed qualified to articulate her ideas.
When she experienced "a strong emotion" which she feared weakened

her delivery, she attributed it to the momentousness of the occasion (she was the first to pose the great question of women's civil and political rights before an electoral meeting) and to her "inexperience with parliamentary forms." That inexperience came from situations such as the one she faced at the outset of the meeting, when those who invoked the ancient privileges of the strong tried to silence the voices of the weak. With the end of such injustice, all individuals would learn to address public meetings with equal facility. In the performance of public duty, in the exercise of political right, men had no monopoly.

The fact of being a woman and acquitting herself well in a forum said to be not suited for (and off limits to) her sex gave Deroin's action its political force. She overcame her "natural timidity," she explained, because she was acting in the service of a higher cause, because she was "devoted" to the fulfillment of her duty: "When M. Eugène Pelletan told me one day that I was acting as if I had fired a gun in the street to attract attention, he was right. But it was to attract attention not to myself, but to the cause to which I was devoted."[93] Whether for herself or the cause, the inescapable point was that attention was drawn to a woman in public space. Simply the fact of asking for the floor at an electoral meeting of democratic-socialists was to draw attention to herself, as if she "had fired a gun in the street," that is, as if by acting as men did (by appropriating the phallus) she had created a disturbance and broken the law.

Although the disturbance was actually created by those reacting to her, Deroin was indeed trying to break the law in order to expose its contradictions and ultimately to change it. No matter that she deemed the law unjust and therefore violable; even those among the democratic-socialists who were sympathetic to her candidacy (some fifteen delegates voted to place her name on the electoral list) agreed in the end that it was unconstitutional. Here Deroin, and feminists more generally, reached the limit of their improvisations, the limit of their ability to redescribe the concepts (woman, the feminine, the individual, rights and duties) that made their difference incompatible with equality. Without legal recognition, there was no way for a woman to qualify as a citizen, to achieve the status of an individual. In the political context established by the constitution, the abstract individual was de facto embodied as a man, and only those identical with him were allowed to vote or to serve as elected representatives of the people.

Even when it came to taking responsibility for her own political actions, the rules of law in the political context of her time made Deroin's position untenable. She had been one of the founders, in the summer of 1849, of the Association of Associations, a group that coordinated various socialist worker efforts at producer and consumer autonomy. The plans called for replacing money with systems of credit, for ownership by workers of the means of production, and for the guarantee to men and women alike of "the right and the means to live by the product of their labor, they, their children, and their families."[94] The Association of Associations had attracted membership from some 400 other groups by May 1850, when its leaders were arrested during a meeting at Deroin's house. (By this time there were strict limits on political meetings and on the number of people who could associate for any reason, and this gathering was deemed to be in violation of those rules.) Although there seems to have been a measure of gender equality practiced in the Association before the arrests, as well as acceptance of the fact that wage labor was the condition of workers of both sexes, in the preparations for the trial Deroin was persuaded to deny any leadership role.

> I had been urgently begged, in the name of the Association, not to acknowledge that I was the author of the project . . . The prejudice that still prevailed in the associations was exacerbated by the preeminent role that a woman, devoted to the cause of women's rights, had taken in this work. Not wanting, in the presence of our adversaries, to start a debate among socialists . . . I contented myself with answering the question that was put to me: No, I have had nothing to say about the associations.[95]

Deroin's tactical willingness to accept subordinate status did not prevent her being sentenced to six months in prison for her role in the illegal meeting. Like Olympe de Gouges she was subject to laws that denied her the rights of a political subject. But as she contested them, she appealed to a higher truth: "I must protest against the law by which you want to judge me. It is a law made by men; I do not recognize it."[96] Man-made law at once established the possibility for her protest and

its limit. In this sense it constituted the very subversiveness of her
feminism, its place in history.

———————■———————

Even from jail Deroin sought to defend women's rights. When, in the
course of considering limits on the right of petition, a deputy proposed
to the Assembly that women be denied that right altogether, Deroin
petitioned to protect this right of last resort for those excluded from
direct representation. (There was constitutional precedent for granting
petitioner rights to the unrepresented in the Constitution of 1791, and
because of that precedent women's right to petition was ultimately
allowed to stand.) She supported Leroux's futile effort to extend the
suffrage to women gradually by letting them vote in municipal elections, and she continued to write about the need to include women in
politics. But it was clear, especially after Napoleon III's coup d'état in
December 1851, that women had lost access to whatever public forum
they had had. With her newspaper shut down and many of her associates already in exile, Deroin departed for England.

She continued to work for the feminist cause, editing a bilingual
journal, the *Almanach des femmes,* from 1851 through 1853. She ran a
school for children of expatriates, practiced vegetarianism, and was
increasingly drawn to spiritualism as the years passed. She maintained
her socialist affiliations, however; she was active in the group around
William Morris, who delivered the eulogy at her funeral in 1894.[97]
Though firmly a feminist to the end of her life, Deroin came to believe
that the moment for her kind of work had passed. In 1849 she had
inscribed herself in a feminist history that began with Olympe de
Gouges. De Gouges, she told readers of her "Cours de l'émancipation
de la femme," "like all the creators of a new idea . . . had cleared the
road without achieving her goal." The February revolution, she went
on, had permitted the likes of her esteemed friend Pauline Roland to
expose the lie of a universal suffrage that excluded half of humanity.
Then, "in 1849, a woman again knocked at the door of the city to claim
for women the right to participate in the work of the Legislative
Assembly. She did not address the old world . . . The moment has come
for woman to take part in the social movement, in the work of regeneration that is taking shape."[98] Deroin had seized the tribune and had

managed to escape with her life, but she had not thereby won for women the right of access to the public forum. Nevertheless, she had made history; indeed hers was, she pointed out, the first such effort by a woman to run for office. Deroin had devoted many columns in her newspaper to chronicling women's long struggle for emancipation; now she wrote herself into an account that recognized women's capacity for making history—a capacity denied by many male historians of the time who saw women's role as timeless and transcendent, and only men's as productive of change.[99]

The revolutionary moment had passed without achieving its end, but this fact did not diminish Deroin's belief in democracy or her commitment to the feminist cause. When suffragist Hubertine Auclert, intent on documenting a historical tradition for feminists of her day, wrote to her in London in 1886 (eight years before her death), Deroin thanked her for her wishes for a long life. "I wish for that too and hope to realize it, not because I expect to see the complete triumph of our cause in my lifetime, but because I want to work toward it a bit more before I am taken to the next life."[100] Still, she declined Auclert's request for help on the grounds that her approach was no longer appropriate for the times. With feminism and a republic more institutionalized than had been the case in her day, something else was called for: "Now there is no longer a need for impulsive and reckless pioneers; instead it is necessary to join talent to devotion, to adorn truth with the beauty of style; that is why I cannot offer you my useless assistance."[101]

This modest demurral was also a claim to a pioneering place in the history of French feminism, as well as the closing of a chapter in that history. The inner conviction that supported faith in the face of opposition, that provided solace and motivation for Deroin's generation, now required something more: dedication and devotion for the long haul. (In the context of Deroin's comment, devotion connotes a long-term commitment and contrasts with the impulsive, risky behavior of those who expected immediate results. Deroin, of course, exemplified such devotion, but it had not been part of her strategy in the heady days of the revolution.) The simple exposure of truth was no longer enough to win adherents to the cause; now truth must be ornamented by "beauty of style," presumably to make it more appealing, and thus more successful. Deroin seemed to be endorsing subtle persuasion as a substitute for the stark announcement of truth. And she seemed to suggest that persuasion of that kind was not suited to the abilities she had developed in the course of her activism in 1848.

In her letters to Auclert, Deroin not only conveyed a firm sense of herself and other women as historical actors; she also conceived of feminism as a political force inspired by its connection to women's actions in the past. With this conception she contributed to the building of a notion of a subversive feminist tradition and to a commonality of purpose among women past, present, and future. This conscious effort to insert women into history at once constituted a feminist identity and infused the movement with a sense of purpose. At the same time, Deroin was aware of the influence of time, and therefore of changing political contexts, on the thoughts and actions of successive generations of feminists. Indeed, she clearly disavowed the notion that the substance and strategy of one generation of feminists ought to serve as a model for the next.

For this reason Deroin would probably not have been surprised, as I initially was, to find herself evoked in Madeleine Pelletier's autobiographical novel in 1933 as the *nom de guerre* for a young feminist activist.[102] Pelletier was, like Deroin, a socialist (although the term had new meanings in the twentieth century), but her feminism rejected most of what Deroin advanced: the irreducible difference of women, the necessary complementarity of the sexes, the religiously inspired vision of social regeneration accomplished by the loving influence of the mother. Instead Pelletier, with entirely secular reasoning, proposed the elimination of all traces of gender difference as feminism's best route to equality. Deroin might have understood this as a response to a new set of conditions in which she was ill equipped to intervene. By her lights, feminism could not be detached from its historical moment. And yet, of course, she also saw it as a changing quest based on the enduring truth that Woman was Man's complement and his equal, and on her ability—her duty—to exercise political rights.

The tension between Deroin's sense of the impact of history on feminist tactics and her commitment to a timeless idea of woman exemplifies the dilemma posed for feminists (and their historians) by the naturalized notions of "sexual difference" used both to justify and to protest women's exclusion from politics in this period. Men engaged in politics and made history; they were understood as beings shaped in the course of time. In contrast, the essence of woman was given; it was as unaffected by history as history was thought to be impervious to women's actions. To enter politics was, for Deroin, to enter history. It was also, although she did not acknowledge it as such, to open "woman"—now conceived in absolute terms as a loving mother—to the changing influences of time. In the process of claiming the rights of the person understood to be "woman" in 1848, the very category of "woman" was reconceived. Paradoxically, and unavoidably, Deroin's advocacy undermined the very woman in whose name she spoke.

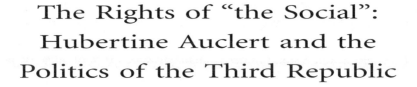

The Rights of "the Social": Hubertine Auclert and the Politics of the Third Republic

The letters exchanged between Hubertine Auclert and Jeanne Deroin in 1886 were an attempt to bridge not only geographic but also temporal distance. An example of the concrete way in which links in the chain of feminist history were forged, they also provided inspiration to the readers of Auclert's suffragist newspaper, *La Citoyenne*. Although Deroin's romantic, spiritual language must have seemed quaint to readers who were used to Auclert's more direct, rational style, there could be no doubt that the women shared a mission: to expose "the lie" (in Deroin's words) of a republic that refused political rights to women. But despite a deeply shared commitment to emancipation, there were also important differences between the two women, differences that, as Deroin so gently pointed out, had everything to do with history. Hubertine Auclert literally came to politics with the Third Republic; at age twenty-five she migrated to Paris from the department of the Allier in 1873 in order to participate in the growing—and now legal—women's movement. The politics of the new Third Republic were radically different from those of 1848. As a result, not just the strategy but the very substance of her feminism were different from Deroin's.

Hubertine Auclert's activism spanned more than four decades of the Third Republic, from the early 1870s until her death in 1914. Even when other feminists urged a more moderate approach, she consistently argued for women's right to vote, in speeches, newspaper articles, petitions, and electoral campaigns. Her arguments were a running commentary on the changing policies and theories in the political arena. Some of Auclert's speeches are dazzling for their combination of diverse and inconsistent appeals: wherever she found openings in arguments, she inserted her claim for women's right to vote. Through her one can track the changing and ambiguous political currents in the Third Republic, as well as some of its persisting contradictions and concerns.

———————■———————

If the conflict between formal political rights and substantive social rights was a dilemma for the Second Republic, the Third faced "the social question" in new terms: What was to be the role of the state in addressing problems of poverty and economic inequality? And how was that role to be legitimated? On the first question there was more agreement than the debates among republicans and socialists would initially indicate. Socialists argued that "a social republic"—a state that enacted and enforced social and economic equality—was the only kind of republic worth having, and they depicted it, often in familial terms, as resulting in better care for the wives and children of workers, as well as for the sick and unemployed.[1] Republicans, partly in response to the growing socialist presence at the polls, in trade unions, and in strike activity, eventually came around to the idea that the state must address "the social question" by attending to those casualties of capitalism who, through accident, weakness, or vulnerability, could not care for themselves. Although this vision was far from the egalitarian one of the socialists, it too was conceived in familial terms. Indeed, common to both positions was the assumption that the state owed care to its constituents in the way a family, out of duty and affection, cared for those who had nowhere else to turn.

On the second question there was far more disagreement. Socialists still used the rhetoric of sovereignty as they sought to represent the working class interest at all levels of government. For many, socialist leader Jules Guesde's call for ballots, not bullets, was still a call to revolution; the conquest of city halls and seats in parliament by socialists in the 1890s was depicted as an effort not only to make the government more responsive to the social question, but also to give "the social" direct representation in decisions of state.[2] Republicans were more ambivalent and divided on the question of popular sovereignty. Many of the architects of the new republic (among them large numbers of monarchists and conservatives) thought that appeals to popular sovereignty must be avoided at all costs, since the experience of the Paris Commune (the revolutionary uprising against the conservative leadership of the new republic in 1870–71) had demonstrated its dangers.[3] If the republic was taken as the representative of its people, and if those people felt that the state's actions misrepresented them, then by right they could dissolve the government; logically, in fact, it had already dissolved itself by failing to represent them. To avoid such reasoning, as well as the anarchy and social warfare that they thought followed from it, these politicians felt it was necessary both to refrain from discussing rights in the enabling legislation of the Third Republic and to restrict the suffrage to those whose property gave them a real stake in the nation's future. Other more liberal or radical republicans thought it would be impossible to have a republic without universal (manhood) suffrage given the precedent established in 1848, and their views eventually prevailed.[4]

But the existence of universal suffrage was not a concession to the idea that the government reflected or embodied the will of the people. Instead of restricting suffrage, the legislators and those who shaped public opinion sought to undermine the doctrine of popular sovereignty by arguing that the state did not represent the people and so could not be legitimated as an expression of their will. Instead it had a managerial function to arbitrate and balance different and conflicting interests. At the same time, the legislators set out to establish the consensus necessary for political stability by producing citizens who represented themselves as republicans, and so could not think of destroying the form of government that had established their identity. Under the Ferry laws (passed in 1881, 1882, and 1886 and named for the minister of education, Jules Ferry), education was free, compulsory, and secular. Schools were to inculcate "that religion of the Fatherland . . . that cult and that love at once ardent and reasoned, with which we want to penetrate the heart and mind of the child."[5] Children were to become not just patriots, but reasoning, scientific, logical thinkers—republican subjects, exemplars of the republican ideal.[6]

As the relationship between the state and the people was reconceived, the social question was separated from political rights. A definition of "the social" in Emile Littré's 1877 dictionary offered as fixed a definition that would continue to be contested for the next decades: "The Social. Used, in opposition to politics, for conditions that, apart from the form of governments, relate to the intellectual, moral, and material development of the popular masses. The social question."[7] This formulation excluded "the form of governments" as a condition for the improvement of the popular classes and "politics" as a means for achieving such improvement. Exercising the vote, in other words, was considered neither a means to social reform nor the expression of popular sovereignty. It was rather a process of consultation that made a gesture to democratic ideas of rights. "The social" was, in this conception, an object of the state's attention. For, in the name of order, progress, particular interests, and the general welfare, the state might well address the "intellectual, moral, and material development" of the masses of its people.[8]

The social had neither direct political representation nor independent agency. But it could be addressed by the state, as it was increasingly in the course of the Third Republic. The state regulated wet nursing in order to lower infant mortality in 1874, provided tutelage for "morally abandoned" children in 1889, and enacted protective legislation for working women in 1892. It also monitored sanitary conditions in the homes of the poor to prevent the spread of contagious disease.[9] Beginning in the late 1890s, it enacted laws requiring employers to provide compensation for industrial accidents, the first of the measures that brought into being the welfare state.[10]

The notion of the social, although it was associated most frequently with the "popular classes," involved a more general rethinking of the meaning of the individual. What made state intervention plausible was that it aimed at regulating the interdependent actions of individuals, defined now as members of groups. While the privacy and singularity of individuals became an ever more prominent concern (evident in the popularity of photographic portraits, the fascination with the new science of graphology—the analysis of the unique features of individual handwriting—and the paradoxical public attention to the intimacies of private life),[11] in political discourse the individual was being defined not in opposition to society, but as a preeminently social being.[12]

The sociologist Emile Durkheim, writing at the end of the century, summed up a line of thought that rejected the "moral egoism" of Rousseauian individualism (with its autonomous, self-willing actors whose antithesis was society) and put in its place an individual who was social by definition, since the bonds that linked him to others predated his birth and could not be severed. According to this thinking, there was no contract (nor had there ever been one) entered into by individuals that could be broken. Instead society *was* the human condition. "The individual self [*le moi*] is, in fact, a we [*un nous*]; that permits us to understand why the social we [*le nous social*] can be considered a self [*un moi*]."[13] Durkheim argued that the self was not an entity, but a perception, a "coalescence" of disparate impressions integrated into "a more or less definite" sense of wholeness. Any sense of wholeness—whether of a society or of a self—was an achievement (and not a stable one), built on the functional interconnectedness of disparate parts. (In society, the social division of labor—a description Durkheim offered to replace the socialists' class struggle—consisted of this same complementary interrelationship of disparate parts.) To secure the self, an other was required and continuously internalized: "the image of the one who completes us becomes inseparable from ours . . . an integral and permanent part of our consciousness, to such a degree that we can no longer separate ourselves from it" except in the presence of the object the image represents.[14] The point was to acknowledge the relation to an other as integral to the constitution of the self: the whole (whether the individual or society) consisted of differentiated parts.

The legal theorist Léon Duguit, who had suggested that property should not be considered an individual right, emphasized the group aspect of individual identity:

> Man is a social animal, as was said long ago; the individual, then, is all the more man for being socialised, I mean for being part of social groups. I am tempted to say that it is only then that he is a superman. The superman is not at all, as Nietzsche made out, he who can impose his individual all-powerfulness; it is he who is strongly tied in to social groups, for then his life as a social man becomes more intense.[15]

And another legal scholar, René Worms, wrote: "Society is not composed directly of individuals, but of groups of which individuals are members."[16]

Although this theorizing of a new kind of individual was offered by those who considered themselves the political enemies of socialism, it shared with socialism an emphasis on the importance of collective identities and on the relational nature of those identities. Socialists, who were increasingly visible and well organized in the 1880s and 1890s, understood these collective identities as warring classes; hardworking producers faced off against their exploiters, the "bloodsucking" capitalists.[17] Republicans offered instead the idea of functional social divisions of labor, hierarchies of complementary differences, which Durkheim dubbed "organic solidarity." Conflict was replaced by mutual attraction as Durkheim made the analogy between social groups and individuals: "If one of two people has what the other has not, but desires, in that fact lies the point of departure for a positive attraction."[18] Similarly, occupational differences provided the basis for social intercourse.

Whereas the socialists imagined a world in which divisive class differences would end with the triumph of the will of the sovereign people, republicans tended to see difference as a permanent aspect of social life. Whatever the value placed on it, however, difference was a factor to be reckoned with in the political discourse of the period. Acknowledging the primacy of social difference provided a new basis for citizenship; the abstract individual—autonomous, independent, rights-bearing—no longer served to typify man, the citizen. In his place were interdependent members of groups, whose differences gave them an interest in political participation. The right to participate was given by the vote, which signified formal equality among different interests. Thus socialists argued that it was in the interests of the workers to use the vote as an arm of class struggle to achieve economic equality, while republicans pointed to the vote as a sign of that human equality which preceded asymmetries of function and power in the social division of labor. In this vein, Léon Bourgeois described solidarism as a system of "free and rational interdependence, based upon equal respect for the equal rights of all." And Charles Brunot argued that not individuals but rights were equal, interchangeable units.[19]

With difference and social identity taken as defining characteristics of individuals and the vote seen as an expression of the different interests those social differences produced, it would seem to follow that women, too, should be allowed to vote. Using the language of functional interdependence and diversity, Hubertine Auclert drew that conclusion in 1881: "Everyone cannot fill the same role; to the contrary, diversity is indispensable for the harmonious working of society . . . The duty imposed on all is different for each. The right inherent in the individual is equal for everyone."[20] But her plea for women's suffrage was systematically denied.

The terms of denial, whether socialist or republican, usually invoked a notion of a functional division of labor that assigned politics to men and domesticity to women. Although the "woman question" was a source of much debate and contest among socialists and although some groups within the workers' movement endorsed calls both for equal pay for equal work and for the vote, there was a great deal of reluctance (and often overt hostility) to taking up women's issues. At best, meetings of socialist workers voted to support women's suffrage and then let the matter drop. The justification, when it was given, was sometimes theoretical: women's emancipation must await the revolution. Sometimes it was practical: since women didn't have the vote, and since socialists wanted to win political power, it would be a waste of time to worry about representing women's interests. At other times socialists maintained that the only natural place for women was at home: "the woman at the hearth [la femme au foyer]" was the slogan of a significant portion of the working-class movement.[21]

The functional division of labor was also the republican justification for denying women the vote. It was an exception (and, Auclert would point out, a contradiction) to the promise that social divisions of labor would not affect political participation. The division of labor between man and wife, unlike divisions of labor among men, was taken to be the division between public and private, intellectual and affective, political and social. Indeed these differences were said to be the results of evolution and thus the mark of civilization.

Emile Durkheim provided a good example of this position, one that was widely subscribed to at the time. In the remote past, he noted, the differences between men and women were hardly apparent. Not only were the sexes of the same size, but they led the same existence. Women had not yet attained their now characteristic weakness and gentility; like certain female animals, they actually took pride in their warlike aggressiveness. Sexual relations were casual ("mechanical"); there was no such thing as conjugal fidelity. The coming of the division of labor changed all this. Woman "retired from warfare and public affairs and consecrated her entire life to her family." As a result "the two great functions of the psychic life . . . [were] dissociated," women becoming specialized in "affective functions," men in "intellectual functions."[22] From this followed "morphological" changes, not only in height and weight, but especially in brain size. Citing studies by the physician/sociologist Gustave Le Bon, Durkheim reported:

> with the progress of civilization the brain of the two sexes differentiates itself more and more. According to [Le Bon] this progressive chart would be due both to the considerable development of masculine crania and to a stationary or even regressive state of female crania. "Thus," he says, "though the average cranium of Parisian men ranks among the greatest known crania, the average of Parisian women ranks among the smallest observed, even below the crania of the Chinese, and hardly above those of the women of New Caledonia."[23]

The morphological evidence had a powerfully naturalizing effect on the whole argument; it established a natural history for the social process of the division of labor and a social history for the evolution of sexual difference. Both of these were taken as signs of the progress of civilization. In the contemporary world, they distinguished civilized societies from the savage: "There is even now a very great number of savage people where the woman mingles in political life."[24]

The evolutionary account sought not only to reconcile the social division of labor with the exclusion of women from politics, but also to protect the masculinity of the citizen as popular sovereignty was undermined as a basis for the republic's legitimacy. For the story of women's withdrawal from politics can be read as a parable about popular sovereignty more generally. In this reading the emergence of the social as the object of state concern diminished the importance of the individual as the source of the republic's legitimacy. The vote was then a vestigial instrument, signifying the public power of men (fathers and husbands) as a means of affirming the paternalistic rule of the state. In an odd inversion (given the historic refusal of individuality to women), the diminution of the importance of the individual as a public actor was represented by the withdrawal of woman to the private sphere, the realm of the personal, the affective. The individual, now elided with the social (as woman was ensconced in the family), was to be taken care of by the state.

The state established its legitimacy in this scenario not just by the votes of its citizens but by analogy with the fathers of families. Motivated by benevolent concern for the moral and physical well-being of his loved ones, the good bourgeois *père de famille* acted always on their behalf. The identification of male citizens with this state made its interventions into their own lives less evident and less intrusive; or at least it confounded the possibility of making clear distinctions between the sanctity of the family and the disciplinary role of the state. The analogy between the state and a father, and the restriction of citizenship to men, also served to align masculinity and politics, but in a new way. As theorists turned away from the ideas of an originary social contract and of the sovereign, independently willed individuals who concluded it, they dropped the notion that the shared maleness of citizens provided the foundation for the state. Whereas maleness had been the prior common bond of those who spoke for the nation in 1789, and of those who held property rights in their labor in 1848, by the 1890s it was the other way around: the state conferred masculinity on its citizens. While such a conception secured the loyalty of citizens to the republic, it also suggested that the lines of sexual difference were less transparent, and hence less secure, than many believed them to be. Evolution, a naturalized explanation of sexual difference, was an attempt to establish masculinity as a fact prior to and independent of state action.

But evolution could not entirely dispense with the contradictions for democratic theory created by a republic that no longer relied on popular sovereignty for its legitimation. It is here that feminism enters the analysis, exposing and embodying the contradictions. Hubertine Auclert provides the case in point.

Auclert refused to accept evolution as an explanation for the exclusion of women from politics, because it contradicted the republican promise of equality for all regardless of social/functional differences. If women were excluded, then political inequality *was* an effect of the social division of labor. And that had serious implications for the whole question of rights, and not just those of women: "Before being invoked by the adversaries of votes for women, the idea of subordinating the exercise of a right to a question of role was used as an objection to universal suffrage for men."[25] Those men who tolerated the exclusion of women, she warned the National Workers' Congress at Marseilles in 1879, were always in danger of losing their own rights. "A republic that keeps women in an inferior condition cannot make men equals."[26]

Auclert sought an alliance with socialists who held to the doctrine of popular sovereignty by arguing that the "social republic" was the only authentic form of representative government. She tried to point out that the disenfranchisement of women was tied to the depoliticizing of the social question. And since women were equated symbolically with the social (as vulnerable, dependent, in need of care), she insisted that women's rights were ultimately about popular sovereignty—about the right of the social to represent itself.

———————————

If women (and hence the social) were to be self-representing, they must meet the republic's standards of behavior and belief for its citizens. For this reason, Auclert's feminist subject was a republican subject, a (potential) citizen both "loyal and logical."[27] But constructing such a subject and maintaining her credibility entailed dealing with a number of obstacles.

By her actions Auclert sought to demonstrate her capacity (and by extension that of all women) to answer the call of the republic, to accept its conditions for full membership. She began her suffrage campaign as early as 1876, three years after her arrival in Paris, where she had come (supported by a small inheritance from her father) to join the struggle for women's rights. (She was inspired, she said, by Communards Louise Michel and André Léo and by Maria Desraimes and Léon Richer, founders of the Association for the Rights of Women in 1870).[28] She waged her battles in the pages of her newspaper, *La Citoyenne;* in hundreds of petitions she circulated and sent to the legislature; and in a small number of direct actions undertaken alone or under the auspices of feminist organizations.[29] She tried to organize a women's tax revolt and a boycott of the census. In the spring of 1880 she appeared regularly at city halls in the various arrondissements of Paris to urge women not to take the vow to "obey" the men they married. "No, Madame!" she shouted at what must have been an astonished bride.

"You do not owe obedience and submission to your husband . . . you are his equal in everything . . . Live at his side and not in his shadow . . . lift up your head . . . be his friend, his wife, his companion, and not his slave, his servant."[30] After being described as hysterical, likened to the priests who tried to inject religion back into civil marriage ceremonies by disrupting them, shunned by other feminists and by the society of freethinkers whose name she invoked to justify her behavior, and threatened with arrest by the police, she wrote articles in which she urged women not to take their husbands' names and to insist on separate property arrangements in their marriage contracts. "For a woman, possession of her name and her income or wage—that is the foundation of liberty in marriage."[31] She overcame her own reluctance to marry only when her lover, Antonin Levrier, became fatally ill. From 1888 to 1892 she lived as his wife in Algeria, where he was a magistrate, returning to Paris and to feminist activism after he died. In 1904 she joined a group of feminists on the hundredth anniversary of the promulgation of the Civil Code to burn a copy of the document that "enslaved" the women of France. And in 1908 she overturned a voting urn in the Fourth Arrondissement. In court she defended her action not as a crime against the republic, but as an exercise of politics in the name of republican liberty. She had been inspired, she told the judges, by the historical precedent of past revolutions, when "men had erected barricades in order to be able to vote."[32]

Auclert's public actions covered a wide range of possibilities, most of them tailored to meet republican standards of citizenship, and thus to prove that women could be citizens. The masthead of the early issues of *La Citoyenne* provided a graphic illustration of her intentions. Centered just below the newspaper's title, and in type almost as large, was Auclert's name; the effect was to proclaim her the exemplary female citizen. Such a self-representation accorded with her belief that the realization of her goals required their enactment. "One must act," she wrote, "as if one can do everything."[33]

She offered her action as empirical evidence that gender had nothing to do with the exercise of rights. "All sorts of scientific research is done," she pointed out, but "never has anyone tried to take a set number of children of both sexes and submit them to the same method of education, the same conditions of existence."[34] All that now existed was an empty claim lacking any basis in science. "The objection made that women know nothing about public life is invalid, since it is only through experience that one can be initiated into public life."[35]

Enacting citizenship in standard political terms was a risky business for women in the Third Republic. They could try to prove their likeness to men by demonstrating competence as journalists and orators, petitioners and organizers, strategists and reasoners, and by finding the right balance between persuasion and pressure, logical argumentation and direct action. But they also had to establish their difference from the women who had come to symbolize all that was politically dangerous for the republic. These figures of women were so deeply rooted in the political imaginary of the republic, so fully equated with the meaning given to "woman," that they could be evoked even by activities that were considered reasonable when undertaken by men.

There were two tropes that depicted women as inimical to the republic. The first was that of the unruly, sexually dangerous woman, the perpetrator of irrational violence, who was often used in popular iconography to represent the Paris Commune. This figure had a long history, dating at least from the French Revolution. For the Third Republic, the image of the *pétroleuses*, the torch-wielding furies who supposedly set out to raze Paris during the last days of the uprising against the newly established government, equated women's excesses with the excesses of revolution.[36] During the Commune women had indeed demanded their rights and played a role in political mobilization. After the Commune these activities became a sign of the entire movement's subversiveness; indeed the Commune itself was depicted as an incendiary woman whose raging passion threatened to burn up the systems of property and government that were the bases of social order. Thus one observer wrote: "the women behaved like tigresses, throwing petroleum everywhere and distinguishing themselves by the fury with which they fought; a convoy of nearly four thousand passed the Boulevards this afternoon, such figures you never saw, blackened with powder, all in tatters and filthy dirty, a few with chests exposed to show their sex, the women with their hair disheveled and of a most ferocious appearance . . ."[37]

When the imagery was taken literally, the Commune became a demonstration of the "facts" of women's nature. Even feminists participated in this discourse. When Maria Desraimes pleaded for the commutation of the death sentences of the women accused of arson, she excused them as women "whose passions were overstimulated, who in their frenzied state joined the most profound ignorance to the corruption they had experienced from the cradle."[38] For Desraimes (as for many of those who opposed her calls for reforms of women's legal status), ignorance and corruption were not the sole causes of the actions of the *pétroleuses;* rather they permitted something in the nature of women—their tendency to overexcitement and frenzy—to emerge.

The second representation of woman as a danger to the republic was that of the pious, superstitious handmaiden of the priest. A great deal of the resistance to women's suffrage rested on the belief that, since women were disproportionately susceptible to the influence of priests, their votes would enhance the power of the antirepublican, proclerical right. First articulated in 1845 by Michelet, this view gained enormous popularity, becoming almost axiomatic during the Third Republic.[39] Ardent republicans, many of them supporters of educational and legal reforms for women, drew the line at the vote. Among them was Léon Richer, a leader of the women's rights association and editor of its newspaper, *L'avenir des femmes.* Richer argued that women needed extensive education to be weaned from "the black peril" of the clergy. "Among nine million women who have attained their majority, only several thousand would vote freely; the rest would take their orders from the confessional."[40] Another republican, the solidarist philosopher Alfred Fouillée, reiterated these fears at the turn of the century: "There are already so many unqualified people in politics that I cannot foresee without anxiety women throwing themselves into the fray of political parties. In Catholic countries, the vote of most women would be that of their confessors, who themselves receive their orders from Rome. Instead of contributing to progress, it would lead, I think, to a setback. Let us wait; the question seems premature to me."[41] In 1907 Radical Party leader Georges Clemenceau reiterated this opinion more strongly. "The number of those who escape the domination of the clergy is ridiculously low," he warned. "If the right to vote were given to women tomorrow, France would suddenly jump backwards into the middle ages."[42]

The belief in women's propensity to religiosity deployed older notions about female superstition, irrationalism, and fanaticism to equate women as a group with clerical antirepublicanism. Since their presence would endanger the continued life of the political community, it was argued, their exclusion was justified. These arguments were double-edged. On the one hand, they usually attributed women's views to a lack of secular education and thus granted the possibility of change through the extension of secular education to women. On the other hand, the explanation of women's attraction to the church invoked not only institutional but psychological causes, said to be rooted in the submissive nature of woman. This explanation precluded the possibility that education would have any effect, and thereby definitively ruled out granting women the vote.[43] Although Fouillée's objection came after several decades of education for women and when numerous women teachers were successfully educating schoolchildren in the secular values of the republic, the figure of the pious woman in thrall to her confessor continued to serve as the most widely used justification for denying women the vote. It served also to equate masculinity with secularism, scientific reasoning, and independent thinking—the prerequisites for citizenship in the republic.

Despite their apparent differences, the tropes of the pious, obedient fanatic and the sexually frenzied revolutionary were two sides of the same coin. Both depicted women as subjected to and bringing to bear influences that were outside the bounds of rational control, a control women were incapable of exercising. Both considered women's susceptibility and lack of discipline dangerous to the republic. Even at home, a woman might be an agent of priestly subversion, but in the political realm the damage she could do was much greater.

Auclert tried to present an alternative to these images. Accepting the Third Republic's reverence for rationalism, positivism, secularism, and science, she displayed an eminently rational self, disciplined through the force of logic. The word "logic" recurred throughout her writing. She called on women to show "more logic" than those who oppressed them, and she denounced unequal treatment repeatedly as "neither just nor logical."[44] She submitted to logical tests the arguments made against women's rights: Would anyone suggest that the specialized functions of the baker denied him the vote? she asked. "It would be as logical" to do that as to exclude women from these rights because they did housework and cared for children.[45]

For Auclert, women deserved rights because they were logical beings,

not the undisciplined fanatics of republican fantasy, nor, for that matter, Olympe de Gouges's individuals constructed through imagination,
or Jeanne Deroin's loving mothers. Feminists by virtue of their campaigns for the vote and their own identification with a constructed or
"invented" tradition, these three were separated by the differences of
their historical contexts—differences that were matters not simply of
background events, emphasis, or detail, but of the discursive arenas in
which the very meanings of "women" and their rights were constructed.

Auclert's method was scientific according to the standards of her
time; truth, for her, was a matter of fact. And fact, she considered, was
self-evident. Although Auclert believed that the assertion of fact in a
logical argument could dispel contradiction, her own arguments—like
those of Olympe de Gouges and Jeanne Deroin—did not avoid paradox.

Routinely she concluded vehement denunciations of the harmful
effects of women's disenfranchisement with offers of empirical proof:
"We can support this allegation with facts."[46] Numbers were even more
persuasive, she thought. Whenever she could, she provided them to
support her position. If anyone doubted that women's tax contributions were appropriated for men's uses, for example, they need only
consult the state budget and compare the allocations for women and
men: "Numbers are eloquent; they prove better than words that we
have reason for mistrust."[47] As social investigators made their cases for
legislation or regulation with data gathered from statistical surveys,
Auclert countered with facts to support her recommendations for
reform.[48] Why not pay women for housework? she asked at one point.
Since, when a wife died, her husband had to hire a nurse for his
children, wasn't this clear evidence of the monetary value of wives'
domestic work? To those who maintained that paid work was destructive to women's physical and moral well-being, she offered a consideration of the low level of women's wages. "It is not work, but poverty,
that kills women."[49]

To the head of the typographers' union, Jacques Alary, who in 1883
insisted that admitting women to the printer's trade would destroy not
only the women themselves but also French civilization, she retorted
that printing was indeed an appropriate trade for women. In an inflam-

matory pamphlet, Alary had predicted that a woman who undertook
to work in a printing shop "will be deformed by taking on the look,
the voice, and the gross mannerisms of the men she associates with in
the shop; she will finally fall into a state of nature and become simply
female." That becoming "simply female" was a return to animality,
worse even than slavery or barbarism, was clear: "Where is the negress
from Havana or the Turkish harem girl who would agree to exchange
the Spanish hacienda or the Turkish household for a place in a printing
shop?" Since the condition of women was a test of the progress of
civilization, and since only domestic confinement kept women "delicate" and "elegant," French civilization rested on "la femme au foyer."[50]
In response to Alary, Auclert pointed firmly to the "facts" of women's
employment. Could the work of a compositor possibly be any more
tedious than shopkeeping, which required women to stand all day, or
more dangerous than laundering, which had women plunging their
hands into scalding water and lifting heavy, sizzling irons? Would the
high wage of the printer be more of an inducement to moral corruption
than the impossibly low wage of the pieceworker who sewed boots and
had to supplement her insufficient earnings by prostitution? The facts
of women's working life patently contradicted the assertions of printers,
she maintained. Those who refused to be persuaded by these facts were
acting out of either self-interest or bad faith.[51]

One of these motives was clearly the explanation for those who
justified women's exclusion from politics in the name of protecting the
republic from its religious enemies. There was a double contradiction
in their argument, Auclert said, so flagrant that its tolerance could be
attributed only to hypocrisy. Women were surely no more committed
to the clerical cause than were priests, and yet priests voted. If fear of
religious influence was the issue, why let those vote whose profession
was religion? There was only one obvious answer: "Of course M. le curé
is a man." In addition, the republican justification for excluding women
was based ultimately on biblical teaching about the sins and punishment of Eve. "Man has made these laws, and even in our era of atheism
and free inquiry, he conserves them religiously."[52]

Having established that these contradictions prevailed because they
perpetuated men's power, Auclert nevertheless sought to disprove them
by scientific means. She called upon women who held secular views to

put them into practice, in order to demonstrate that religious belief was a matter not of sexual identity but of political affiliation. To counteract prejudices against them, women must furnish the proof of their antagonism to the church. "To offset the troublesome influence of reactionary women, the salutary influence of republican women is necessary."[53] As early as 1877 she urged women to support her call for the expulsion of the Jesuits. If they remained indifferent or mute, she warned, they would be accused of making common cause with the clergy in their obscurantist work, thus justifying prevailing opinions. "Let us show that we are not with them. Let us rise up, and let our cry of protestation be heard from one end of France to the other. Let us say loudly to the world that we want enlightenment, liberty."[54]

Given all these facts and demonstrations, Auclert's attempt to offer proof in the face of hypocrisy was paradoxical, since hypocrisy, by definition, is an interested denial of what is known to be the truth. In a way, this strategy worked to her advantage anyway, for it marked her own position as truthful and disinterested. At the same time, she recognized the difficulty of using logical reasoning to construct a political subject. If interest was the obstacle, no amount of reason could persuade. In the end, both reason and force were the answers. When Auclert announced the formation of her National Society for Women's Suffrage in 1883, she declared her commitment to rely not on force but on "persuasion," by which she meant the power of logical reasoning.[55] And in the same article she urged that women create a counterforce to male power: "one cannot demand of human nature more perfection than it has; as long as men alone make the laws, they will make them for themselves and against us."[56]

The historical record showed how intent men were on preserving their power, she said. Women's support for revolutions in the past had been no guarantee that men would share power once they won it. Dismissing the promise of some "alleged socialists" that women would receive rights in a future new society, Auclert pointed out that that was an old ploy of revolutionaries who had no intention of keeping their "holy promises." One had only to remember the experience of Olympe de Gouges at the time of the Great Revolution; women then had naively worked for political change only to be ridiculed and punished for their efforts by the very men they had helped to victory. In 1848 the experience was repeated; by proclaiming the rights of *tous les français* and then restricting them to only "half the nation," men displayed their true "selfishness." Things were no different now, she maintained. Why should a Chamber of Deputies consisting entirely of men, and living off revenues from women's taxes, give up their right to be sole judges and masters of women? The only correction to this situation was the mobilization of women against them. Argument alone would never prevail; women must organize a counterforce to achieve emancipation.

In Auclert's articulation of feminist political goals, however, the choice between force and persuasion was never clear-cut. This dilemma was not hers alone. It was part of the prevailing tension among liberals, conservatives, radicals, and socialists about how much political conflict could be permitted without endangerment to the life of the republic. When did mobilization on behalf of a specific interest or to express opposition to government policy cross the line separating persuasion from force? The issue of trade unions was an example, and their legalization in 1884 amounted to an acknowledgment that economic pressure might be an acceptable way to "persuade" employers. But the willingness of the government to intervene against strikers (and the bloody confrontations that resulted in the 1890s and 1900s) was clear evidence of the indeterminacy of the distinction between legitimate means of persuasion and unacceptable uses of force.[57]

The tension between persuasion and force was exacerbated for Auclert by the fact that it was a *female* political subject she wanted to create. Any allusion to "force" could conjure up the harpies of the Commune; for that reason she often emphasized "persuasion" and did not use the word "force" even when that was what she had in mind. But persuasion also had its limits. In order to persuade, women had to be considered parties to political discussion, and they had to express themselves within the existing terms of debate.[58] But because they could not vote, they were excluded from discussion, hence disqualified from using persuasion. More difficult still, they were not included in the terms of discussion used by others. As a result they were doubly absent: they could not enter politics to represent their interests, *and* those interests were not represented in the debates.

Thus it was that language inscribed women's inferiority or rendered women invisible, Auclert said. For certain occupations or functions there wasn't even a word that designated a female. How could feminists demand the right for a woman to serve as a witness, an elector, or a lawyer, she asked, when those words existed only in the masculine gender? It would not do to say that gender was neutral in these cases, that women could be included under the male designation. If they were, there was no way to represent them—they could not even be included in statistics (the primary means of securing objective representation). "Isn't it through the force of saying certain words that one ends by accepting the meaning they literally denote?" Auclert called for a "feminization of language," the introduction of specifically feminine equivalents of hitherto exclusively masculine nouns. "The first feminization is that of language, because if the feminine is not distinctly established, it will always be subsumed by the masculine."[59] Auclert pointed to the power of language to change material reality—in this case the sexual division of labor—that language was supposed only to describe. For those committed to a conversation that took sexual difference as a natural premise, Auclert's suggestion could never be persuasive.

Even more troubling about associating persuasion with women, however, was establishing their capacity for logical reasoning. When Auclert used the term "persuasion," she meant the systematic repression of a contrary proposition. But persuasion had other connotations that contradicted the notion that it was a process in which truth prevailed over error. It denoted eloquence; it was an appeal not to the mind but to the soul; it inspired conviction through the "beauty" of its performance. Religion persuaded as well as science, and a woman's tears moved a man to action as easily as a scholar's ideas. Persuasion might rest on error as well as on truth; there was nothing self-evidently good or true about beliefs one had been persuaded to accept.[60] Moreover, like the notions of imagination or androgyny in earlier periods, persuasion was gendered. The use of beauty, eloquence, and emotion to persuade was most often described in terms of the ploys of women. Indeed, rhetoric was considered the "feminine" counterpart to "masculine" philosophy. The persuasive woman was more typically a threat to logical reasoning than an incarnation of it.

Thus, when a woman claimed to be engaged in logical reasoning in order to persuade, as Auclert did, she drew a complicated response. On the one hand, she offered the possibility that women could persuade

by means and for ends usually not associated with them; in this way
she demonstrated a capacity for reasoned argument and so effectively
challenged prevailing stereotypes. On the other hand, since a logical
woman was an illogical combination, her persuasiveness had to be
attributed to other factors. In this vein, commentators noted with a
certain ambivalence Auclert's "eloquence" and her ability "to provoke
emotion" in her audience.[61]

For the female political subject, then, persuasion was at best ambiguous. Her logical reasoning abilities might be better addressed to those
who shared her interests than to those whose interests were unalterably
opposed to her own. Excluded from both the arena and the language
of politics, women had no access to the means and terms of persuasion
and thus no recourse but to embrace the idea of force. It was thus that
Auclert appealed to women to challenge the right of those in power to
speak for society as a whole, reasoning that the interests of women
could be known to and represented by only themselves.

Auclert's attempt to constitute the female political subject as an
exemplary republican exposed the limits of the very project of establishing republican subjects. The goal of consensus and homogeneity,
embraced most fully in the educational curriculum, ruled out of order
any dissent that was fundamental. In that way, politics legitimated the
rule of the powerful, expanding to include only those who agreed to
play by the rules. Women were the sign of irreducible difference in this
system, but not its only possible articulation. (Workers, too, represented
and enacted unacceptable dissent.) Feminist demands for inclusion
required either that such difference be admissible—that revolution be
entertained as a serious possibility—or that women not be considered
fundamentally different. But the latter alternative was no less revolutionary, since it called into question the law—the constitutional equation between masculinity and citizenship. Either way, therefore, in the
symbolic structure of politics, the female political subject was a revolutionary subject—however legalistic her actions, however reasonable
her words.

Auclert's main line of argument was that there was a connection between women's interests and the interests of the social. Functionalist
thinking had given more credence to the notion of a women's interest

during the Third Republic, not only among the growing numbers of women organized in suffrage societies, but also among legislators willing to support bills in favor of the vote. (From 1906 on, support for these bills increased in the Chamber of Deputies, although after 1919 and until 1944 the far more conservative Senate regularly defeated them.)[62] Supporters of women's suffrage argued that women had an "interest" that must be taken into account and a specialized knowledge that was required if the welfare of the nation was to be properly administered. (Welfare and women were often taken to be the same thing.) Women's interest must then be represented by a women's vote. Ferdinand Buisson, deputy for the Seine and president of the Chamber's commission on universal suffrage, called in 1911 for women's "social collaboration" through the vote: "It has been observed that in public life there are a great number of interests that a woman is as qualified as, more qualified than, a man to look after and to serve."[63] These interests had to do with "the family, public assistance, hygiene, protection of young girls and children"—in short, with the social.[64]

Auclert appealed to this "women's interest" as she articulated a feminist political identity. But the ambiguities of the term presented an enormous challenge to her, for interest connoted particular advantage, selfish motivation, and profit, as well as empathy or concern for, curiosity about, even attraction to, others. It pitted individuals and groups against one another when their interests were opposed, but it also drew them together when common interest created a shared identity; it was at once divisive and binding.[65] Beyond this, the notion of interest implied the prior existence of the subject whose interest was being invoked. "Women's interest" conjured up a subject with an abiding set of needs and attributes, what we would now call an essentialist conception of women. It also ran the risk of so particularizing women that their exclusion from the general body politic was affirmed.

Auclert tried to avoid esssentializing and particularizing women even while appealing to "women's interest." She did so by explaining that women's particularity was the historical effect of constitutional laws (beginning with the constitution of 1791) that stripped all women of the political rights that some women (depending on their birth and marriage) had enjoyed in the past. The legal exclusion of women as a group, she argued, created their agency as advocates for the restoration of a lost justice.

While she insisted on the historical origins of women's interests, Auclert maintained that women's interests were in fact not particular at all; they were consonant with the general social interest. Yet again, however, she sought to avoid the complete conflation of women's interest with the general interest, lest she lose the ability to appeal to women's separate political identity. Here was the paradox of "sexual difference" exemplified; there was no clear way to make the case for a specific women's interest when general equality with men was the goal.

In 1881 Auclert explained the need for a newspaper and an organization devoted to women's interest: "To those who accuse us of being exclusionary, of making the question of women a separate question, we answer that we will be obliged to pose the question of women as long as women are placed in a separate condition; and that, until woman has the power to intervene to defend her interests wherever they are at stake, any change in the economic or political condition of society will not ameliorate her condition."[66] It is unclear in this statement whether women's interests are the result of discrimination against them or whether that discrimination prevents them from defending their already existing interests. That lack of distinction actually grounds women's collective identity, making it both the cause for and the product of a concerted mobilization.

What were "women's interests"? Auclert rarely elaborated on them except to make the vote both an interest and the means of defending other interests. And usually she contrasted these other interests with what she referred to as men's "interest of sex [*intérêt du sexe*]." That selfish desire to dominate socially and sexually led to monopolies of male power in the trades as well as in politics, to a corporate defense of particular investments necessarily at odds with the general good. Auclert regularly posed one kind of interest (particular, selfish, sexual, male) against the other (general/human, selfless, loving, female). She identified men with war and death, women with peace and the preservation of life, men with waste and instability, women with economy and social harmony. It was women who knew how to economize, establish workable budgets, impose order, and realize "social harmony." And women could be counted on to represent the nation as it was: "the national housekeeper will acquit her office with more humanity than glory."[67] Women, in this view, were the social and its representative; the call for their enfranchisement was a repudiation of the benevolent paternalism of the republican state.

Women's identification with the social was by definition not particularistic; indeed Auclert saw no difference among the various groups of adults who looked to the state for justice and welfare. Women, she argued, were structurally and socially like workers, and workers were like women. In consequence, there was a natural alliance to be made between the working class and feminist movements; both groups had the same issues at stake. Auclert first proposed this idea in a speech to the National Workers' Congress at Marseilles in 1879, one of the early attempts to organize a socialist workers' party in France.[68] She came to the Congress as the delegate of two organizations, a cooperative of women workers, Les Travailleuses de Belleville, and of her feminist association, called at that date Le Droit des Femmes. If, as the liberal theorists suggested, she said, the sexual division of labor was a paradigm for the social division of labor, then workers and women must make common cause. But, she continued, the liberals were wrong about the consequences of complex social differentiation, and the socialists were right. The increasing division of labor in society had brought not the harmony of friendship, but the strife of conflicting interests, of oppressed versus oppressor, exploited versus exploiter; in similar fashion, the increasing division of sexual labor had proletarianized women. "I am here, full of esteem for this great assembly, the first group of freely elected worker-delegates in France in centuries that has permitted a woman, not because she is a worker, but because she is a woman— that is to say, one who is exploited—the slave delegate of nine million slaves, to present the demands of the disinherited half of the human species."[69]

"Woman—that is to say, one who is exploited," collapsed the distinction between worker and woman, since in the language of the nascent labor movement workers were by definition those who were exploited. Auclert evoked the difficulties of women's lives in terms that workers shared: both groups needed work, subsistence, and wages to enable them to support others as well as themselves; both needed access to law and political rights to advance and protect their interests. At the same time she described women's situation as a more extreme version of workers', since women were still "slaves" because they lacked the

vote. These were issues that workers, themselves oppressed and mis-
treated by their bosses, should understand; there would be no real
liberty or fraternity for them until women had achieved economic,
social, and political emancipation. In the final analysis it was illogical
and immoral for working men to take on the role of oppressors,
becoming one with their own bourgeois enemies in order to dominate
women; the two groups were, after all, equivalent, perhaps even the
same: "We address ourselves to you, proletarians, our comrades in
misfortune, to support our right to emancipation. You are voters, you
have the power of numbers; all of you are women at heart [*tous vous
êtes femmes par le coeur*], you are our brothers. Help us to liberate
ourselves." [70]

There was no difference, at heart, between women and working men.
In order to range the "proletarians" on her side, Auclert likened their
values and sentiments (desire for happiness, reform, peace, intimacy,
and love) to those of women, and in opposition to aggressive, competi-
tive, warlike bourgeois men, "our common oppressors." She at once
obliterated the line of sexual difference between working men and all
women and reconstructed it to distinguish the unemancipated from
their bourgeois exploiters. Her speech borrowed its rhetoric and de-
meanor from the orators who usually spoke to groups of laborers,
articulating an identity for them as members of a working class. As she
passed "from polemic to appeal, from lyricism to caustic irony, from
repeated denunciation to exalted peroration," Auclert, too, articulated
that class identity.[71] But she stripped it of its masculine pretension, both
by the content of her speech and by the fact that a woman was
delivering it.

The camaraderie she appealed to and enacted was premised on
likeness, not on difference, on the mutual recognition of the powerless.
The interests of workers and women were the interests of the exploited,
those members of the social body that it was the job of the state to
defend and protect. Unless the exploited were able to represent themselves in the government, however, the state would fail to fulfill its
responsibility. For the state was not a neutral instrument, but—analo-
gous as it was to the patriarchal bourgeois family—a form of class and
gender domination.

The alternative, for Auclert, was not to abandon the idea of a relationship between the state and the social, but to reconceive it and the familial model on which it was based. The analogy between state and family kept a place for a separate women's identity, an identity Auclert had to maintain if she were not to see the interest of women subsumed within that of (male) workers in the logic of her own appeal. In the place of paternal rule she offered parental cooperation: both partners represented and governed the social needs and interests of its members. "It is not possible to be man and woman at the same time," she wrote in a 1908 pamphlet. "It would be considered strange for a man to play the role of father and mother in a family, and yet it is permitted to men to play this double role in the legislature."[72] Indeed the representation of women was the only guarantee of wholeness and "virility" for the republic. It was not simply that women's domestic expertise was needed in the "large household," "la cuisine administrative," now so poorly managed by men; the issue was far more serious than a simple division of social labor.[73] For a republic that refused women the vote was "mutilated," as "impotent" as an amputee missing an arm or leg. Its gait was limping, its one-eyed vision distorted. It lacked the generative power that could come only from the coupling of men and women in the political realm.[74] Not only was the general welfare compromised by the exclusion of women, but so were men's health, their masculinity, their very life.[75] Auclert compared the excision of women from the social body to the bodily mutilation practiced by Saints Jerome and Cyprian. Like them and for the same irrational reasons, "the free-thinking legislators mutilate the social body, cutting off half its limbs to spare themselves impure feminine contact."[76] Such actions were not only abnormal but also self-defeating, for without the explicitly heterosexual partnership of women, men could fulfill neither their own nor society's destiny. Indeed, without the presence of women, men lacked the phallus that guaranteed their masculinity. Women, then, were the phallus— the source of men's power.

Thus Auclert argued that denial of the vote to women called into question the state's ability to ensure the masculinity of its citizens. The vote for men alone, she cautioned, was a ruse, creating the illusion of sovereignty when in fact it constituted a cession of power. The subordination of women was symbolically and actually the subordination of the social to the political and the state (and working men were included in the social). As long as the social remained the object of legislation and could not speak on its own behalf, men (especially working men) as well as women were denied a fundamental right of self-representation (even if men had the vote). The dissociation of the social and the political, mothers and fathers, women and men, was achieved by the denial of citizenship to women. Denying the social an active role on its own behalf made substantive rights and social justice matters of administrative regulation rather than of politics. When this happened, male citizens were rendered impotent as representatives of their own social (and economic) interests.

The interest of the social, then, was women's interest, not because women literally cared more about health, welfare, and justice, but because those areas, like women, were deemed extraneous to politics. "French women have a sense of utilitarian democracy. When they are voters and candidates, they will force administrative and legislative assemblies to understand human needs and to satisfy them."[77] For Auclert, the enfranchisement of women would be the enfranchisement of the social and the restoration of the potency of citizenship—a potency realized only when men's (sexual, social, symbolic) need for women was acknowledged by the recognition of women's political rights.

The notion of a parental rather than a paternal state also informed Auclert's discussions of French policy in Algeria, where she lived for four years as Levrier's wife. In articles sent to Parisian newspapers from 1888 to 1892 (and in 1900 gathered into a book) she linked the plight of "les femmes arabes en Algérie" to her campaign for suffrage. She was quite sure that if French women had anything to say about colonial policy, their Algerian sisters (the more accurate analogy was probably daughters) would never be as exploited and degraded as they now were. French women's interest, in this case, was not only in the social problems of Algerian women, but also in the general improvement of colonial rule. Auclert accepted the view that France's mission was to "civilize" the more primitive natives, enlightening them with republican secularism and modern science. She found it puzzling, therefore, that the French tolerated Koranic law, since it was both religious and arbitrary. And she was even more disturbed by the licentious practices this law seemed to encourage, practices that seemed to her particularly degrading to Muslim women.

In her book on Algeria, Auclert likened prejudice against women to racial prejudice; in both cases the undervaluation of the innate capacity of those excluded (women, natives) delayed the advance of "civilization." The absence of white women from the councils of French administration prevented the uplifting of a naturally "gifted and beautiful race."[78] The scorn of French men for all Arabs resulted in the perpetuation of ignorance and superstition instead of its banishment; in this way the French mission undermined its own ends.

> It is by observing how racial prejudice dominates everything in Algeria that one understands the absurdity of sexual prejudice. Thus it is that the Arab race, so beautiful and well endowed, is scorned absolutely by Europeans, who, however, are rarely as handsome or possess as many natural abilities as the Arabs. And here is the contradiction. The French conqueror says to the Muslim: "I scorn your race, but I abase my law before yours; I give the Koran precedence over the Code."[79]

In what we would now call a classically "orientalist" approach, Auclert regarded Algeria and its women as exotic, lush, and sensual.[80] The images she offered were physical and erotic: she described exhausted and exploited bodies, men and women copulating in the streets, young girls forced to have sex, women dying from the strain of bearing too many children, mothers with disfigured and empty breasts nursing their babies with their blood. (The exploitation of French women, in contrast, was discussed abstractly in terms of institutions, social resources, legal codes, and political power.) The danger of the situation, as she saw it, was not simply that Algerian women's condition undermined the progress of "civilization," but also that it corrupted the colonial administrators and, by extension, the high standards of civilized France. For if French men participated even indirectly in the degradation of Algerian womanhood, what was to stop them from "forgetting" their training and treating French women in the same way? Only the moralizing presence of French women could set the situation right; if French women voted and participated in colonial affairs, native women would receive the same education as men, Algerians would be allowed to develop the virtues of secular republicanism by voting—the "civilizing mission" would be set on its proper course. As things now stood, she wrote several years later, "cultivated white women" were denied the vote while "savage blacks" were given it. And although she supported the right of "natives" to the vote in a republic, she considered their preferential treatment over white women "an insult to the white race."[81] Indeed, racial prejudices were primary in this argument. "Civilized" French women, already triumphant over the instincts and passions of their bodies, were finally the most reliable agents of French colonial policy. Like mothers in a family, they would provide discipline and morality for the nation and all its members. Like mothers, too, they would raise their dependent children to become loyal citizens of the republic. (When it came to children and "natives," the family analogy, redefined to equalize the roles of mother and father, retained all its connotations of hierarchy and dependence.)

Auclert made women's interest most fully synonymous with the national interest in her discussion of Algerian women, but her argument there was not uncharacteristic. The objective was to bring women's knowledge of the social to bear on the formulation of policy; to make women full partners in the administration of the nation; and to end the separation between the political and the social, without, however, fully dissolving the differences between men and women. The identity of women as a definable political constituency was achieved in critical opposition to existing policy and understood as the result of that policy. At the same time, the particularity of this identity was denied by making "women's interest" synonymous not only with the social interest, but with the goals of the republic itself. "When women, who have the same interests in the State as men do, are, like them, armed with the rights necessary to protect themselves, to defend themselves, to improve their lot, France, in possession of the sum total of its mental forces, will take its place as a world leader."[82]

Like the socialists whose support she sought, Auclert refused to abandon the notion of popular sovereignty. If genuine equality was to be achieved, she maintained, the state could not be construed as a father (however generous and caring), and citizenship could not remain an all-male affair.

Auclert had long denounced the equation of masculinity and politics as selfish and antisocial. She characterized the evolutionary story of women's withdrawal from politics as a fable that masked an unwarranted expulsion, accomplished by means of law.[83] She looked upon the use of state power to protect male power as a calculated usurpation, contrary to the republic's stated purpose. In this regard she had labeled unacceptable the call of typographers' union leader Jacques Alary for government legislation to "put insuperable obstacles in the path" of women who sought employment as compositors.[84] Alary argued that if women became printers they would become like men and then, inevitably, men would become women: "It is unacceptable that men should have to live like drones and stay at home to care for the household."[85] To live like a drone was to have value only as a source of sperm for the queen, only as an agent of reproduction. To live like a drone was to live like a human female, to be degraded as a man. No truly republican government would permit such degradation, according to Alary. In his view, law was the guarantee against such degradation. Auclert called this use of this power an abuse of the state in the selfish interests of men.

Auclert denounced the association between the republic and the masculinity of its citizens, but its persistence was evident in the reaction to one of her protests in 1908. Along with feminists Caroline Kauffmann and Madeleine Pelletier, she entered a polling place in the Fourth Arrondissement on election day and knocked over a voting urn while denouncing the "lie" of "unisexual suffrage." Testifying later, one of the election officials reported that witnessing this scene had produced in him an awful stillness, as if he had gazed on the Medusa.[86]

It is impossible, since Freud, to read that account without thinking about castration. And if one takes Freud as the reader of a certain cultural logic, then his analyses can illuminate what in this case seems an exaggerated (and irrational) response by the election official. Freud took the decapitated head of Medusa, the monstrous symbol reflected on Athena's shield, to signify castration.[87]

> To decapitate = to castrate. The terror of Medusa is thus a terror of castration that is linked to the sight of something. Numerous analyses have made us familiar with the occasion for this: it occurs when a boy, who has hitherto been unwilling to believe the threat of castration, catches sight of the female genitals, probably those of an adult, surrounded by hair, and essentially those of his mother.[88]

By extension, Athena, who bears the horrible head on her shield, becomes "a woman who is unapproachable and repels all sexual desires—since she displays the terrifying genitals of the Mother." She is "a representation of woman as a being who frightens and repels because she is castrated."[89] The recognition of the horror of castration, however, carries with it a certain reassurance for the boy, which is the basis for his comprehension of sexual difference. Freud writes:

> The sight of the Medusa's head makes the spectator stiff with terror, turns him to stone. Observe that we have here once again the same origin from the castration complex and the same transformation of affect! For becoming stiff means an erection. Thus in the original situation it offers consolation to the spectator: he is still in possession of the penis, and the stiffening reassures him of the fact.[90]

The Medusa, then, has a double effect: it is at once a threat to male sexual power and a confirmation of it; by embodying the horror of what might be, the image intensifies a desire to preserve what is.[91]

In the official's account, the violent interruption of the exercise of the vote (Auclert trampled the ballots as they spilled onto the ground) was experienced as the threat of castration. By questioning the legitimacy of one of the boundaries between the sexes, Auclert was taken to be questioning sexual difference itself. But at the same time, the fact that her action was illegal (she was arrested by the police and fined by a judge) ruled her questions out of order, thus reassuring the official that the vote (like the phallus it signified for him) belonged to men alone. It was exactly this association between the phallus and the vote that led an irate journalist to refuse Auclert's demand for women's suffrage in these terms: "Is it our resignation as men that dame Hubertine asks of us? Let her say it frankly."[92]

Auclert rejected this association of masculinity and the vote in the name of the social division of labor. She pointed out that not all social divisions followed the lines of gender: "to be man or woman matters no more in the distribution of social functions than it does to be tall or short, brown-haired or blond, fat or thin."[93] Sexual divisions in the social/political fields were arbitrary impositions, she added, designed to protect men's monopoly of certain jobs and of political power, their "interest of sex." When women had access to law, they would represent more than their own interest, she argued; they would represent the social interest. Indeed, only when women voted would the social achieve the kind of importance politicians and sociologists already attributed to it. "By becoming a citizen, the French woman will fulfill her duty even better, since her role as educator will extend to the entire human collectivity and her maternal solicitude will encompass the whole nation."[94]

Auclert's vision was far more democratic than that of the theorists and politicians whose discourse she invoked. In her version of republican politics, women (who stood for the social) were not the passive recipients of assistance; they were active agents and their agency was symbolized by the vote. Even if the sexes had fundamentally different natures (she talked of "the rough nature of man . . . the soft character of woman"), even if only women could bear children, the social value of men's and women's contributions to the nation were equivalent and must be recognized as such.[95] Women reproduced the nation while soldiers defended its life. In fact, if the sheer investment of time were taken into account—a few weeks of training versus nine months of gestation—"it would be infinitely less easy for men to be mothers than for women to be soldiers."[96] Auclert had endorsed the proposals offered by the slate of women who ran for office in 1885 that there must be compulsory military service for men and compulsory humanitarian service for women. "Defense of territory to men—care for children, the old, the sick, and infirm entrusted to women."[97] Different tasks, but equally vital functions, warranted political equality.

Only political equality, she argued, would meet the goal of justice to which the republic had pledged itself. Then women's participation as voters and elected representatives would transform "the minotaur State" into "the maternal State," she wrote in 1885.[98] In these metaphors, the half-human predatory monster who demands tributes of money and blood is replaced by a wholly human figure, solicitous of the welfare of everyone: strong and weak, rich and poor, young and old, sick and well. The humanization of the state is also its feminization, the displacement of the father by the mother. In Auclert's figuration the repressed returns: the object of state concern (the social) becomes the subject of its own care, restoring a form of exactly that popular sovereignty which the paternalist republican state sought to contain.

And it was, indeed, as a popular mobilization of the social that Auclert ultimately defined her suffrage campaign. Although she counseled persuasion as a feminist tactic, Auclert concluded that reasonable arguments were not enough to defeat men's "interest of sex."[99] What was required was a counterforce that could bring public pressure on women's behalf: "If men are strong it is because they unite and reunite. Let us do as men do [*Faisons comme les hommes*]!"[100]

"Faisons comme les hommes" was a call to political action, an urgent summons to women to emulate the socialists, whose claim to represent the interests of the working class had, since the late 1880s, won them increasing numbers of seats in the Chamber of Deputies and on municipal councils throughout the nation. "Faisons comme les hommes" was an endorsement of the idea that collective interest (and not individual will) was the engine of political participation. But it was also a repudiation of the prevailing terms of the social/sexual division of labor and of the role of the state in perpetuating them. It treated law not as a means of regulating natural phenomena, but as an instrument of (male) power. Auclert's battle cry announced an intention both to share and to seize that exclusive power. In either case the result would be the same: to strip citizenship of its ability to confer or confirm masculinity and thus to deprive the state of its role as the representative father.

If women could indeed do what men did in politics, how could the differences between the sexes be discerned? how could the role of the state be made acceptable? By forcing her contemporaries to confront these questions, Auclert exposed the tenuous relationship between sexual difference and politics. This was the source of the hostility to her and of the critical strength of her feminism.

———————■———————

In the annals of French feminism, Hubertine Auclert has been remembered less as a pioneering figure than as an outspoken and sometimes troublesome militant. Her insistence on direct action, while it earned her the sobriquet "the French suffragette," neither galvanized a large following nor won for her the retrospective renown of an Olympe de

Gouges or of activist counterparts such as the Pankhursts in England and Susan B. Anthony in the United States. As the women's suffrage movement gained a mass following, it eclipsed Auclert's efforts rather than celebrating them. Her early call for the vote was more often deemed premature than prescient by the women who took up the feminist cause at the turn of the century. They stressed the need for respectability, explicitly (and ironically, given her own disavowal of particularity) rejecting Auclert for her "particularism." Bitterly, Auclert dubbed these newcomers opportunists who endorsed the vote only "after studying the weather vane for a long time," while they "pretended that they invented the movement."[101] She derided their timidity and resented their usurpation of what she considered to be her rightful place in history.

In a way she was right. Auclert's funeral, in April 1914, drew large numbers of feminists, who listened appreciatively to more than a dozen speakers; accounts of the event (which praised her extraordinary "ardor and perseverance") were front-page news at the time.[102] An obituary in *La femme de demain* (Woman of tomorrow) stated that she had earned the right to the title of "mother of women's suffrage on the day when it becomes a reality in our country."[103] But when the vote did come, Auclert was rarely given this kind of credit by her successors. Although she drew renewed attention as feminists in the 1970s began to compile histories of the women's movement, the first biography of her was written by an American historian and published only in 1987. His account honors her desire to be remembered for her uniqueness, as a martyr to the more backward thinking of the moderate and legalistic mainstream of the French suffragist movement. "At the society Suffrage des Femmes, we have tried to force the development of feminist ideas as gardeners try to force the flowering of plants," she wrote in a note to herself, "but . . . forcing does not produce new convictions. It takes, alas! time to make flowers bloom, as it does to change *mentalités*. But time is long and life is short!"[104]

Auclert did not achieve, either in her lifetime or subsequently, the kind of historical recognition she sought. This fact is not entirely surprising. For one thing, the size of the movement and the diversity of its strategic positions in the period 1870–1914 offered many more examples of active, articulate feminism than had been available earlier.

For another, the movement's divisions and the inability of any of its factions to deliver the vote contradicted the tenets of teleological history. All sides might agree that Olympe de Gouges, allowed to die for beliefs she was forbidden to utter in the public forum, embodied the ironic fate of feminism; but they did not agree on much more, including whether Jeanne Deroin's illegal run for office was an appropriate precedent for women in the Third Republic.

Auclert repeatedly corrected the historical accounts of her own role (and that of others) written by journalist Jane Misme (editor of *La Française* and a latecomer to suffrage, who founded the French Union for Women's Suffrage in 1909). But despite her reference to the slow germination of new ideas, she did not produce a linear, evolutionary story of women's defense of their political rights. Rather, the actions of women in the past—as far back as Jeanne de Navarre and Jeanne d'Arc—provided evidence for the enduring capacity of women to engage in politics and proof that the first revolution's constitution, which had equated citizenship with masculinity, had introduced distortions into previously more equitable social arrangements. Her account of the present was a defense of her own embattled actions, which were depicted not as the products of an inevitable and cumulating historical development, but of the logic and moral purpose of her thought. Feminism, in this view, involved the detection and elimination of those contradictions in the theory and practice of republicanism that led to the unjust (and unjustifiable) subordination of women. Its history was about repeated efforts to resolve an enduring contradiction, not about progress based on accumulated wisdom and ever more effective strategy.

Auclert's craving for an identifiable place as one who opened a new chapter in an evolutionary story of French feminism was at odds with her own inability to write that kind of history. She insisted that the vote was an instrument of social progress if universally applied: "Suffrage is a machine for progress . . . Like many other modern inventions, which become useful only with the help of certain arrangements, suffrage needs all the feminine and masculine energies of the nation in order to become an evolutionary instrument capable of transforming the social order."[105] But she did not conceive of feminism itself in evolutionary terms. It was rather a strategic intervention driven by a moral purpose; and its adherents were more or less adept at hunting down contradiction, in whatever form it took at a particular time.

Auclert's wish to be remembered as having opened a chapter in feminist history had a great deal to do with the vision of history of her age. She lived at a time when monumental histories were being written from many different political perspectives, and few of these granted any positive agency to women. Indeed many of them placed women outside history entirely, assigning them to timeless, natural, transcendent realms. Auclert, who made the case for politics, was also making the case for women's role as historical actors. It followed, therefore, that lue, if not the success, of her efforts would be measured by the attainment of a distinctive, even unique, place in history.

But the attainment of such a place is necessary only if agency is itself conceived ahistorically, as an attribute of individual will rather than as the effect of discursive attribution, that is, of the designation of specific characteristics tied to special social functions or roles (such as "woman," "mother," "feminist," "father," "worker," "citizen"). Auclert's historical account of the origins of feminism is about just such discursive attribution (albeit in different terms). Before 1791, she argued, women were indistinguishable from men as members of society; it was legal mistreatment (the exclusion of women from politics) that inaugurated their collective political identity. Feminists thus entered history as excluded political subjects.[106] Their agency was produced as a contradiction within the discourse of the universal rights of man.

Auclert's self-conscious attention to contradiction and the difficulty she had in conceiving of feminism teleologically make her an ideal site for exploring the history of feminism in its changing discursive contexts. And it is finally as such a site that she achieves historical visibility. She becomes exemplary not of the achievements and frustrations of a particular brand of feminist, but of the continuing dilemma of feminism *and* of the specific contradictions it embodied in the period of the Third Republic. Reading Auclert in this way does not deprive her of seriousness or significance, but neither does it confer on her the uniquely individual status she sought. Rather (and perhaps far more importantly) it allows us to place her, and feminism more generally, clearly and centrally in the large histories of politics from which they typically have been excluded.

5

The Radical Individualism
of Madeleine Pelletier

Madeleine Pelletier presented herself as an individualist among feminists in the early decades of the twentieth century. A generation younger than Hubertine Auclert (she was born in 1874 and died in 1939), she could nonetheless be found with Auclert in the ranks of militant suffragists: invading polling places in 1908; editing a newspaper, *La Suffragiste*, irregularly from 1907 to 1914 and again briefly in 1919; writing feminist articles, brochures, and, in her later years, plays and novels; running for office on the socialist ticket in 1910; and agitating for the equality of women in the organizations of Freemasons, socialists, anarchists, and (from 1920 to 1925) Communists. But unlike many of her associates, she sought political rights not as a means of collective emancipation, not as a way of representing some presumed women's interest in the public realm, not in order to win recognition and respect for women's difference. For Pelletier, the goal in relation to women's identity was entirely negative: "not to be a woman in the way society expects."[1] From this perspective, formal rights meant access both to liberty and to power, since these were the psychological prerequisites for any enunciation of individuality. "Give to a woman, even an inferior one, the right to vote, and she will cease to think of herself exclusively as a female and feel herself instead to be an individual."[2] Rights were, in Pelletier's view, not the recognition of a preexisting subject, but the means by which an autonomous subject could be brought into being.

Although Pelletier invoked the language of equality she scorned the leveling uniformity it could imply. For her, socialism was about fairness, not about sameness. She believed in a meritocracy of intellectuals, in the superiority of the intelligentsia over the pliable masses. Because intelligence knew no boundaries of class or gender, she thought, its possessors must have access to positions of influence and leadership. This access could be guaranteed only if the right to politics were genuinely universal. To claim the universal right to politics did not imply the homogeneity of citizens. Rather, it offered the possibility of thinking oneself an independent, self-realizing individual, wholly sufficient, uncompromised by any dependency.

Pelletier's feminism cannot be read, as Auclert's certainly could be, within the discourse of the "social" that made women both agents and objects of reform.[3] Instead, it drew its force from critiques (on the right and left) of rationalism, mass democracy, and parliamentary reformism. It was a radically individualistic feminism. Pelletier's objective was to unsex the subject of rights, to detach individuals from the categories of social identity that constrained their creativity, and so to leave them free to shape their own destiny. "The sole duty of society is not to interfere with anyone's activity; let each person find his own bearings in life as he pleases, with all its risks and perils."[4]

Madeleine Pelletier's feminism confounds the arguments of those who presume that a preexisting and self-evident group interest lies behind women's claims for political rights, that women's politics reflect their collective experience. For Pelletier it was precisely the other way round: feminism was not a means to enhance the social status of women, but a way of dissolving the category entirely. Her example supports the thesis that historically there have been feminisms "without women."[5] For Pelletier feminism offered not only an escape from the demeaning passivity of most women's lives, but an alternative to avowing the identity of "woman." In possession of political rights, a woman's identity would be transformed: "She will be an individual before being a sex."[6]

Madeleine Pelletier was early (and for most of her adult life) affiliated with socialism. She joined the newly unified French Section of the Workers' International (Section Française de l'Internationale Ouvrière;

SFIO) in 1905, went with the Communists in 1920 when the socialist party split, and affiliated with the Party of Proletarian Unity when she left the French Communist Party in 1925. But she was never enthusiastic about Marx's political and economic theories (despite having been made to read *Capital* by her teacher, the anthropologist Charles Letourneau), and although she liked the idea of central economic planning and state provision of education and child care, she distrusted anything that subordinated individuals to social regulation. Her interest in social justice she found best expressed, she said, in the doctrines of Robespierre. Her goal was the "suppression of inheritance; free instruction at all levels; generous assistance for children, the old, and the sick; no more class distinctions; no more worship of money. Intelligence and work the only means of success."[7]

Philosophically, she is best described as a liberal. She read John Stuart Mill enthusiastically and followed the teachings of Henri Bergson with interest. Politically, she was attracted to anarchism, but not for its pledge to destroy the state. It was the endorsement of individualism that drew Pelletier to the anarchist fold (and its aggressively masculinist style that drove her away). More broadly, Pelletier's feminism was articulated within the discourse of individualism, which had changed in important ways since its first formulation during the Enlightenment.[8]

At the beginning of the twentieth century individualism did not carry the same clear democratic promise it had at the end of the eighteenth. Always defined in a contestatory political relationship, the enemy of the "individual" in the eighteenth century had been the fixed social identities of feudalism and special legal privileges that attached to them. By the end of the nineteenth century, the individual was opposed to the crowd, the product of the egalitarianism of mass democracy. At the same time, there were continuities between the eighteenth- and twentieth-century notions of the individual: in both cases the ultimate opponent of the individual was the state, his freedom was secured outside the law though protected by it, and in both cases he was figured as masculine.[9]

The early twentieth-century individual was distinguished from the common crowd by superior intellect. This individual was not a conformist, but a creative spirit, whose mind controlled his body and therefore his actions. The mind/body distinction did not necessarily

translate into a rational/unconscious opposition. Although individualism in this period was clearly a facet of the "discovery" of the unconscious by psychologists, it was not a simple defense of the rational
subject. Indeed, while some theorists of individualism extolled the
unconscious as a "vital force," others reviled its pathological influences
and feared its political manifestations, citing as dangerous examples the
Boulanger Affair of 1886, the Dreyfus Affair, and the growing appeal
of right-wing nationalism.[10]

Early twentieth-century apostles of individualism cut across political
lines. They included revolutionary syndicalists, conservatives such as
the popularizer of crowd psychology, Gustave Le Bon, and nominal
republicans such as the philosopher Henri Bergson. Bergson and Le
Bon seem to exemplify the discourse of individualism in its complexity
and contradiction. Despite the diversity of their programs, the propo-
nents of individualism sought an alternative to what seemed an oppressive social homogeneity associated with bourgeois political institutions and cultural forms. They rejected solidarism's insistence on
interdependent divisions of labor, insisting instead on the absolute
autonomy of persons, by which they meant both a self disciplined by
reason and an authentic self that existed prior to its signification. The
role of language was crucial to these theorists of individualism. They
attacked anything that imposed meaning on a self from outside itself.
Bergson, for example, taught that no symbolic figure could adequately
signify the reality of life. And he warned against the use of categories
that reduced individuals to groups. For radical revolutionary syndicalists and for conservatives such as Le Bon, "citizen" was such a category.
A citizen was an interchangeable part in the passion-driven machine
of mass democracy. Its antithesis was the individual, expressing his own
uniqueness of mind and/or spirit. But of what did such expression
consist? Was an individual's language a direct emanation of his being?
Did reason fully control such expression? And what of the fact that
language was necessarily shared, originating not internally but socially?

The issue of the unconscious—so pressing to professional psychologists and the general public alike at the turn of the century—complicated any simple reply.[11] Like the eighteenth-century imagination, the
unconscious was a force that both defined reason (as its antithesis) and
threatened to compromise its operations. It appeared in or as language

and so affected the possibility of pure, rational expression by individuals. However psychologists and philosophers valued it—as a dangerous influence to be controlled at all costs or as a positive force for individual liberation—they concurred on the elusiveness of the phenomenon.

Le Bon viewed the unconscious as dangerous. He warned that "visible social phenomena appear to be the result of an immense, unconscious working, that as a rule is beyond the reach of our analysis . . . The part played by the unconscious in all our acts is immense, and that played by reason very small. The unconscious acts like a force still unknown."[12] He compared its destructive impact to "microbes which hasten the dissolution of enfeebled or dead bodies."[13] The Belgian philosopher (and disciple of Bergson) Georges Dwelshauvers was far less anxious but equally convinced of the elusiveness of the unconscious. He described "certain ensembles of conditions that determine conscious acts without necessarily being known to consciousness."[14] Bergson himself was entranced with the remarkable possibilities the unconscious presented for thinking about the mind. He described the unconscious as "all that can appear in a conscious state once that magnifying instrument [the analogy was to a microscope] we call attention intervenes, so long as the meaning of this last word is greatly expanded and we understand by it a broadened and intensified attention that no one person possesses in full."[15] For these theorists, the unconscious began at a point before cognition or where it failed; it was the invisible, that which eluded analysis, that for which there was no adequate name.

For Le Bon this was the point at which the crowd overwhelmed the individual. "From the moment that they form part of a crowd the learned man and the ignoramus are equally incapable of observation."[16] The crowd was "the slave of the impulses which it receives." In the crowd individuals were swayed by words that evoked images "quite independent of their real significance." These meanings were, moreover, vague, unstable, and transitory. Their effect was hallucinatory and influential: "They synthesize the most diverse unconscious aspirations and the hope of their realization."[17]

Historians have commented on Le Bon's descriptions of the hysterical, impulsive, credulous, and suggestible crowd, but they have not connected these descriptions to his preoccupation with language.[18] Yet it was precisely the problem of signification that was at the heart of Le Bon's preoccupation. He thought that language was "the outcome of the unconscious genius of crowds," so there was no way of stabilizing it or calling it back to some true or fixed meaning.[19] Instead, the individual who would dissociate himself from the crowd, who would escape its power, was he who knew the difference between words and things and could therefore manipulate signification to his own ends. "The art of those who govern . . . consists above all in the science of employing words." "One of the most essential functions of statesmen consists . . . in baptizing with popular, or at any rate indifferent words things the crowd cannot endure under their old names." In this way, Le Bon pointed out, the Consulate and the Empire had brought back the institutions of the past in new clothing, creating an appearance of change "without, of course, laying hands on the things themselves."[20] It was their intellectual ability to resist the illusory power of words and the emotions they evoked—to stand outside language—that separated individuals from crowds: "the isolated individual possesses the capacity of dominating his reflex actions, while a crowd is devoid of this capacity."[21]

This capacity separated not only individuals from crowds, but also men from women. "The simplicity and exaggeration of the sentiments of crowds have for result that a throng knows neither doubt nor uncertainty. Like women, it goes at once to extremes."[22] By referring to a literal, naturalized gender, Le Bon here grounded his observations about crowds in words whose meaning he took to be unmistakable. In this way he avoided the contradiction implicit in his own argument: if language could speak the (national or racial) unconscious, then how could an individual who stood outside it, who reflected on it and resisted its power, fully control his speech? Le Bon took the position (not his own, but one available in the current discourse on language and the unconscious) that made a distinction between different kinds of words, between representation and reality, taken as antithetical. Unlike the hypnotic words uttered by Napoleon or General Boulanger, "masculine" and "feminine," "men" and "women" were terms that transmitted characterological and physical facts. The validity (the transparent and therefore prelinguistic status) of the terms of Le Bon's "science of crowd psychology" was secured by its invocation of gender.

"Crowds are everywhere distinguished by feminine characteristics, but Latin crowds are the most feminine of all" was not a statement mediated by language, but a statement of scientific fact that separated Le Bon, the cognizant intellect, from the crowd.[23]

In Le Bon's writing, "women" was a metonym for the crowd. Their well-known irrationality and susceptibility to affective disorders (witness the propensity of women to hysteria and the ease with which they were hypnotized) not only led him to justify their exclusion from juries; he also used their disenfranchisement to signify the worthlessness of mass voting. Le Bon felt that citizenship had become a crowd phenomenon as a result of universal manhood suffrage, which gave numerical strength to "inferior elements" and voice to the unconscious "needs of the race."[24] For practical reasons he did not advocate abolishing the vote or restricting it, since that would not change the inherently collective nature of electoral processes and governments. In any case he thought that the "dogma" of universal suffrage was so powerful that only time could erode its standing. But he had no faith in citizenship. In effect, "electoral crowds" were like women; there was no individuality or independence in them, and they were as powerless to articulate and realize a sense of rational purpose. Democratic political representation, then, was another kind of misrepresentation, for it undermined the individual power that citizenship was once meant to enshrine. In the teeming, homogeneous, feminine mass, men lost not only their reasoning capabilities but their very selves. This loss of self was equated with a loss of masculinity.

The literal reference to gender served to ground Le Bon's argument as science, and science in this period served to invoke a "reality" that was outside language. But the figurative usage of gender contradicted that grounding. The crowd was feminine, so was the unconscious, so was language. The masculine was the individual, the conscious "reality." Le Bon argued that the power to shape words rather than be shaped by them—to maintain one's individuality, to possess one's self—was the achievement of superior intellects. Intellect was the triumph over the misleading power of words, figured as the feminine. But since this was precisely a figurative, not a physical reference, it left open the possibility that women could stand in the masculine position and so become individuals.

Although he came at the question from a different perspective, Henri Bergson can be located within the same discursive field as Le Bon. Bergson was among the most popular philosophers of his day. His course of lectures at the Collège de France from 1903 to 1907 attracted large audiences of "students, clerics, intellectuals, and society ladies."[25] Subsequently his books sold widely and he gained an international reputation. Like Le Bon, Bergson was an apostle of individualism; unlike Le Bon he considered unconscious, intuitive processes to be the key to individuality. These processes or feelings lost their uniqueness once they were named, for words could only misrepresent (by generalizing) the authenticity of the inner soul. Like Le Bon, Bergson offered a critique of signification that stressed the distorting effects of symbolic categories. But unlike Le Bon, Bergson considered language to be the product of reason, the tool of cognitive analysis. It was the rationalist attempt to name emotional impulses that confined their evolving, temporal existence to a fixed, categorical space, one that obscured the unique sensibility—the reality—of any individual. The reflexivity that for Le Bon was the self-defining power of the individual was for Bergson a destructive (collective) exercise that substituted necessarily approximate representations for the real thing: a ceaselessly mobile process, preconscious, prelinguistic, in which emotion was the active force (the analogy was to music, which expressed and aroused deep feeling without words). The truly free individual was in a constant state of becoming; reflection, as well as the acceptance of ready-made ideas and "acquired habits" (mechanistically imposed by society in the interests of order), limited freedom and prevented the full enactment of one's self.[26] Categories and habits were conveyed by language, the collective attempt to subdue individuality. But they only stifled the creative impulse, the "élan vital" that expressed the essence of the human. The individual came into his own when he transcended language and simply existed. The implications of this philosophy were that no symbol, no category adequately captured the ever-evolving reality of any individual: "We shall see that the contradictions inherent in the problems of causality, liberty, and personality have no other origin, and that to solve them it suffices to substitute the real self, the concrete self, for its symbolic representation."[27]

Logically, gender might be considered one of those symbolic representations, those "acquired habits," that hindered perception of any individual's "real self." But Bergson did not extend his critique to the question of gender. This became most explicit when he responded to virulent attacks on his philosophy's "feminine" style and content by, on the one hand, defenders of rationalism such as Julian Benda, and, on the other, Action Française leader Charles Maurras. Bergson's reply invoked categorical distinctions between the sexes, which were implicit in his philosophy, not just a tactical defense against his critics. "A psychology that places so much emphasis on sensibility" might be dismissed disdainfully as "feminine," he acknowledged, but such a dismissal would be mistaken.[28] For the dynamic, creative emotions he described, those that "vivified, or rather vitalized, the intellectual elements with which they combine" were different from the more superficial feelings experienced by women. "Without wanting to undertake a comparative study of the two sexes," Bergson played a variation on an accepted theme. He granted (against prevailing opinion) that men and women were equally intelligent. Women, however, were "less capable of emotion." The comparison was between the profound sensitivity of the male and the "surface stirrings" of the female.[29] Here sentiment became the power of (male) creativity in its uniquely individualized form, and reason was not only a lesser, commonly held human attribute, but that which prevented the full expression (and sensation) of self. In this defense of Bergson's philosophy, sexual difference appeared as a natural difference, prior to its signification—in just the way that Le Bon invoked it. But it also functioned as one of those categories that reduced individuals to membership in a group. It was Bergson's point that the mark of individuality was its spiritual resistance to or transcendence of collective representation. But the definition of men and women in terms of their sexed bodies operated as just such a representation.

Whether defined against the unconscious (as in Le Bon) or as its realization (as in Bergson), the notion of the individual rested on a refusal of collective, conventional forms of representation. Individuals were those who could shield themselves—by virtue of superior intellect or sensibility—from the oppressive massification created by these collective designations. "The thought [of any individual]," wrote Bergson, "remains incommensurable with language."[30] And it called all those forms into question by relativizing their meanings. (Thus Le Bon: "Words . . . have only mobile and transitory significations which change from age to age and people to people.")[31] At the same time, individuality was established through a set of oppositions grounded in the presumed naturalness of gender, so gender's own status as a linguistic representation never became a question.

Or at least it never became a question for those unaffected by the equation of maleness, masculinity, and individuality. Those affected by it experienced this exclusionary construction of individuality as a contradiction, and they used the individualist critique of language to state their claim. The feminism of Madeleine Pelletier can be understood in exactly this way: as an attempt to make the precepts of early twentieth-century individualism consistent with its own philosophy. Pelletier referred to sexual difference as "psychological sex," an imagined, socially imposed set of acquired habits that had nothing to do with physiology.[32] She argued that her contemporaries' equation of women with their sexed bodies contradicted the very notion of individuality as a transcendence of collective identification. And she called upon women to become individuals by rejecting any identification with the feminine. As she sought to demonstrate the immateriality of the sexed body for the concept of the individual, however, Pelletier found she could not transcend signification entirely. When it came to sexual difference there was no neutral language. So in order to dissociate herself from the feminine, Pelletier endorsed the masculine; she continued to operate within the terms of the signification of a naturalized "sexual difference." Her espousal of radical individualism thus embodied and exposed the way in which the concept of the individual rested on the repression (but not the resolution) of the contradiction posed for it by sexual difference. Pelletier's attempt to use individualism for feminism made explicit that repression and so functioned as a critique of the very philosophy upon which it was based.[33]

Madeleine Pelletier was trained as a psychiatrist. In 1902–03 she waged a successful and highly publicized campaign to be allowed to take the examinations for a psychiatric internship in a mental asylum. (The rules until then had stated that candidates for the position "must enjoy their civil and political rights," an impossibility for a woman.) She not only sought entry for women into a profession that had previously excluded them; she also undertook research that established the contingent and changing nature of ideas, including ideas about the self.[34]

Pelletier thought that the feminine identity accepted by most women was a psychological, not a physical phenomenon. It was a form of internalized oppression, the effect and the cause of their subordination. "The mentality of slaves revolts me," she wrote, echoing Nietzsche; "I do not like women as they are."[35] Her life's work was aimed at transforming that psychology by re-presenting women free of the degrading signs of their differentiation from men. The goal was to realize the possibility of individuality; but since individuality was figured as masculine, since masculinity was as close to universalism as one could get, the refusal of feminine difference became synonymous with an avowal of the masculine. Pelletier's solution was to detach femininity and masculinity from the physical bodies of women and men, making masculinity a possibility for both sexes. She urged feminists to "virilize" themselves and to clothe their daughters "en garçon." "It is necessary to be men socially," she wrote.[36] And yet, of course, for women to become "socially men" did not resolve all the problems posed by their difference.

The project of re-presenting women was the focus of Pelletier's work from her earliest student days. As a young medical student, under the tutelage of the physical anthropologists Letourneau and Léonce Manouvrier, she demonstrated that attempts to use sex or race to explain differences in brain size and attempts to use brain size to measure sexual and racial differences in intelligence were fundamentally misguided. In a study of male and female Japanese skeletons published in 1900, she measured cranial size in relation to bone mass, particularly the femur. She found that female skeletons tended to have larger cranial capacity in proportion to their height and weight, but she did not claim superior female intelligence as a consequence. Instead, she mockingly dismissed the idea that there might be "a mysterious law, a special arrangement of bony tissue which would have a relationship to sex as strange as it was unknown"; arguing instead that differences of physical stature, not of sex, were at issue. "If woman's cranium is heavier than her femur it is not because she is female; but because she is a slighter being whose muscle tissue and bones are less developed than man's."[37] In fact, she went on, the differences between small and large skeletons were far more significant than those between males and females or among different races.[38] Finally, she disputed the notion that brain size had anything to do with intelligence anyway; how could an ensemble of conscious and unconscious sensations, including temperament, energy, and the speed or slowness of perception—"this kind of mental chemistry whose reactions are as yet unknown"—be reduced to a matter concerning the organic mass of the brain?[39]

The crucial point—that sex and race were anthropological classifications that mistakenly turned certain apparent physical differences into generalized explanations of character and behavior—recurred throughout her work, long after she and other scientists abandoned craniometry. She attacked any social policy—whether it took the form of differences in women's educational and occupational opportunity, of prohibition from military service, or of restrictions on contraception and abortion—that reinforced the impression that women could be classified by their physical sex. But Pelletier thought that since law was the privileged locus of power, political disenfranchisement must be addressed first because it confined women to a collective identity by denying them the possibility of recognition as individuals. The vote, she thought, would have a "virilizing" effect on women by eliminating one of the more powerful structural supports of female/feminine difference.

Although the vote was an important aim of her feminist strategy (especially in the period before World War I), and although she sometimes conceded the priority of structural change, Pelletier stressed the importance of psychology.[40] "The deep trench that separates the sexes psychologically is above all the work of society."[41] She sought to close the gap by eliminating feminine difference in the behavior and subjectivity of women. Since femininity consisted only in its enactment, and since women perpetuated their subservience by accepting regulatory norms and enacting the difference of their femininity, the goal of feminists must be to eschew feminine behavior. "Observation of small children at play shows that in early life both sexes have the same mentality; it is the mother who begins to create psychological sex, and the feminine psychological sex is inferior."[42] Wearing long skirts and hats adorned with flowers and birds, adopting a mincing gait, behaving flirtatiously or with exaggerated modesty, displaying excessive delicacy of language and feeling, refusing to go out at night because it was improper, or suffering thirst rather than entering a café—these seemingly minor behaviors ("tous ces menus usages") "together form all the psychological differences of the sexes."[43]

Feminism's major task, as far as Pelletier was concerned, was to provide an analysis of this behavior and an alternative to it. Like the psychoanalyst, the feminist must bring reason to bear on unconscious acts (acts that were so routinized as to be outside conscious reflection), and so forge a new subjectivity for women, one free of the taint of femininity. Here Pelletier took a firmly rationalist stand. As in any movement, she thought, the educated (those who had escaped the social categories of identity into which they were born) must lead the masses. ("In the long run, and under the influence of individuals of the elite, social evolution takes place.")[44] Feminist mothers must inculcate a different psychology in their daughters, she wrote in an advice manual, L'éducation féministe des filles, in 1914. The cultivation of a new psychology would be achieved by giving girls names that could be shared with men (Paul/e or André/e or René/e, for example), by not showering them with affection or feeding them too much sugar, and by teaching them to tolerate pain by inflicting it on them. In addition, Pelletier recommended that girls be tutored by men, who, despite their misogyny, were more demanding teachers than women. Girls were also to be given a rigorous physical education that included learning to use a revolver. The gun would not only permit them to go out alone safely but would also increase their self-confidence and courage. The gun in a girl's (or woman's) hand was tangible evidence of her power, a phallic prosthesis that made her feel the equal of men. "Apart from the uses it has in cases of danger, the revolver has a psychodynamic power; simply the fact of feeling it on one's self makes one braver."[45]

Inner confidence and physical strength were only part of Pelletier's program. The re-presentation of women also, and perhaps primarily, involved exchanging the clothing of servitude for the garments of freedom. Pelletier extended the arguments of the League for Women's Emancipation and of individual feminists who had petitioned as early as 1896 for an end to enforcement of an ordinance of 1800 prohibiting cross-dressing by women.[46] These groups argued that pants permitted women to engage in sports and more healthful activities because they allowed for freer movements. Pelletier, in addition, stressed the psychological effects. Wearing men's clothing made it clear that women were not primarily objects of male desire, but beings unto themselves.

She had nothing but contempt for feminists who argued that they must "remain women" in order to win broad-based support for political emancipation. She ridiculed their feminine wiles. Their fashionable, low-cut dresses meant to attract men enraged her. She was exasperated by a suggestion for a suffrage parade in which beautifully dressed women would toss flowers to the crowds from decorated carriages. She created a mocking image of a feminist preparing for a demonstration in the parliament by embroidering a hat to attract notice (and presumably sympathy) from a handsome young deputy. "If all feminists were of this stripe, those who want to maintain masculine prerogatives would sleep calmly for a long time."[47] She once declined to perform an abortion for a woman in the postal service who had been raped by a fellow worker while both were involved in a strike. Pelletier questioned the woman's avowal of feminism because she curled her hair, wore feathered hats, used lipstick, and was heard to say that "women should remain women" and not try to "become men": "I thought she got no more than she deserved. May all feminists who are only half-feminists be treated the same."[48] This deep hostility to any display of femininity by professed feminists is evident in Pelletier's mocking depiction of the appearance at an international congress of some of the most eminent socialist-feminists of the day:

> Naturally the socialist women were very careful not to appear sexually liberated. Rosa Luxembourg wore a long dress, long hair, a small veil and flowers on her hat. Clara Zetkin did the same. In those days hats were held on with large pins, and when Clara Zetkin spoke from the podium, her broad gestures made the hat flop from right to left—the effect was comic. Laura Lafargue, daughter of Karl Marx, was named vice-president of the congress. She appeared with her face swathed in a thick veil; from afar she looked like a package of cloth.[49]

In Pelletier's view, veils, like dresses, hats, and flowers, made a spectacle of feminine sexuality; they were the demeaning mark of difference that was the source of women's subordination. They covered women and obstructed their vision. Veils were as demeaning as the low-cut dresses she abhorred (perhaps because the female body, whenever it wore explicitly feminine clothes, was already objectified). "I do not understand," she complained to her friend Arria Ly about the rage for décolletage, "why these ladies don't see the vile servitude that lies in displaying their breasts. I will show off mine when men adopt a special sort of trouser showing off their ———."[50]

This comparison was telling precisely because it went to the heart of the relationship between clothing and sexual difference. Women's difference consisted in the display of all parts of their bodies and in the (then fashionable) flirtatious veiling of the face, all designed to signal sexual availability. This clothing constituted them as objects of male sexual desire, revealing their lack of power. The clothing of the socialist women undermined the power that public speaking, and the content of their speeches, were meant to claim. Men's power, in contrast, came from covering up the one part of their body that mattered—the penis. Men's clothing constituted them as desiring subjects. It was only through suggestion that the fantastic identification between masculinity (the physical penis) and phallic power could be maintained. "The phallus," Jacques Lacan has written, "can only play its role as veiled."[51] Male privilege, he suggests, is based on the fantasy (the mistaken notion) that the anatomical penis is the symbolic phallus and that men, therefore, are powerful, autonomous individuals. In fact, he continues, men have relinquished autonomy by subordinating themselves to the law (the Law of the Father, imposed through the threat of castration). They are linked as brothers by their acceptance of the law and by their imaginary identification with its power. Male identity is achieved positively through such things as male citizenship (membership in the polity confirms possession of the phallus) and negatively through the exclusion of women, who are defined as the Other because their lack of a penis is mistakenly understood as the lack of the phallus. But male identity is always unstable, for it must maintain the illusion that men have the phallus (the symbolic power that the penis cannot assure) while covering up for its absence. "Appearing," according to Lacan, "gets substituted for the 'having' so as to protect it on one side and to mask its lack on the other."[52]

In this ambiguity about "appearing" and "having," Pelletier located not only the source of masculine power but also an opportunity for women to claim it. Symbolically this claim could be asserted when women put on masculine attire. To re-dress the female body "en homme" was to signal its autonomy and its individuality (there was no neutral, genderless style). The process should begin as early as possible. Little girls, she urged feminist mothers, should have short hair and boys' clothing. Feminists, in their own costumes, must abandon the signifiers of femininity. She herself wore closely cropped hair, a starched collar, tie, and suit coat long before these had become fashionable attire for "modern" women after World War I.[53] (She also wore trousers on occasion, although these were still forbidden women in early twentieth-century Paris.) She understood her transvestism as a transgression of prevailing norms, a way of establishing her individuality in the face of a disapproving crowd: "Those who wear false collars and short hair have all the liberty, all the power. Well! I also wear short hair and false collars in the face of fools and wretches, braving the insults of the hooligans in the street and of the slave-woman in an apron."[54] Cross-dressing was an integral aspect of her feminist politics. "I like exteriorizing my ideas, carrying them upon me as the nun carries her Christ, or the revolutionary his red rose. I wear these exterior signs of liberty in order that they may say, that they may proclaim, that I desire freedom."[55] In 1919 she wrote: "My clothing says to men, I am your equal."[56]

When Pelletier occasionally succeeded in "passing" as a man, she was delighted, even though in several instances her appearance endangered her. At a meeting of the SFIO executive committee (of which she was a member from 1909 to 1911, and the only female) she "realized an old dream" when she came dressed in men's clothing; but she was taken for a police spy and only narrowly avoided a beating. (She did not shirk these encounters, but responded aggressively—like a man—hurling insults in slang and exchanging blows with those who attacked her.)[57] In 1914, while working for the Red Cross in Nancy, she was identified as an enemy agent: "My masculine appearance sufficed to call up a crowd of some two thousand persons howling around me; an old woman seized me violently by the jacket; I owed my rescue to climbing into an officer's car."[58] These experiences taught her a certain caution.

In 1921, when she hoped to cross Europe unnoticed because she was traveling to the Soviet Union without a passport, she compromised her usually adamant stance by attempting to pass as "a woman like any other," wearing a wig, stockings, and a skirt as part of her disguise.[59] (This feminine presentation was no more comfortable for her—perhaps even less so, since it belied her sense of her own identification.)

The experience of "passing" was a permanent feature of Pelletier's situation: whether dressed "en homme" or "en femme" she flouted convention and concealed the discrepancy between her socially attributed identity and the one she desired.[60] But passing is never an entirely successful venture. "By playing the personality as one wants to appear," she noted, "one finishes by becoming it a bit [*un peu*] in reality."[61] The "a bit" expresses the ambiguity of the enterprise. Its ambiguity was, for Pelletier, the source of desire and pleasure. Donning men's clothing and walking through red-light districts at night, Pelletier was gleeful when prostitutes mistook her for a man. "They call me 'big boy [*mon gros*],'" she reported to her friend Arria Ly; "I'd like it better if they called me 'slim,' but one is as one is."[62] Here her performance reproduced the terms of masculine identity as sexual difference (even as she adamantly denied any "libidinal" investment): the desire of a woman worked to confirm that she had the phallus she appeared to have. The re-presentation of herself "en homme" thus paradoxically depended on the gendered opposition she sought to disrupt. Her mimicry expressed a longing to be a man. ("Oh, why am I not a man? My sex is the worst misfortune of my life," she wrote to Ly.)[63] But at the same time it exposed the fragility of *any* phallic appearance. In Pelletier's case there was a dissonance of which she was all too aware: the clothing of masculinity covered a discernibly female body: "I am short and fat; I have to disguise my voice and walk quickly through the street so as not be discovered."[64] The figure of the "femme en homme," by at once revealing and disguising its lack, by playing on the ambiguity of the necessarily veiled phallus, repudiated the association between the physical body and symbolic power (the penis and the phallus).[65]

By her own account, Pelletier's adoption of masculine dress proclaimed the social and political irrelevance of her physical body, but it inevitably raised the question of her erotic inclination.[66] When she sent

Arria Ly a portrait of herself as a man, she warned her teasingly not to fall in love. "The trip to Lesbos doesn't tempt me any more than the trip to Cythera."[67] Although police reports referred to Pelletier as a lesbian, she did not frequent the circles that made Paris "the capital of Lesbos" in the early twentieth century.[68] And she insisted that she was entirely celibate. Although she sometimes argued that celibacy was not synonymous with chastity, in her own case Pelletier was quite clear: "I haven't wanted to educate my genital sense," she wrote to Ly in 1908; "my choice is the consequence of the unjust situation of women."[69] Twenty-five years later, when there was greater license for women's sexual expression, she was even more vehement: "Certainly I consider that a woman is free in her body, but these affairs of the belly [de bas ventres] disgust me profoundly."[70] Perhaps if Pelletier had encountered something like Monique Wittig's startling assertion that lesbians are not women, she would have taken a different position on the question of lesbian identity.[71] As it was, to declare oneself a lesbian in early twentieth-century Paris meant, in Pelletier's estimation, either to exaggerate one's femininity (in the upper-class style of Natalie Barney and Colette) or to emphasize one's sexuality, however "inverted" (in the manner of Radclyffe Hall, Romaine Brooks, and the Marquise de Belbeuf).[72] Neither of these options was acceptable, since what demeaned femininity in Pelletier's view was precisely that it functioned to make women debased objects of sexual desire.

In addition, she seems to have shared the prevalent view of homosexuality as an abnormality (which nonetheless must be tolerated); its cure, she thought, lay in a more just society. Lesbians, she wrote in her utopian novel, Une vie nouvelle (A new life), in 1932, were either single women who could not find a suitable male lover or married women so oppressed by their husbands that they sought tenderness from other women, by default. When women gained "la liberté sexuelle"—that is, total equality with men—"sapphism" would gradually disappear.[73] But the near identity between men and women, in dress and deportment as well as in subjectivity, also might lead to the disappearance of distinctions between heterosexuality and homosexuality. When the individual replaced the family as the "social cell [cellule sociale],"[74] and when individuals were no longer differentiated by "psychological sex," when men were virile and women "virilized," then might not all sexual relations be, in effect, homosexual relations? Pelletier probably had a more complex notion of desire in mind, one that took difference to be necessary, but more flexible than the strict categories of sexual difference allowed. Still, by tying the achievement of political and social equality to the elimination of all sexual difference, Pelletier revealed the connection between heterosexuality and inequality within the terms of the individualism to which she appealed.

But she did not opt for or project a utopian homosexual future, although in *Une vie nouvelle* she imagined a time when homosexuals would be "given the rights of the city." The leaders of the future understood that homosexuality wasn't "normal," but they "nonetheless found it archaic and arbitrary to regulate caresses, to designate what was permitted and what forbidden."[75] Despite this gesture of toleration, homosexuality was a marginal issue for Pelletier; the real question was whether heterosexual relations could be reformed.

In principle, Pelletier thought they could be. Women, after all, were sexual beings. However scandalous the idea might seem to her contemporaries, "Woman desires; the sexual instinct calls in her, too."[76] And sex, she wrote in 1931, "is very powerful, Freud has shown that it is much more powerful than we had previously believed."[77] As sexual beings, women had "a right to love." And the exercise of that right need not be degrading. "The liberated woman does not feel diminished by a sexual initiation that she wants . . . The sexual act is not the giving of one's person. It is the temporary meeting of two beings of different sexes; its aim is pleasure."[78] With neither marriage nor domestic cohabitation to constrain her, and entirely self-sufficient economically, a woman might take her pleasure as a man's equal. "If there were no longer cohabitation, all these family hatreds so well described by Freud would end."[79]

Despite her desire to obscure the issue of the sexed female body, Pelletier repeatedly had to confront it. If individuality was to be achieved, and if individuality meant full autonomy, there was no evading the relationship between the self and its phenomenological expression in the body. The guarantee of women's integrity in the sexual act ("the sexual act is not the giving of one's person") and in all her relationships rested on the disposition of her body. The absolute right over her body was the physical expression of a woman's individuality;

it could not be compromised without a loss of self: "Individualism has taught that each person belongs only to himself and cannot give himself away to anyone."[80] Thus Pelletier warned that reproduction must be treated as a function of the female body, but not as its essential meaning. She condemned what she took to be misguided feminist attempts to elevate women's status by celebrating maternity. In the end this strategy simply confirmed women's inferiority, for it located all their value in a physiological function that compromised the coherence and autonomy of the body: "Never will childbirth give women a title of social importance. Future societies may build temples to maternity, but they will do so only to keep women locked up inside."[81]

If women were to bear children (a necessity for the reproduction of the species and sometimes the unintended side effect of pleasurable liaisons), maternity must be a choice, not an obligation. There could be no interference by the state, no law to inhibit women's freedom of choice. To that end Pelletier was an active member of the neo-Malthusian organization led by Paul Robin and Nelly Roussel, and she campaigned for full legalization of abortion in the first trimester of pregnancy. Even a state's interest in population could not ultimately interfere with a woman's control of her bodily functions, she maintained. "Above all, the individual is sacred . . . he has the absolute right to live as he pleases, to procreate or not to procreate. In wishing to put a brake on individual liberties in the national interest, one always does more harm than good."[82] As for the fetus, the idea that it had rights was absurd. "The child once born is an individual, but the fetus in the uterus is not one; it is part of the mother's body."[83] As part of the mother's body, the fetus had no autonomous existence. "The pregnant woman is not two persons but one, and she has the right to cut her hair and her nails, to get thin or fat. Our right over our bodies is absolute."[84] If the absolute right over their bodies was a guarantee of women's individuality, it was also a bar to their full absorption into the (masculine) ranks of the abstract individual, since the body in question must be accepted and protected in all its female difference.

To avoid this contradiction Pelletier looked for a way to overcome sex entirely. Although she spoke tolerantly of sexual drives and imagined a time when pleasure would be the sole motive of equal partners, she also looked forward to the day when human evolution would advance beyond its animal inheritance. The sexual function "is a physiological function, like nutrition or circulation," and ought to occupy the same place in the scale of human values—necessary, but not of the highest order. "Sexuality is a natural function, but it is not a noble function."[85] She thought that Freud overemphasized the power of sexual drives to determine behavior (and like most of the French psychiatric profession, she strongly objected to his theories of infantile sexuality). Far more important were human intellectual capacities, which, when properly developed and deployed, were the true source of happiness: "The gamut of animal pleasures is quickly traveled . . . But the life of the mind is infinitely more varied."[86] When she suggested that "the cerebral family" should replace "the sexual family," she offered this illustration of its impact on women: "Instead of being a female perched on her brood like a mother hen, woman will be a thinking being, the independent artisan of her own happiness."[87] The contrast is between animal and human, the sexual and the cerebral, mother and artisan, a being in the service of her body and one whose mind shapes her destiny.

This distaste for the physicality of the body led Pelletier to suggest the possibility of doing away with sex entirely. She often introduced celibacy as an alternative. In this connection she reassured feminist mothers that it was a perfectly appropriate choice for their daughters. "Doctors who have written about the dangers of chastity have considered only men; women don't have the same imperious sexual drive." The only drawback to a chaste life was loneliness, but this could be avoided if a young woman lived in common with several others.[88] In Pelletier's autobiographical novel, *La femme vierge* (The virgin woman), the heroine refuses the lure of amorous entanglements and, as a result, is able to live a truly independent life. When she notices that certain novels provoke sexual feelings, she stops reading them. From time to time "she had an erotic dream,"[89] but her health never suffered.

> Certainly, she wasn't without sex; she, too, experienced desires, but she repressed them in order to be free, and she did not regret it . . . Marie had replaced love with the life of the mind; but how few are capable of doing that. In the future, woman will be able to liberate herself without

renouncing love. It won't any longer be base . . . Woman will, without being diminished by it, live her sexual life.[90]

Marie's superior intellect enables her to sublimate her sexual drive with no regrets. Repression establishes her superiority to others ("but how few are capable of doing that"). "In the future" things may be different, but that future seems indefinitely postponed. The route to the brave new world is through the assertion of individuality, the triumph of mind over body, reason over desire, masculine over feminine. It is a route open to those women of superior intellect who choose to take it, and whose choice begins a slow but inevitable process of change.

In *Une vie nouvelle*, her attempt at utopian fiction, Pelletier pursued her thinking on this issue to its final logic. The hero, Charles Ratier, at the beginning of the novel a sensuous man with many mistresses, culminates his career by giving up sex for the study of science. He learns how to regenerate human organs, thus conquering death (and diminishing even further the need for reproduction). The progress of science, coupled with a general tendency for population to decline, promises a future in which individuality will be increasingly possible. "Depopulation," she had written earlier, "far from being an evil, is an essential good, the corollary of the general evolution of beings; it is the expression of the victory of the individual over the species."[91] An even greater victory is portended by the settlement that astronauts discover on the moon, presumably a glimpse of the life that lies ahead for those on earth: "All individuals were the same and there was no sex. Reproduction was achieved with eggs obtained by individuals from a special establishment that was maintained at a warm temperature."[92]

"All individuals were the same and there was no sex." Where there is neither sexual difference nor sexual congress there are individuals; where there is sex there are not individuals. Individuals can be represented as individuals only if they have no sex. On the moon the contradiction between the necessary duality of sexual difference and the requisite singularity of individuality can be resolved; on earth it can only be repressed. Madeleine Pelletier's frustrating quest for individuality named the repression of sexual difference as a strategy and so made visible its hitherto hidden role in representing the individual as the transcendent human. The need to accept the masculine as the universal individual, on the one hand, and her insistence that individuality transcended sex, on the other, was a paradox she could not resolve.

———————■———————

When Pelletier wrote of the sameness of individuals, she meant specifically that they were not differentiated by sex, but her notion of individuality did not abandon the idea of natural hierarchy. Although sexed bodies were irrelevant, minds were crucial for differentiating among people; intelligence, understood as the power of rational control, separated individuals from the crowd. Intelligence was not a universal attribute of humans; indeed it was limited to a few; but Pelletier thought that the chance to display it ought not to be categorically denied on the basis of sex. The mind was, after all, beyond the reach of the body, although intelligence was innate. There was "an original intellectual inequality,"[93] which could be overcome only partly by education, and it was the only acceptable basis for making social distinctions. Unlike aristocracies of wealth, birth, or gender, "the aristocracy of reason" was natural, inevitable, and salutary.

The sign of superior intelligence was individuality, and it consisted in originality, the refusal to conform to conventional behaviors and manners, the ability to transcend "the imaginary bonds" of society and to affirm instead the exclusive reality of the self. "I am, and I am alone," she wrote in a deliberate reference to Descartes. "Before reflecting on it, I believed myself tied to men and to things by all sorts of bonds . . . Upon reflection, I have understood that all these bonds are illusory and that I am truly alone, the only reality."[94]

"I am alone, and everything is outside me."[95] The self was a private property that lay beyond the control or influence of others, but its perception depended on the existence of those others. Pelletier operated within the terms of a discourse in which individuality rested on the presence of its massed opposite—the crowd, the community, the social body, the nation—and on a hierarchical positioning of the relationship between self and society. The individual was not only opposed to the crowd; he also called into question the ruling precepts of republicanism: the beneficence of electoral majority rule and of regulatory law imposed in the name (or for the good) of the majority. The leveling effects of these laws were antithetical to individuality. "Individualism is in contradiction with democracy as it is understood by the common people."[96]

Pelletier attempted to articulate her theory of individualism in 1919, at a moment when she was profoundly disillusioned by the power of nations to mobilize the masses for futile and devastating wars. "Duty, devotion, sacrifice, I do not know you; you are words, and I know that they wish only to fool me with words."[97] But her argument went much further than an attack on patriotism, invoking as it did the discourse of individualism. The elitism expressed in Pelletier's 1919 book was evident throughout her long career—in her description of feminism as the achievement of a small elite in 1906, in her discussion in 1912 of social progress as "the triumph of the best people," in her comment in 1914 that social change was a process influenced by "individuals of the elite," in her devastating portraits of the enduring nature of working-class men's brutality and women's subservience and of the masses' jealousy, fear, and hatred of "superior intellects," and in her characterization (in her 1922 account of her journey to the Soviet Union) of the masses as "the amorphous dough good only to take the shape that a small number of intelligent and daring people wish to give it."[98]

In *Une vie nouvelle* Pelletier described the earliest days of her imagined revolution as the chaotic unleashing of masculine sexuality. Until a benevolent dictator imposed law, there was no safety, especially for women. "At night, bands of drunken men roamed the streets exposing their organs and shouting obscene propositions."[99] Here the display of the male organ was a revelation of the lack of the phallus, of its absence socially and politically, not of the possession of its power. Women's defense, Pelletier adds, was to don men's clothing, to obscure the question of what they had or appeared to have, so they would not become the rapists' prey. The new costume, which stuck, then enabled women, as men, to identify with the phallus when a Father emerged to declare his Law. But when a dictator took over and organized the reconstruction of society, "politics in the narrow sense of the word" disappeared. (And sex was returned to its proper sphere. Animality, Pelletier felt, was best indulged, like other necessary bodily functions, in private.)[100] People were so content with life that they accepted being governed by a minority; they had no desire to emulate the Father. "The masses were not interested in public affairs."[101] Only the elite voted, and their intelligence legitimated their power. The phallus was now possessed by only a few—a few of both sexes. And virility signified higher qualities of the mind.

Skeptical of the operations of mass democracy, Pelletier nonetheless campaigned for women's citizenship. She was fully aware of the limits of her position: in order to gain the individuality that was "the only reality," women must have political recognition as women. Historically, citizenship was taken as the recognition of the rights of preexisting individuals. Pelletier's position reversed this causality, exposing the way in which citizenship created both rights and individuals. Her call for women's suffrage acknowledged the defining and inescapable power of representation (things were brought into being by the words that signified them; women became citizens when so designated by law), but also its instability and its vulnerability.

Yet there was more to it than that. In earlier periods, citizenship was taken to be the sure sign of individuality; by the early twentieth century that correspondence had come into disrepute. Citizenship was now seen by many to have reduced the individual to an indistinguishable member of the mass or crowd; it signified the loss of individuality rather than its assertion. Pelletier was in the position of asking for precisely that which subsumed individuals in order eventually to free some of them. She tried to explain to her anarchist friends that "political suffrage, in spite of being perhaps an illusory goal, was a stage women must pass through to free themselves."[102] The issue was at once practical and symbolic: Women as a group had to become legitimately, legally, part of the (electoral?) crowd, indistinguishable from its male members, in order for some of them to be able to rise above it. Transcendence was possible only if one was already included within the terms of representation one wanted to transcend. It was no accident, then, that Pelletier referred to suffrage in evolutionary terms, as a "stage" women had to pass through. The tension in her own position came from trying to realize two historically different (and inconsistent) meanings of "individual" in the same historical moment. The tension was sometimes relieved, sometimes intensified by the fact that as individuals both the eighteenth-century universal citizen and the twentieth-century singular intellectual were symbolically identified as masculine.

This tension perhaps overdetermined Pelletier's masculine self-presentation. For she wanted to assert both her right to citizenship and her intellectual superiority to any crowd (whether of women, feminists, socialists, workers, or party militants)—a paradoxical and doubly masculine effort! Her appearance and behavior distinguished her in any organization she joined. Anarchists and socialists, calling her back to her body as the ontological ground of her identity, urged her to let her hair grow and to wear dresses. One of her socialist mentors, Gustave Hervé, offered Louise Michel as a model—Michel had "arrived" at leadership in the party without giving up her femininity, he argued; why could Pelletier not do the same?[103] Although Pelletier reported these conversations with scorn, she also relished the impression of singularity she created. She was anomalous, neither a feminine woman like her feminist colleagues, nor fully a man like her socialist comrades. Even among the vanguard, she was unique; and this sense of uniqueness was also a sense of superiority. One sees her repeating this attempt to establish her individuality throughout her political itinerary.

Pelletier was most active politically in the years before World War I. She was initiated into a mixed-sex "obedience" of Freemasons in 1904 (the regular lodges of Freemasons excluded women), attracted by the intellectual climate, the exchanges of ideas among republicans and socialists, and the possibility of further opening the masonic movement to women. In a frenzy of activity, she delivered lectures and wrote articles on many topics, including women's rights to abortion and to suffrage. Her success in introducing Louise Michel into her lodge was a great coup that brought her both attention and praise. Pelletier's stated goal was to gain full access for women—citizenship in the eighteenth-century sense of the term. At the same time she wanted to preserve the elevated atmosphere of Freemasonry, including its rituals and hierarchies. "There is no need to conceal the fact," she asserted in a 1904 lecture, "that our civilization . . . is the achievement of a restricted elite." The masses were as incapable of having the kind of "profound" thoughts expressed by masons as they were of changing society. So there was no point in bringing them into the movement. "My conception of the masons would be that of an enlightened oligarchy strong enough to force the government to take account of it, and which would not have the defects of other oligarchies since its ranks would be open to all intelligent persons."[104] Intelligence was a guarantee, she thought, not only of decency but also of justice and benevolence.

Pelletier's intelligence and her extraordinary energy won her admiration but also enemies among Freemasons, many of whom feared that her campaign to bring women into regular all-male lodges would succeed. She was eventually disciplined for her excesses (including threatening someone with a revolver) and suspended from her lodge. And although she remained a Freemason all her life, by 1906 she had transferred her energy and attention to socialist and feminist organizations.

In 1906 Pelletier agreed to take over from Caroline Kauffmann the leadership of a small feminist organization, Women's Solidarity (La Solidarité des Femmes). In the same year she joined the SFIO, the newly unified socialist party. In those organizations, as in Freemasonry, the tension between her universalist claims for women's rights and her elitism was apparent. Indeed, although some historians have depicted this period in Pelletier's life as a prototypical example of the "unhappy marriage" of feminism and socialism, in her case this characterization misses the point. It was the tension between an engagement in emancipatory politics (on behalf of women, citizens, workers), on the one hand, and the pursuit of individuality, on the other, between universalism and elitism, that troubled Pelletier's political experience in this period. How was one to enact the individualism of the feminist subject in the age of mass politics? Pelletier's avowal of both socialism and feminism enabled her to distance herself from the engulfing claims of either.

Among feminists, she took a stand against femininity; among socialists she denounced misogyny. She criticized the "absurd ideas" put forward under the banner of feminism, but stressed the importance of feminist organizations for women who entered political parties. These organizations made it possible for women to "know how to affirm themselves," she wrote in an astute 1908 pamphlet, *La femme en lutte pour ses droits*. Women must enter political parties in order both to prove their capabilities and to bring feminist influence to bear. (They must not, however, campaign only for feminist goals, for that would call their party commitments into account; a woman must instead act as "a good militant," "un bon militant." When issues relating to women came up, they must of course speak out.) Feminist groups taught women to speak, a crucial ability, since "in a political group, he who doesn't speak doesn't exist."[105] But such an existence, though necessary, was only ephemeral. "Have no illusion about it; if a party raises you [to a prominent position] it is because it has an interest in doing so. Their sexual feelings apart, women feel kindly for men, but men in general feel nothing but indifference to and hatred for women."[106]She counseled women never to give a political party "your heart, because this heart is ours; it belongs to our feminist organizations, the only ones that work for our emancipation." She then referred to feminist organizations as women's only true "home," using the English word to underscore her point.[107] It is tempting to see here a pun on the French word "homme" and to suggest that Pelletier meant that feminist organizations allowed women to be at home—"homme," that is, as men, human, free of the attribution of demeaning feminine characteristics, free of the need to define their existence in accordance with the desires of men. Feminist organizations, in Pelletier's view, functioned less to solidify a shared female identity than to strengthen the resolve of any woman engaged in political activity to resist the pressures that would reduce her to her sex.

In Solidarité des Femmes Pelletier argued against those who saw feminism as the political expression of women's identity. In the SFIO she presented herself as "un bon militant" (using the masculine form of the term). And in that capacity she eventually won election (the only woman to do so) in 1909–1911 to the executive council as the representative of the left-wing insurrectionist faction led by Gustave Hervé. But "bon militant" that she was, her sex and her feminism distinguished her from other of the party leaders.[108] In 1906 she argued for the vote at the party congress at Limoges, and she subsequently negotiated with Jules Guesde, Jean Jaurès, and others to have implemented the party resolution that had passed in favor of women's suffrage. Although she carefully avoided feminist advocacy while a member of the executive council, she did write on behalf of the feminist cause, at one point infuriating Hervé with an article for his newspaper, *La guerre sociale,* advocating women's service in the military. (Hervé countered by telling her of the unnaturalness of the proposition: "if women go to the barracks, men will have to make soup and babies.")[109] If socialist activism took her beyond the confines of a women's movement, feminism gave her a distinctive position among socialists. When she ran for a seat in the legislature in 1910 on the socialist ticket, Pelletier stressed her own exemplary uniqueness. As a crowd of domestic servants gathered to hear her speech, she told them "all about the evolution of women towards independence . . . [and] I presented myself as an example of this evolution."[110] And in 1922, while she acknowledged the need for separate organizations of women workers and peasants within the Communist Party, she insisted (as a feminist) that fully evolved intellectuals like herself be included on the same terms as men.[111]

Although Pelletier stayed in the SFIO until it split in 1920, she also worked hard to advance the neo-Malthusian program in these years. She wrote *L'émancipation sexuelle des femmes* in 1911, republished its chapter on the right to abortion as a separate pamphlet in 1913, and then included it as a chapter of *La rationalisation sexuelle* in 1935. In addition she regularly lectured on the issue of birth control, debating its merits in public forums, especially at the Club du Faubourg in the 1930s. And she seems to have performed abortions as part of her medical practice.[112]

Her advocacy of population control through contraception and abortion rested on a belief in the importance of the individual's responsibility for the economic and social conditions of his or her life—a belief antithetical to most socialist analyses of the structure of capitalism.[113] (Hervé's exceptionalism in his support of the neo-Malthusians appears to have been one reason for Pelletier's association with his faction of the socialists.) Here was a cause that fulfilled both the eighteenth- and twentieth-century conceptions of individualism by making control over one's body the literal expression of (and the precondition for) the unfettered possession of property in the self. It was a cause that also shifted the emphasis of her individualism, making the state and its laws, not the crowd or the mass or social convention, that which must be opposed if the individual was to exist.

And it drew attention to the female body in its (troubled) relationship to any individual woman's quest for a nonsexed identity. There was a paradox in Pelletier's commitment to a politics centered so concretely on the female body. The woman who insisted that mind, not body, was the key to individuality, who deemed sexual difference a matter of acquired psychological habits, who dismissed the affairs of "the lower belly" as decidedly inferior to the higher activities of the mind, was involved in a campaign to theorize and bring about the autonomy of women in relation to their physical (and necessarily sexed) bodies. Pelletier's work on behalf of abortion rights revealed the interdependence of the mind/body opposition she held to so tenaciously: the autonomous self (even in her thinking about it) was not just a cognitive achievement; it was a material entity, an integral body.[114] And the issue of sexual difference was crucial in relation to this body; even as abortion transcended the limits maternity placed on women, it drew attention to the body whose influence was to be denied.

Laws prohibiting abortion had been on the books since 1810; article 317 of the penal code punished both those who sought and those who performed abortions. In July 1920, riding a wave of pronatalist agitation that linked France's recovery from the devastation of World War I to an increased birthrate, legislators toughened these penalties and also outlawed even the publication of contraceptive information. Pelletier was defiant before and after the new laws. She considered the criminalization of abortion a denial of women's individuality, another aspect of the denial of citizenship. With these laws the state both reduced women to their wombs and violated their bodily integrity. It appropriated women's reproductive functions for state interests in the same way that men used women's bodies as "an instrument" to satisfy their sexual needs and (through family and property arrangements) to maintain patriarchal power.[115] The state infringed its own commitment to protect the liberty of its people by illegally dispossessing women of an inalienable possession: their bodies, their selves.

The remedy, Pelletier thought, was not only to insist on the vote for women, but also to challenge the illegality of the law. After 1920 her speeches and writings provided such a challenge. One of her pamphlets, L'amour et la maternité, was published in 1923 by the Group for Propaganda by Pamphlet. But Pelletier seems also to have practiced propaganda by deed in good anarchist fashion, using her medical expertise and her position as a doctor (from 1906 on she was a physician in the postal service and also had a small neighborhood practice) to perform clandestine abortions (although she never acknowledged the fact).[116] Through this activity she constructed herself as a dedicated individual, putting her scientific knowledge (her education and training) to work on behalf of those unable to help themselves (unable even to control their bodies). "Law and morality are for ordinary men and circumstances," she had one of the scientists say in her 1920 play, *In Anima Vili, or a Scientific Crime; "we* are extraordinary men . . . let us rise to the heights where we find ourselves placed."[117] In freeing the bodies of women from the most oppressive aspect of the law, Pelletier transcended the law. This transcendence was, in effect, the enactment of her own individuality. But, paradoxically, it was a thoroughly masculine individual she enacted: the doctor-scientist-intellectual defined in hierarchical opposition to its object, the reproductive woman's body, and to the external, illegitimate authority of the state. At the same time, by restoring the bodily integrity of the self to women who otherwise had lost it, Pelletier substituted herself for the law. This action had several implications. Not only was she making a point about the absolute liberty of individuals to exist outside state regulation, whether or not they were considered citizens; she was also acknowledging the formative power of law to create or deny individuals.

The end of Pelletier's life poignantly illustrated the defining power of the law and the limits to any individual's control of her self-representation. Her words and deeds had made her a formidable enemy in pronatalist eyes. She was repeatedly denounced as a example of the feminist threat to the future of French civilization. In 1933 she was placed under surveillance and investigated for practicing abortion. In 1935 the Club du Faubourg was sued for promoting pornography because Pelletier had spoken there on a number of topics related to her book *La rationalisation sexuelle;* these included "Is the wedding night legal rape?" and "depopulation and civilization."[118] In 1939 she was arrested, and this time convicted, for having supervised abortions. (A stroke in 1937 had left her partially paralyzed so she could not perform the operations herself.) The state of her health led the judge to sentence her to a hospital rather than a prison. So, although she was mentally quite fit, Pelletier spent the remaining months of her life in an insane asylum. She died in December 1939.

Historians have noted the irony of the fact that the first woman psychiatric intern was, in her last days, incarcerated in an asylum. But

for Pelletier the terrible contradiction was between the legal and personal perceptions of her situation. Her own testimony of sanity had
little effect on her legal status. "You can't imagine how terrible it is to
be in an insane asylum when one has all one's mental faculties," she
wrote to her friend Hélène Brion. "My mind is as vigorous as ever. That
is why I suffer so."[119] In another letter she remarked that someone had
read her a news article reporting on Swiss plans to mobilize women
for the army. She reminded Brion that this had been an idea of hers
many years ago and that Gustave Hervé and everyone else who read
her article had ridiculed her for it. "This is how, in France, women who
distinguish themselves from an intellectual point of view are treated.
[Arria Ly] committed suicide and *I* am in a madhouse."[120] The power
of others (exemplified by the law and its agents) both to confirm and
to deny the existence of individuals was overwhelming. The project of
self-creation, however superior the intellect of the individual, could not
take place without its sanction.

Pelletier's situation in 1939 was the obverse of the courtroom scene
she had experienced so proudly in 1908. Then she had been charged
with breaking the law for throwing stones at voting urns. Her trial was
attended by a number of feminists, all of whom considered the event
a triumph. "The whole group was there . . . even some of H. Auclert's
and Mme. Oddo's groups. It was the first time that feminism appeared
in a court of justice. They wished me courage."[121] Congratulations were
in order because feminism had gained its day before the law. Pelletier's
sixteen-franc fine was as much a mark of legal attainment, of the
coming into being of a feminist subject, as it was a punishment.

The integrity of the self, as of the body (its physical embodiment),
rested finally on its establishment by "exterior" powers. That was why
the vote was the key to the realization of women's individuality. At the
end of her life, despite her distrust of crowds, mass democracy, and the
reductive effects of categories of social identification, Pelletier still
considered citizenship, as signified by the vote, the most important goal
for feminists.[122] Because it was women whose individuality she sought,
Pelletier exposed the otherwise repressed paradox of the theory she
espoused: There was no absolute autonomy of the self outside of
language, no individuality unless represented as such. Representation

by the law, before the law, was at once the antithesis of the individual and the very source of its existence.

———■———

Pelletier's concern with re-presenting women was comprehensive. It extended to history, to the use of past figures as inspirational models for feminists, and to the writing of the history of feminism to clarify the meaning of the contemporary struggle.

In Pelletier's fictionalized autobiography, *La femme vierge*, the protagonist (Marie) hesitates to take on the leadership of the feminist organization La Solidarité des Femmes in 1906. She explains to the group's secretary, Caroline Kauffmann, that she fears she will lose her position as a schoolteacher if she assumes too public a role. Kauffmann solves the problem by suggesting that Marie take a pseudonym—Pelletier recounts the moment as a baptism—and she becomes "Jeanne Deroin, in honor of the famous feminist of 1848." "Strive to show yourself worthy of such a great *patronne*," Kauffmann tells the young woman, using the word in its many resonances to mean at once sponsor, protector, and model.[123]

Pelletier's reference to a baptism evokes the taking of saints' names and suggests such hallowed status for feminist predecessors. It reveals the importance she attached to locating herself within a historical tradition made up of activist heroines. From one perspective, Jeanne Deroin was the perfect namesake for an early twentieth-century feminist. She had engaged in battles that were still being fought: for the suffrage, socialism, sexual autonomy, and women's right to be candidates in national elections. From another perspective, however, Pelletier's choice of Deroin was surprising. For the substance of Deroin's ideas, especially her acceptance of the absolute difference of woman, her stress on the symbolic importance of motherhood, and her attempt to elevate the feminine to equivalent status with the masculine, could not have been further from Pelletier's own. Clearly, it was not because she endorsed Deroin's specific ideas that Pelletier placed herself in the same historical tradition. Rather it was because Pelletier identified Deroin as a quintessential feminist that she used her as an inspiration for the fictionalized version of her self.

What did Pelletier mean by "feminist"? She was unequivocal in defining herself as one: "I can say that I have always been a feminist, at least as long as I was old enough to understand."[124] So begins her "Mémoire." In the course of the memoir she expresses contempt for "women as they are," boredom with the limited range of feminist organizational activity, outrage at other feminists' uncritical embrace of femininity, and pessimism about the future; but she never forswears her identification: "Moreover, I remain a feminist. I will remain one until I die."[125] Feminism was not just advocacy on behalf of women's rights; it was above all a position of defiance, the ability to transcend conventional norms. The point was to break the rules in order, paradoxically, to win legal recognition.

For defiance of the law in the name of women's rights, Deroin was indeed a good predecessor. She was remote enough in time to serve as an abstract model; the specific details of her performance (and the substance of her ideas) were not so current as to confuse the imagination. It was enough to know that she had run for office despite constitutional prohibition; in the process she had exposed the hypocrisy of the republic *and* re-presented women as citizens. For the young Marie to take on the name of Deroin was not only to re-present herself as a feminist, but to commit herself to the cause of the political representation of women.

The vote was the starting point of such a re-presentation; its pursuit provided an otherwise elusive unity in the present and continuity with the past. Pelletier offered it as the rallying point in her first speech to Solidarité des Femmes. She attacked the group's vague ideas about "the social value of the mother and the housekeeper, feminine virtues, and male vices."[126] In their place she offered a common goal: "We want equality, that's all—the right to vote."[127] The reaction of her audience and her excitement at their enthusiasm led her, briefly, to underestimate the difficulty of the task: "A young (woman) lawyer said, 'Lead us to victory!' My heart beat very fast. For a minute, my word, I thought victory had arrived! But that will not happen so soon."[128]

Pelletier learned quickly that her word was not enough, that words uttered by a woman did not guarantee individuality. The issue of who controlled the language of representation was not resolved by a woman's appropriation of language; to be a "speaking subject" required more than uttering words. Even within her group the women did not understand the relationship between the enactment of their femininity and legal disenfranchisement. Marie expressed some of Pelletier's disappointment. After her first meeting of Solidarité, Pelletier wrote, Marie's feelings were mixed: "Certainly, the president was nice, but feminism, in the confused mind of the old militant, appeared to her as something weak, and she had so wanted it to be strong!"[129] For Marie (as for Pelletier) it became as important to re-present feminism as it was to re-present women, to constitute a strong feminist subject who defied social expectations about women.

For this project historical figures could provide stark exemplars. Pelletier talked a good deal about the importance of what we now call role models. She had urged feminist mothers to provide their daughters with literature about unusual and courageous women and men (John Stuart Mill, Jeanne d'Arc, and the mathematician Sophie Germain were examples she cited); for feminists Jeanne Deroin offered such a profile in courage.[130] But in addition to the courage it gave her, taking Deroin's name allowed Marie to add historical legitimacy to her feminist advocacy and retrospectively to cast Deroin (as the apostle of the vote) in her own image.

The fictional Marie expressed not only Pelletier's frustration with other feminists, her sense of uniqueness and isolation ("one could search all of Paris and not find another Marie");[131] she also allowed Pelletier to express her desire to control the meaning of feminism. At one point in the novel, Marie decides to write a doctoral thesis on the history of feminism. (Since she doesn't have a baccalaureate, she enrolls at the Ecole Pratique des Hautes Etudes, "where no diplomas are required.")[132] Pelletier mentions this course of study only in passing, and there is no discussion of why Marie wants to write history. But it seems plausible to speculate that Marie's doctorate was the equivalent (for politics) of Madeleine's medical degree (for science). It established her credentials as activist and scholar of the movement (indeed her scholarship was a form of activism), allowing her to transmit its heritage and its inspiration to future generations, but also to rewrite that history in her own terms. As science was for Pelletier the key to the future of society, so history was for Marie a way of shaping the terms of feminism in the present and the future.

In Pelletier's novel Marie goes on to an illustrious career as a socialist politician in Germany, where women have the vote and use it to improve the lives of women. She is tragically killed at the height of her career, a bystander caught in crossfire between revolutionaries and government soldiers in Berlin. Her old friend, Charles Saladier, a socialist militant who had accompanied her to Germany and become her secretary there, returns to Paris and seeks solace among her former associates. Caroline Kauffmann, now a spiritualist medium, channels a message from Marie. Hearing the dead woman's voice, the terrified Saladier flees. The scene is comic as Pelletier presents it. But Marie's message, (mis)represented by Kauffmann as the authentic voice of the dead heroine, seems to have a more serious function in the novel: "It is Marie. I am not dead; no one dies. I see the new world coming. Strive, strive, work toward the light above the graves; the new world advances." [133]

Spoken by the present and for its own purposes, the voice of history points to the future. As Pelletier understood it the history of feminism was exactly this: an imagined lineage for defiant women, one of the resources they must constitute in their transformation from subjected women to feminist subjects. To see the history of feminism as anything more or less than this would be, in her eyes, to deny its vitality and its enduring purpose.

6

Citizens but Not Individuals:
The Vote and After

French women received the right to vote on April 21, 1944. The Committee of National Liberation, led by General Charles de Gaulle and located in Algiers, simply announced the enfranchisement of women as part of an ordinance setting out the terms by which republican government would be restored. According to one source, the proclamation was greeted with neither enthusiasm nor opposition;[1] in post-Vichy France the voices of the senators who had blocked suffrage bills since at least 1919 were stilled.[2] Women's suffrage was then formally written into the constitution of the Fourth Republic (adopted in 1946). Its preamble reaffirmed the 1789 Declaration of Rights and then added a phrase that would have gratified Olympe de Gouges: "the law guarantees to women equal rights with men in all spheres." The constitution's section on sovereignty spelled out the details. Article 4 stated that "all French citizens and nationals of both sexes . . . may vote under conditions determined by law."[3] De Gaulle noted in his memoirs that "this tremendous reform . . . put an end to controversies that had lasted for fifty years."[4] And Louise Weiss, a feminist who had waged the last campaign for women's right to vote in the 1930s, before the outbreak of war, shared the general's sense of the importance of the action: "The worldwide accession of women to a civil status identical with that of men is without doubt the most important collective phenomenon of the first half of this century. We do not yet know all its consequences, but it pleases me to have had a part in it."[5] As in 1848, a Provisional Government, seeking to impose republican order in a situation of political chaos, granted universal suffrage in order to legitimate its position as the representative of the sovereign people. David Thomson, the historian of French politics, characterizes the sense of the moment thus: "Efforts to establish rather tenuous and fictitious strands of legal continuity gave way to an admittedly Jacobin theory: that there must be early general elections to express the national 'general will' of the sovereign people. The revolutionary tradition was born anew; and the Fourth Republic, instead of being in form a continuation of the Third, was to emerge from a momentous, creative act of national will, exercised though universal free suffrage."[6] Unlike in 1848, however, universal suffrage this time included citizenship for women.

The inclusion of women has been explained as a calculated attempt by de Gaulle and his associates to preclude a feared Communist victory in a new government. Since women were thought to be more conservative than men, it was hoped that they would counter the influence the left had gained during the resistance.[7] But this kind of calculation, if it was made at all, seems to have been only part of the explanation.

More important was that by 1944 the definition of democracy had expanded to include sexual democracy (in the form of the vote for women). Enfranchising women enabled the new government to distinguish itself both from the Vichy regime and from the Third Republic. The weaknesses of the Third Republic were seen by many, including de Gaulle, as having led to its own demise at the hands of Pétain; citizenship for women was one of the ways of signaling the end of an outdated republic and the advent of a more modern one. (As it turned out, since there was little difference in substance between the two republics, women's suffrage supplied one of the few striking contrasts.) Suffrage for women also aligned France (whose democratic credentials had been compromised by the Vichy regime) with the other Western democracies, most of which had long before recognized women's political rights. Describing the committees of women organized by the Free French forces in London in 1942 to prepare legislation to ensure a better status for "the family, women, and children," a supporter stressed the importance of the international context: "These committees maintained contact with similar foreign or international organizations so that France might eventually be restored to her proper place in these respects on the international plane."[8] The vote for women in 1944 brought France into line with the other Western democracies.

In addition, enfranchising women was a way of practically and symbolically resolving national political differences. Practically, the vote was granted to women as a way of eliminating one of the conflicts that had plagued the previous republic. In the years after World War I especially, the Chamber of Deputies regularly sent a suffrage bill to the Senate, where it was just as regularly defeated. By granting women the vote, the Provisional Government ended one of the conflicts between the two legislative bodies, thus asserting national unity in a forceful way.

Symbolically, the vote for women signified the dissolution of all difference. The inclusion of women as citizens, their incorporation into the body politic, was a gesture of national reconciliation, ending divisions among Radicals, Socialists, Communists, and Catholics, among resistance fighters, among members of the councils of the Free French movement, even between colonial subjects and their rulers, as well as between women and men. All were declared the same, and their sameness lay in their membership in the nation. Especially during the life of the Provisional Government, before the decision to create a new republic had actually been taken (in a referendum in April 1945), the population must be a unified nation, with the government representing its single voice and will. De Gaulle's voice repeatedly intoned the message, first from London and then from Algiers: "The French have only one country . . . France is and will remain one and indivisible."[9] In 1848 unity had been achieved by declaring class differences irrelevant to the exercise of political rights (with universal manhood suffrage, it was claimed, there were "no longer proletarians in France"); in 1944, the merger of the sexes into a single citizenry performed at least some of the rhetorical work of national political unification.[10]

———■———

Looking back on these circumstances, in which government leaders found it in the national interest to enfranchise women, Louise Weiss asked a question about feminist agency in her characteristically self-important way.[11] "Without the hard struggle that I led, would French-

women have obtained their political rights at this moment?" Her answer was an unqualified "yes . . . thanks to international contingencies."[12] Among other reasons, she offered the observation that it was
no longer tenable, in a world in which all the other democracies had
long before granted women citizenship, for France to claim to be a
democracy without letting women vote. But she also insisted on the
importance of feminist struggle for defining de Gaulle's action not as
the gift of a benevolent (or self-serving) prince, but as a response to
"an aspiration." She drew an analogy to the landings at Normandy by
English and American troops. Without the participation of the resistance fighters, she argued, France would still have been liberated, but
the event would have been only a strategic victory imposed from
outside. With the participation of the *maquis*, the landing became
somehow exemplary (the idea is not clearly expressed) of the way Weiss
thought history should work, of her belief in the moral necessity of
action by the oppressed, of her conception of the process of democratic
politics.[13] According to Weiss, without feminist struggle women would
have been merely passive recipients of their rights, whereas with such
struggle they could be seen as having actively won their own emancipation.[14]

Weiss understood her role and, more broadly, the issue of feminist
agency within the discourse of individualism also spoken by Madeleine
Pelletier. Although politically the two women were at odds—Pelletier
was a socialist, Weiss a Radical—Weiss believed, with Pelletier, that
"individuals of the elite" could bring about change, and she defined
her actions in these terms.[15] The title of her memoir, *Combats pour les
femmes* (Struggles for, or on behalf of, women), captures something of
her sense of superiority, as does her comment that many of her former
associates were "stupefied" by her decision to agitate for the vote. "[My]
having left the influential [journal] *Europe nouvelle* to dedicate myself
to the unfortunate women who were deprived of all rights, and therefore of any importance, seemed to them a strange folly."[16] Weiss here
understands her turn to feminism, as well as the activities she undertook in its name, to involve a set of personally determined strategies.
For her the story is one set in motion above all by her individual will.
But a different story about Weiss serves as an effective summary and
conclusion for this book. It is an account in which feminism is consti-

tuted by the exclusion of women from politics and by the repression of sexual difference as a political issue; one in which feminism then constitutes the agency of feminists, an agency that "jams the theoretical machinery" of republican political discourse, exposing its limits and disrupting its smooth functioning.[17]

Weiss had not been active in feminist circles before 1934; instead she had worked in the peace movement, editing the magazine *Europe nouvelle,* which sought after World War I to substitute mediation for warfare in international diplomacy. She explained her turn to feminism as a political strategy: if women's votes had to be courted by politicians, then men would be influenced to avoid war by their belief that women preferred peace. (Weiss herself did not accept the essentialist equation of women and peace, but she was willing to entertain the "hypothesis" in order to win support for "my apostleship for peace.")[18] Weiss assumed the position of woman deliberately and subversively; that is, she presented herself as the spokesperson for a group with which she had not previously identified.[19] But having made the identification, she used her own case to point up the limitations of the republic's proclaimed universalism. Through the lens of feminism, the incongruity of her situation became disturbing: here was a prominent journalist who enjoyed a great deal of political influence but did not enjoy formal political rights.

Weiss's campaign sounded a familiar feminist theme: it attacked the inconsistencies in republican ideology and demanded that they be corrected. In the 1930s the republic was under siege from the right and left; in the name of protecting it, she demanded women's right to vote. Each time there was a constitutional crisis, whether it was a dispute about the powers of the president, the actions of the cabinet, or the future of republican forms of government, Weiss pressed for the vote. (Her book is organized in exactly this way, alternating accounts of the crises of the regime with tales of her feminist interventions.) She took to the streets when other political groups did during the Popular Front. She organized demonstrations and marches; imitating the English suffragists, she and a group of women chained themselves to the statue at the Place de la Bastille; and she set up ballot boxes (made of hat boxes) to collect "votes" for women candidates outside polling places. She recognized the dangers of her activities in this period of worsening political instability: "To demand our rights in such a dramatic period seemed inopportune, insolent, dangerous to those professionals who had begun to fear for their future."[20] Indeed, the campaign might well bring down the very regime that could advance women's cause. But she also insisted that the timing was crucial for advancing the cause. The "incompetence of the government" and "the petrifaction" of republican institutions had to be both exposed and exploited; the way to do that was to focus on the use and misuse of the vote by insisting on suffrage for women.[21]

Weiss was particularly proud of the impact her campaign had on the Conseil d'Etat, the highest administrative tribunal in the nation. She felt she had won an official acknowledgment of the rightness of her cause from those whose job it was to reconcile the principles and practices of the law. In May 1935 (as Pierre Laval, the ally of Italian Fascists, negotiated an accord with Stalin that threw French Radicals, Socialists, and Communists into disarray) Weiss ran a protest campaign in the Eighteenth Arrondissement for a seat on the Municipal Council of Paris. She enlisted the members of her organization, La Femme Nouvelle, to sit outside polling places and hand out unofficial ballots, which were to be placed in hat boxes. (The results were then announced to the press—Weiss had a keen sense of the need for publicity—as victories for women candidates and expressions of support for women's rights.) Inevitably, some men mistakenly placed their feminist ballots in the official boxes, but these were discarded during the tally. Weiss maintained that the election was invalid because all votes cast had not been counted. She took her case first to the prefecture of the Seine and then to the Conseil d'Etat.[22]

The Conseil d'Etat turned down her appeal but at the same time conceded the merits of her case and acknowledged the "formal contradiction" she had pointed out: French law was written, not customary, they agreed, and no written law prohibited women from voting. Existing law assumed the universality of rights and the capacity of citizens to exercise them; thus no law was necessary to permit women to vote. "On the contrary, it would be necessary for Parliament to pass a law expressly preventing them from exercising these rights." But the legislature had passed no such law. Therefore, the Conseil admitted, "logically . . . women have the right to vote in all elections." The Conseil stopped short of granting the vote by interpreting exclusion to be the (by implication illogical) intention of lawmakers. But it also recognized the inadequacy of its solution by suggesting that it was bound by "the state of existing legislation." The rapporteur noted explicitly that the insertion of the phrase "the state of existing legislation" was a call for legislative change.[23] Instead of dismissing Weiss's case as folly, the Conseil had conceded its merits. And Weiss clearly considered her success to have been an important conceptual and legal factor in the eventual winning of the vote.

Arguably, the decision of the Conseil d'Etat was as much a sign of the greater openness of some republicans to "sexual democracy" as it was of Weiss's brilliant reasoning. But for our purposes here the question of that kind of causality is beside the point. What is interesting is Weiss's insistence, once she put on the feminist mantle, that the insufficiencies of republican political discourse be exposed and corrected. This attention to inconsistency did not originate with Weiss; it was the hallmark of feminism.

So was the difficulty Weiss faced in declaring herself a "woman," like the others whose emancipation she sought. For her the category had to do with political exclusion and not with sex. In her memoir she swings back and forth between a description of herself as a woman without rights and as the social and intellectual superior (not a woman) of those poor benighted women whose cause she had taken up. Yet speaking from the position of a "woman," however qualified the reference, necessarily evoked her difference from the men whose social and intellectual equal she was in the high diplomatic circles in which she moved.

The reaction to Weiss's campaign by one of her colleagues underscores the difficulty feminists faced, not only in making their points to begin with, but in correcting the historical record. Those who had lived through the turbulent street fighting of the 1930s were particularly insistent on the long-standing republican preference for ballots over bullets. For this reason the militancy of feminists had disturbed Weiss's colleague Marc Rucart. Rucart, a member of Léon Blum's cabinet in 1936 and later of de Gaulle's Committee of National Liberation, told

Weiss many years later how angry her feminist street demonstrations had made him. "The right to vote does away with the right of insurrection, Madame . . . Hadn't you read Victor Hugo?"

Weiss's answer startled Rucart: "Yes, my dear minister. But, tell me, did we then enjoy this right to vote?" Weiss notes that "Marc was stunned. Politically, he could think only as a man."[24]

Weiss attributed Rucart's lapse of memory to his belief that women did not belong in the political sphere, but it is equally likely (since he was a member of the government that granted the vote) that once women were incorporated into the electorate, they seemed to him to have always been there. Having resolved one of the inconsistencies of republicanism meant erasing the fact that it had ever existed. Furthermore, in Rucart's mind feminist militancy still bore the taint of irrationality that its opponents used to discredit it (it was that which justified his anger when he spoke to Weiss so many years later); republicanism, in contrast, was intact, as coherent a system in its past as it had become for him in the present.

In the face of such official interpretations, it is tempting for historians to correct the record by treating feminism as a form of heroic resistance to injustice and by locating this resistance in the wills of individual women. I have been arguing throughout this book that the issue is far more complicated than that. Feminism is not a reaction to republicanism, but one of its effects, produced by contradictory assertions about the universal human rights of individuals, on the one hand, and exclusions attributed to "sexual difference," on the other. Feminism is the paradoxical expression of that contradiction in its effort both to have "sexual difference" acknowledged and to have it rendered irrelevant. Feminist agency is constituted by this paradox. Since the terms of definition of republicanism have changed over time, so have the terms of feminism and feminist agency. Although feminists have been "women who have only paradoxes to offer," they have nonetheless done so in fundamentally different terms.

The historical importance of feminism and the validation of feminist agency, therefore, do not rest on whether or not we can establish that it was feminists who finally brought about the vote (although it is arguable that their actions contributed to the process). It is rather within the changing discourses of individualism, as the nagging reminder of republicanism's insufficient universalism, that feminism has done its critical work and thus ought to find its history.

———————■———————

For feminists the vote was cause for celebration, but it did not end women's status as what Simone de Beauvoir was soon to designate "the second sex." Louise Weiss's experience is once again useful to consider. It did not augur well for the fulfillment of her hopes (although in the long run her political career was indeed that of a liberated woman). Weiss, who joined the Radical Party immediately after the vote was announced, was quickly disabused of her expectations for a place in the new government by Georges Bidault. Bidault consulted her on de Gaulle's behalf for the names of women who might be included when a Constituent Assembly (which would write a new constitution) was organized. When Weiss offered herself, Bidault explained that she was not the type they had in mind. "You! . . . Oh! no. Not at any price. We don't want to embarrass ourselves with worthy women!" She laughed bitterly, she recalled, and then recommended to him a number of widows whose "dead husbands had left them touching names."[25]

As the choice of widows for these first elections suggests, those who formulated the decree granting citizenship to women wanted to continue to consider them as members of families or of collectivities with a particular interest to defend. And they sought to minimize the significance of women's new right to participate in elections, which were, after all, only periodic exercises that need not carry over into other areas of life. Still, citizenship carried with it the promise, if not the immediate realization, of individuality and so opened the way for greater political participation by women. Whatever the intentions of the legislators, women became political subjects with the vote. Ironically, enfranchisement contrasted even more sharply than disenfranchisement with women's continued social/psychological dependence.[26] Instead of eliminating the general problem of sexual difference, the vote drew attention to it with greater force.

This is the relevance of Simone de Beauvoir's *The Second Sex*. Writing in 1949, she referred to the political rights feminists had sought for more than 150 years as (there is a "merely" implied in her use of the terms) "abstract" and "theoretical." Citizenship had made women

men's equals as subjects before the law in a formal, procedural sense, but it had failed to win for them autonomy—social, economic, or subjective. The issue was not that of substantive equality (although de Beauvoir was concerned with securing that too). There was simply no carryover from women's status as abstract individuals to their status as "sovereign subjects," as autonomous beings fully in possession of themselves. In this sense the vote was only a partial victory:

> the period in which we live is a period of transition; this world, which has always belonged to men, is still in their hands; the institutions and values of the patriarchal civilization still survive in large part. Abstract rights are far from being completely granted everywhere to women . . . And abstract rights, as I have just been saying, have never sufficed to assure to woman a definite hold on the world; true equality between the two sexes does not exist even today.[27]

De Beauvoir argued that women would never achieve the status of fully autonomous individuals as long as they continued to serve as "others" to men. Women were the mythic projection of men's hopes and fears, the confirmation of their virility and sovereignty. Although economic freedom was a crucial ingredient in women's emancipation (the concrete dimension that must accompany theoretical rights), the problem was ultimately existential: only man could achieve self-creation through the transcendence of the conditions of his existence. Woman was doomed to the life of immanence; confined to the endless repetition of general feminine functions, she was denied the liberty to live (individually and specifically) as she chose.[28]

> The advantage man enjoys . . . is that his vocation as a human being in no way runs counter to his destiny as a male. Through the identification of phallus and transcendence, it turns out that his social and spiritual successes endow him with a virile presence. He is not divided. Whereas it is required of woman that in order to realize her femininity she must make herself object and prey, which is to say that she must renounce her claims as a sovereign subject.[29]

De Beauvoir believed that the mark of the human was to act as a sovereign subject, to choose the direction of one's life; hence women were being denied the expression of their essential humanity. In her eyes, sexual difference was a secondary phenomenon; it was cultural, not biological. It did not deny the universality (the sameness) of humanity, and it would not disappear when that sameness was recognized or, as she put it, "restored." "Those who make much of 'equality in difference,'" she wrote at the end of *The Second Sex*, "could not with good grace refuse to grant me the possible existence of differences in equality . . . If society restores her sovereign individuality to woman, it will not thereby destroy the power of love's embrace to move the heart."[30]

If these thoughts mark de Beauvoir as an existentialist philosopher and place her on the "equality" side of equality-versus-difference debates among contemporary feminists, they also can tell us something about the effects of the vote on feminism.[31] For, like all feminists, de Beauvoir must be read in terms of the specific political and philosophical discourses of her time. In her case, existentialism and the vote, the idea of the sovereign subject and its legal existence for women, are the crucial discursive contexts. For the vote, instead of resolving the tension between the abstract undifferentiated individual and the individual self defined through difference, had heightened the conflict between the two. In the past the tension between them had been apparently resolved by taking both individuals to be masculine; that resolution no longer worked when women were admitted to the ranks of abstract individuals. Woman's claim to be a sovereign subject was buttressed by her new legal standing as a citizen. De Beauvoir's reference to "renouncing" that claim had to do not only with contravening her inherent humanity, but with violating the law.

As de Beauvoir described it, the acquisition of the vote had not solved the problem of women's subordination, but it had moved the locus of contradiction. There was no longer a question about whether women had rights; when they became legal subjects the universal principles of liberal republicanism could be deemed truly universal. The problem of substantive rights remained, of course; as had been the case with universal manhood suffrage, the limits of formal rights for redressing inequities of economic and social power became more evident. With political rights women could (and did) bring their demands to the legislative arena, pointing up the contradiction between the promise of equality and its realization. But the real tension, de Beauvoir thought, lay elsewhere: Woman "stands before man not as a subject, but as an object paradoxically endued with subjectivity; she takes herself simultaneously as *self* and as *other*, a contradiction that entails baffling consequences."[32] As she pondered the dilemma, de Beauvoir wondered what it would take to achieve the "inner metamorphosis" needed for women to be represented as fully autonomous individuals. "But is it enough to change laws, institutions, customs, public opinion, and the whole social context, for men and women to become truly equal?" De Beauvoir hedged on the answer. She thought, on the one hand, that these changes were a necessary precondition for true equality and would gradually bring it about, but, on the other, that their achievement required the kind of transcendent reach by women that their positioning as objects prevented. "It is not a question of abolishing in woman the contingencies and miseries of the human condition, but of giving her the means for transcending them."[33]

This tension in de Beauvoir's analysis replays some of the tensions about causality and materialism inherent in existentialism's encounter with Marxism. It also marks a new context for feminist critiques, one that was a direct consequence of the vote. When women became citizens the abstract individual appeared to be pluralized; in fact, he was at best neutered, and it is probably more accurate to say that he remained masculine. Women were subsumed into the category, declared to be a version of man for the purpose of exercising the vote. This had the effect of temporarily negating or evading the question that sexual difference had long posed for definitions of the abstract individual. But in de Beauvoir's terms the solution was "theoretical," not actual, because it had no effect on the self/other process by which differentiated individuals were constructed. That process instantiated sexual difference, not as pluralism, but (since the individual was still taken to be a singular type) as hierarchy. When women became citizens they could be represented as (abstract) individuals, but how could they be represented as women?

Post-suffrage feminism was constructed in the space of a paradox: there was the declared sameness of women and men under the sign of citizenship (or the abstract individual), and there was the exclusionary masculinity of the individual subject. On the one side was the presumed equality that followed from the legally guaranteed possession of universal rights; on the other was the inequality that followed from the presumed natural facts of sexual difference. It is in terms of this inconsistency—between the political and psychological meanings of "individual"—that we can understand not only de Beauvoir's difficulties in producing a definitive program for achieving equality, but also the conflicts that have characterized the most recent history of feminism.

Competing feminist visions have taken one side or another of the opposition between the abstract individual (which counts women the same as men) and the individual self defined through sexual difference (which insists on their radical unlikeness). Those who, following de Beauvoir (Elisabeth Badinter is the latest representative of this position), argue for equality take the side of the abstract individual.[34] They insist that sexual difference is irrelevant in the face of the shared human rights recognized by universal principles of liberal democratic law. Those who argue for difference say that sexual difference is the inescapable product of individuation, and that abstract individualism not only represses a difference that can never be overcome, but also perpetuates the oppression of women by making masculinity the norm. ("Equal to whom?" asks Luce Irigaray as she argues against feminists who aspire to identification with the "generic masculine." "This strikes me as quite an ingenuous error since they [women] still lack what's needed to define their own socio-cultural identity."[35] Women, in other words, remain unrepresentable in their own terms.) The goal of the so-called difference feminists is to disrupt the process that objectifies women for the purpose of constituting individual male subjects by making the difference of women the basis for representing an autonomous female subjectivity.[36]

My objective has not been to take sides in these disputes, but to point out that, however intensely felt, they do not signal a defect in feminism (what Theodore Zeldin, citing Louise Weiss's memoirs, referred to as "the bitchiness in the feminist movements.")[37] Rather, the apparent need to choose sameness *or* difference (which can never be satisfied by either alternative) is symptomatic of the difficulty that sexual difference poses for singular conceptions of the individual. To the extent that feminism is constructed in paradoxical relationship to this singular conception of the individual it inevitably reproduces the terms of its own construction.

A rereading of the history of feminism cannot resolve its paradoxes; it is in the nature of paradox to be unresolvable. The study of these paradoxes does, however, introduce a needed complexity into the historical account. I have focused on the history of feminism, but the usefulness of the approach extends beyond feminism to the study of history more generally. It insists on the historical specificity of the paradoxes and contradictions that produce their own disavowals and so on the historicity of what seem to be recurrent or continuous cultural and political expressions. Thus the existence of feminism (or of labor or socialist or antiracist movements, to take only a few other possible examples) is not explained as resistance to a timeless masculinism (or capitalism or racism), or to the fixed limits of liberal political theory. Rather feminism (or trade unionism or socialism or antiracism) is produced, differently at different moments, at sites of historically specific discursive contradiction. Political movements emerge at sites of difficult, sometimes unresolvable, contradiction. And it is the point of historical study to illuminate the specificity of these productions.

The history of feminism has been an important and complex instrument, consciously employed for the ends of feminist politics. My own purpose has been to engage with that history in order to address a set of difficult questions posed by the seemingly endless and often heated debates among contemporary feminists about equality and difference. Like the feminists of the past, my thinking has taken shape within a discursive context I do not fully control (and which others will have to analyze), but I have also drawn consciously on bodies of theory that deal with difference, paradox, and the discursive formation of subjects.[38]

These theories have provided me with a different understanding of the reasons for the intractability of the dilemmas feminists have confronted and for the necessarily paradoxical responses to them they continue to have. But they have not and cannot resolve the dilemmas or make them less intractable. Indeed, in the case of feminism, the problem that has been deemed so central (equality versus difference) cannot be resolved as it has been posed. But can it be posed otherwise?

Would there be feminism without the discourse of individual rights that represses sexual difference? I think not. Can there be a feminist politics that exploits that tension without expecting finally to resolve it? I think so; the point of this book has been to say that feminists have been doing just that for at least two centuries.

If my answers to these final questions are still tentative ("I *think* not" "I *think* so") it is because they are meant to provoke discussion, not to end debate. This discussion is not just necessary for maintaining a vigorous movement (both scholarly and political); it is unavoidable. Historically, feminists have had to confront problems which are central to the ideological organization of their societies, and which are therefore not meant to be seen or even considered as problems. No sure or single solution has been or is possible in the face of that kind of challenge; hence the inevitablity of continued debate.

Subjecting our own paradoxes to critical scrutiny is a way of appreciating the enormity of the problems feminists have faced, the creativity with which they have addressed those problems, and the need for ways of thinking that do not insist on the resolution of opposites. It was, after all, the drive to such resolution that made "sexual difference" an intractable problem for theories of political representation. And it was as a critique of those theories, which attempted to banish the problem of sexual difference by excluding women, that feminism found its unstable raison d'être.

Notes

1. Rereading the History of Feminism

1. Histories of French feminism include Léon Abensour, *Histoire générale du féminisme: Des origines à nos jours* (Paris: Slatkine, 1979); Maïté Albistur and Daniel Armogathe, *Histoire du féminisme français*, 2 vols. (Paris: Editions des Femmes, 1977); Patrick K. Bidelman, *Pariahs Stand Up! The Founding of the Liberal Feminist Movement in France, 1858–1889* (Westport, Conn.: Greenwood Press, 1982); Suzanne Grinberg, *Historique du mouvement suffragiste depuis 1848* (Paris: H. Goulet, 1926); Steven C. Hause with Anne R. Kenney, *Women's Suffrage and Social Politics in the French Third Republic* (Princeton: Princeton University Press, 1984); Laurence Klejman and Florence Rochefort, *L'égalité en marche: Le féminisme sous la Troisième République* (Paris: Editions des Femmes, 1989); James F. McMillan, *Housewife or Harlot: The Place of Women in French Society, 1870–1940* (New York: St. Martin's Press, 1981); Claire Goldberg Moses, *French Feminism in the Nineteenth Century* (Albany: State University of New York Press, 1984); Charles Sowerwine, *Sisters or Citizens? Women and Socialism in France since 1876* (Cambridge: Cambridge University Press, 1982); Evelyne Sullerot, *Histoire de la presse féminine en France, des origines à 1848* (Paris: Librairie Armand Colin, 1966); Marguerite Thibert, *Le féminisme dans le socialisme français de 1830 à 1850* (Paris: Marcel Girard, 1926); Louise A. Tilly, "Women's Collective Action and Feminism in France, 1870–1914," in Louise A. Tilly and Charles Tilly, eds., *Class Conflict and Collective Action* (Beverly Hills: Sage, 1981).

2. *New York Times*, December 31, 1993. The book is Françoise Gaspard, Claude Servan-Schreiber, and Anne Le Gall, *Au pouvoir citoyennes! Liberté, égalité, parité* (Paris: Seuil, 1992).

3. On this question see Geneviève Fraisse, "Quand gouverner n'est pas représenter," *Esprit*, no. 200 (March–April 1994), pp. 103–114.

4. Cited in Charles Sowerwine and Claude Maignien, *Madeleine Pelletier: Une féministe dans l'arène politique* (Paris: Les Editions Ouvrières, 1992), p. 102.

5. Olympe de Gouges, *Le bonheur primitif de l'homme* (Paris, 1788), p. 23: "Si j'allois plus avant sur cette matière, je pourrois m'étendre trop loin, et m'attirer l'inimitié des hommes parvenus, qui, sans réfléchir sur mes bonnes vues, ni approfondir mes bonnes intentions, me condamneroient impitoyablement comme une femme qui n'a que des paradoxes à offrir, et non des problèmes faciles à résoudre."

6. For the uses of the terms "paradox" and "contradiction," see the Petit Robert *Dictionnaire de la langue française* (Paris, 1986), pp. 1353 and 380, respectively.

7. On the history of French republicanism see Rogers Brubaker, *Citizenship and Nationhood in France and Germany* (Cambridge, Mass.: Harvard University Press, 1992); Peter Campbell, *French Electoral Systems and Elections since 1789* (London: Faber, 1958); Claude Nicolet, *L'idée républicaine en France (1789–1924): Essai d'histoire critique* (Paris: Gallimard, 1982); Siân Reynolds, "Marianne's Citizens? Women, the Republic, and Universal Suffrage in France," in Reynolds, ed., *Women, State, and Revolution: Essays on Power and Gender in Europe since 1789* (Brighton: Wheatsheaf Books, 1986), pp. 102–112; Pierre Rosanvallon, *L'état en France: De 1789 à nos jours* (Paris: Seuil, 1990) and *Le sacre du citoyen: Histoire du suffrage universel en France* (Paris: Gallimard, 1992); David Thompson, *Democracy in France: The Third and Fourth Republics* (London: Oxford University Press, 1958).

8. *Encyclopédie, ou dictionnaire raisonné des sciences, des arts et des metiers,* 17 vols. (Neufchâtel, 1751–1765; cited hereafter as *Encyclopédie*), vol. 8, pp. 684–685: "Pierre est un homme, Paul est un homme, ils appartiennent à la même espèce; mais ils different *numériquement* par les différences qui leur font propres. L'un est beau, l'autre laid, l'un savant, l'autre ignorant, et un tel sujet est un *individu* suivant l'étymologie, parce qu'on ne peut plus le diviser en nouveau sujets qui ayent une existence réellement indépendante de lui. L'assemblage de ses propriétés est tel, que prises ensemble elles ne sauraient convenu qu'à lui."

9. *Lettres d'un bourgeois de New Haven à un citoyen de Virginie* (1787), in *Oeuvres de Condorcet,* 12 vols. (Paris, 1847–48), vol. 9, p. 14; cited in Cheryl B. Welch, *Liberty and Utility: The French Idéologues and the Transformation of Liberalism* (New York: Columbia University Press, 1984), p. 11.

10. An example of how this abstracting process works can be seen in the Comte de Clermont Tonnère's comment on the Jews at the end of the French Revolution: "One must refuse everything to the Jews as a nation and grant everything to Jews as individuals . . . They must be citizens as individuals"; cited in Brubaker, *Citizenship and Nationhood,* p. 106.

11. Stephen Lukes, *Individualism* (New York: Harper and Row, 1973), pp. 152–153. See also Uday S. Mehta, "Liberal Strategies of Exclusion," *Politics and Society* 18 (December 1990), 427–453; and Marcel Gauchet, "De l'avènement de l'individu à la découverte de la société," in *Annales: Economies sociétés civilisations* (cited hereafter as *Annales E.S.C.*) 34 (May–June 1979), 457–463. On French liberalism,

see Stephen Holmes, *Benjamin Constant and the Making of Modern Liberalism* (New Haven: Yale University Press, 1984); Welch, *Liberty and Utility;* William Logue, *From Philosophy to Sociology: The Evolution of French Liberalism* (De Kalb: Northern Illinois University Press, 1983); François Bourricaud, "The Rights of the Individual and the General Will in Revolutionary Thought," and Jean Rivero, "The Jacobin and Liberal Traditions," both in Joseph Klaits and Michael H. Haltzel, eds., *Liberty/Liberté: The American and French Experiences* (Washington, D.C.: Woodrow Wilson Center Press; and Baltimore: Johns Hopkins University Press, 1991). On feminism and liberal political theory see Christine Fauré, *La démocratie sans les femmes: Essai sur le libéralisme en France* (Paris: Presses Universitaires de France, 1985); Michèle Le Doeuff, *Hipparchia's Choice: An Essay concerning Women, Philosophy, Etc.,* trans. Trista Selous (Oxford: Blackwell, 1990); Wai-chee Dimock, "Criminal Law, Female Virtue, and the Rise of Liberalism," *Yale Journal of Law* 4, no. 2 (Summer 1992); and Dimock, "Rightful Subjectivity," *Yale Journal of Criticism* 4, no. 1 (1990). On democratic theory and the exclusion of women, see Geneviève Fraisse, *Muse de la raison: La démocratie exclusive et la différence des sexes* (Aix-en-Provence: Editions Alinéa, 1989).

12. Lukes, *Individualism,* p. 146.

13. Welch, *Liberty and Utility.*

14. Pierre-Jean-Georges Cabanis, *Rapports du physique et du moral de l'homme,* 2 vols. (Paris, 1802). I am grateful to Andrew Aisenberg for this reference.

15. Condorcet, "On the Admission of Women to the Rights of Citizenship" (1790), in *Selected Writings,* ed. Keith Michael Baker (Indianapolis: Bobbs-Merrill, 1976), p. 98.

16. This is not to say that the individuality of white men was not also established by contrasts of color or "civilization," just to point out that gender was crucial to the conceptualization of *masculine* individuality, as it became an increasingly important dimension of social and personal identity from the late eighteenth century on.

17. My attention was drawn to the contradictions within the notion of the individual by the pathbreaking work on American individualism and individual identity of literary historian Michael Warner. Warner argues that, in the nineteenth-century American context, heterosexuality was the resolution of the contradiction. See "Homo-Narcissism: Or, Heterosexuality," in Joseph Boone and Michael Cadden, eds., *Engendering Men* (New York: Routledge, 1990), pp. 190–206; "The Mass Public and the Mass Subject," in Craig Calhoun, ed., *Habermas and the Public Sphere* (Cambridge, Mass.: MIT Press, 1992), pp. 377–401; "New English Sodom," *American Literature* 64, no. 1 (March 1992), 19–29; "Thoreau's Bottom," *Raritan* 11, no. 3 (Winter 1992), 53–79; "Walden's Erotic Economy," in Hortense J. Spiller, ed., *Comparative American Identities: Race, Sex, and Nationality in the Modern Text* (New York: Routledge, 1991).

18. Cited in C. L. R. James, *The Black Jacobins: Toussaint l'Ouverture and the San Domingo Revolution,* 2nd ed. (New York: Vintage Books, 1963), pp. 140–141.

19. Jean-Jacques Rousseau, *Discourse on the Origin of Inequality*, in *The Social Contract and Discourses*, trans. G. D. H. Cole (New York: E. P. Dutton, 1950).

20. Emile Durkheim, *The Division of Labor in Society* (New York: Macmillan, 1933), p. 62. In some popular writing sameness was thought to give rise not merely to the conflation of identity and the loss of boundaries, but also to hatred. The socialist Jules Vallès, for example, feared that schools and colleges for women would lead to "le coeur engarçonné, et de cet engarçonnement peut nâitre je ne sais quel mépris de l'homme"; cited by Eugénie Pierre in her reponse to socialist Jules Vallès in *La Citoyenne*, December 26, 1881.

21. Durkheim, *The Division of Labor*, p. 56.

22. Cesare Lombroso and G. Ferrero, *La femme criminelle et la prostituée*, trans. Louise Meille (Paris, 1896); cited in Elissa Gelfand, *Imagination in Confinement: Women's Writings from French Prisons* (Ithaca: Cornell University Press, 1983), p. 50.

23. On this question for contemporary feminism, see Anne Snitow, "Gender Diary," in Marianne Hirsch and Evelyn Fox Keller, eds., *Conflicts in Feminism* (New York: Routledge, 1990), pp. 9–43. Examples of contemporary efforts to get beyond this dilemma of "equality versus difference" include Cécile Dauphin et al., "Culture et pouvoir des femmes: Essai d'historiographie," *Annales E.S.C.* 41 (March–April 1986), 271–293; Martha Minow, *Making All the Difference: Inclusion, Exclusion, and American Law* (Ithaca: Cornell University Press, 1990); Gisela Bock and Susan James, eds., *Beyond Equality and Difference: Citizenship, Feminist Politics, and Female Subjectivity* (London and New York: Routledge, 1992); and the special issue of *Futur antérieur*, "Féminismes au présent" (1993). On the problem of equality and difference for democratic politics, see William E. Connolly, *Identity/Difference: Democratic Negotiations of Political Paradox* (Ithaca: Cornell University Press, 1991).

24. On coherence, see Jacques Derrida, "Structure, Sign, and Play in the Discourse of the Human Sciences," in *Writing and Difference*, trans. Alan Bass (Chicago: University of Chicago Press, 1978), pp. 278–294.

25. Luce Irigaray, "The Power of Discourse and the Subordination of the Feminine," in Margaret Whitford, ed., *The Irigaray Reader* (Oxford: Blackwell, 1991), pp. 118–132, esp. 122–125.

26. Denise Riley, *"Am I That Name?" Feminism and the Category of "Women" in History* (London: Macmillan, 1988).

27. On citizenship, see Rosanvallon, *Le sacre du citoyen*. See also Carole Pateman, "Promise and Paradox: Women and Democratic Citizenship" (The New York Lecture, presented at York University, Ontario, October 1990); Michèle Riot-Sarcey, "De l'historicité du genre citoyen," in Hans Ulrich Jost, Monique Pavillon, and François Vallotton, eds., *La politique des droits. Citoyenneté et construction des genres aux 19e et 20e siècles* (Paris: Editions Kimé, 1994); J. M. Barbalet, *Citizenship: Rights, Struggle, and Class Inequality* (Minneapolis: University of Minnesota Press, 1988); and Catherine Wihtol de Wenden, ed., *La citoyenneté* (Paris: Fondation Diderot, 1988).

28. This book is an attempt to elaborate the point about agency I tried to make in my critique of Linda Gordon's *Heroes of Their Own Lives*. See my book review and the exchange with Gordon in *Signs* 15 (Summer 1990), 848–860. The most concise statement about the kind of agency I propose is still Parveen Adams and Jeff Minson, "The 'Subject' of Feminism," *m/f* 2 (1978), 43–61. See also Michel Foucault, *The History of Sexuality*, vol. 1: *An Introduction*, trans. Robert Hurley (New York: Vintage Books, 1980), p. 93: "One needs to be nominalistic, no doubt: power is not an institution, and not a structure; neither is it a certain strength we are endowed with; it is the name that one attributes to a complex strategical situation in a particular society."

29. In politics, those who offer only paradoxes are often taken to be cranks or quacks; their inability to choose either one position or another seems to justify their exclusion. When feminists designated themselves "pariahs" (as they did repeatedly in the course of the long nineteenth century), they were describing a position they had both chosen and been consigned to. On feminists as "pariahs" see Michèle Riot-Sarcey, *La démocratie à l'épreuve des femmes: Trois figures critiques du pouvoir, 1830–1848* (Paris: Editions Albin Michel, 1994).

30. Cited in Felicia Gordon, *The Integral Feminist: Madeleine Pelletier, 1874–1939* (Minneapolis: University of Minnesota Press, 1990), p. 85.

2. The Uses of Imagination

1. M. J. Sydenham, *The French Revolution* (New York: Capricorn Books, 1966), p. 63.

2. Elisabeth G. Sledziewski, *Révolutions du sujet* (Paris: Méridiens Klincksieck, 1989), especially part 2, "La femme, sujet civil et impossible sujet civique," pp. 63–128.

3. On the history of women and feminism (two different topics) in the French Revolution, see Maïté Albistur and Daniel Armogathe, *Histoire du féminisme français*, vol. 1 (Paris: Editions des Femmes, 1977); Paule-Marie Duhet, *Les femmes et la Révolution, 1789–1794* (Paris: Julliard, 1971); Jane Abray, "Feminism in the French Revolution," *American Historical Review* 80 (1975), 43–62; Jeanne Bouvier, *Les femmes pendant la Révolution* (Paris: E. Figuière, 1931); Olwen Hufton, "Women in the French Revolution," *Past and Present* 53 (1971), 90–108; Hufton, "The Reconstruction of a Church, 1796–1801," in Gwynne Lewis and Colin Lucas, eds., *Beyond the Terror: Essays in French Regional and Social History, 1794–1815* (Cambridge: Cambridge University Press, 1983), pp. 21–52; Scott Lytle, "The Second Sex" (September 1793), *Journal of Modern History* 26 (1955), 14–26; Jules Michelet, *Les femmes de la Révolution* (Paris, 1854); R. B. Rose, "Women and the French Revolution: The Political Activity of Parisian Women, 1789–94," *University of Tasmania Occasional Paper* 5 (1976); David Williams, "The Politics of Feminism in the French Enlightenment," in Peter Hughes and David Williams, eds., *The Varied Pattern: Studies in the Eighteenth Century* (Toronto: A. M. Hakkert, 1971); Darline Gay Levy, Harriet Branson Applewhite, and Mary Durham Johnson, eds.,

Women in Revolutionary Paris, 1789–1795 (Urbana: University of Illinois Press, 1979); Marilyn Yalom, *Blood Sisters: The French Revolution in Women's Memory* (New York: Basic Books, 1993).

4. On representation, see Hanna Fenichel Pitkin, *The Concept of Representation* (Berkeley: University of California Press, 1972); Jacques Derrida, "Sending: On Representation," trans. Peter and Mary Ann Caws, *Social Research* 49 (1982), 294–326; Lynn Hunt, "Hercules and the Radical Images in the French Revolution," *Representations* 2 (Spring 1983), 95–117; Keith Michael Baker, "Representation," in Baker, ed., *The French Revolution and the Creation of Modern Political Culture*, vol. 1: *The Political Culture of the Old Regime* (Oxford: Pergamon Press, 1987); and Paul Friedland, "Representation and Revolution: The Theatricality of Politics and the Politics of Theater in France, 1789–1794" (Ph.D. diss., University of California, Berkeley, 1995).

5. Léopold Lacour, *Les origines du féminisme contemporain. Trois femmes de la Révolution: Olympe de Gouges, Théroigne de Méricourt, Rose Lacombe* (Paris, 1900), pp. 6–29. For biographical treatment, see Oliver Blanc, *Olympe de Gouges* (Paris: Syros, 1981); Benoît Groult, "Introduction: Olympe de Gouges, la première féministe moderne," in *Olympe de Gouges: Oeuvres* (Paris: Mercure de France, 1986; cited hereafter as *Oeuvres*); E. Lairtullier, *Les femmes célèbres de 1789 à 1795 et leur influence dans la Révolution* (Paris, 1840); and Hannelore Schröder, "The Declaration of Human and Civil Rights for Women (Paris, 1791) by Olympe de Gouges," *History of European Ideas* 11 (1989), 263–271. De Gouges's "Mémoire de Madame de Valmont" (1788) is the source of the allegation that she was the illegitimate daughter of the marquis. It is reproduced in *Oeuvres*, pp. 215–224.

6. "Procès d'Olympe de Gouges, femme de lettres (12 brumaire an II)," in Alexandre Tuetey, *Répertoire général des sources manuscrites de l'histoire de Paris pendant la Révolution française*, vol. 10 (Paris: Imprimerie Nouvelle, 1912), pp. 156–164.

7. Jacques Derrida, *Of Grammatology*, trans. Gayatri Chakravorty Spivak (Baltimore: Johns Hopkins University Press, 1976) part 2. See also Paul de Man, *Allegories of Reading: Figural Language in Rousseau, Nietzsche, Rilke, and Proust* (New Haven: Yale University Press, 1979); and Linda M. G. Zerilli, *Signifying Woman: Culture and Chaos in Rousseau, Burke, and Mill* (Ithaca: Cornell University Press, 1994), chap. 2.

8. "Je me suis peut-être égarée dans mes rêveries . . ."; Olympe de Gouges, *Le bonheur primitif de l'homme, ou les rêveries patriotiques* (Amsterdam, 1789), p. 1.

9. "Je veux moi, ignorante, essayer de m'égarer comme les autres"; ibid., p. 4.

10. De Gouges, *Départ de M. Necker et de Madame de Gouges* (1790), in *Oeuvres*, p. 94; de Gouges, *Le bonheur primitif de l'homme*, pp. 124, 126.

11. "Je suis un animal sans pareil; je ne suis ni homme, ni femme. J'ai tout le courage de l'un, et quelquefois les faiblesses de l'autre"; de Gouges, *Réponse à la justification de Maximilien Robespierre, addressée à Jérome Pétion* (Paris, 1792), p. 10.

12. "Je suis femme et j'ai servi ma patrie en grand homme"; de Gouges, *Oeuvres de la citoyenne de Gouges* (Paris, n.d.), vol. 1, p. 10.

13. "L'homme dont l'imagination est si fort blessée, qu'il se croit malade, quoi qu'il se porte bien"; "Imagination," in Pierre Richelet, *Dictionnaire de la langue françoise . . .*, 2 vols. (Paris, 1740), vol. 2, p. 234. I am grateful to Paul Friedland for this reference and for his many helpful suggestions on this chapter.

14. "Tous les objets des rêves sont visiblement les jeux de l'imagination"; "Rêves," in *Encyclopédie*, vol. 14, p. 223.

15. Jean-François Féraud, *Supplément du dictionnaire critique de la langue française par l'abbé Féraud*, 3 vols. (facsimile ed.; Paris: Ecole Normale Supérieure de Jeunes Filles, 1987–88), vol. 1, p. 175.

16. Jean-Jacques Rousseau, *Emile, or On Education*, trans. Allan Bloom (New York: Basic Books, 1979), p. 81.

17. "Imagination" (article by Voltaire), in *Encyclopédie*, vol. 8, p. 561.

18. Philippe Lacoue-Labarthe, *Typography: Mimesis, Philosophy, Politics* (Cambridge, Mass.: Harvard University Press, 1989), pp. 263–264; Denis Diderot, *The Paradox of Acting*, trans. Walter Herries Pollack, in William Archer, *Masks or Faces?* (New York: Hill and Wang, 1957), p. 18.

19. "Quand elles ont du génie, je leur crois l'empreinte plus originale qu'en nous"; Denis Diderot, *Sur les femmes* (1772), in *Oeuvres* (Paris: Brière, 1821), vol. 3, p. 440.

20. Something like a notion of passive imagination operates in Condillac's warning of the dangers of novel-reading for young women, who will imagine themselves into the stories they read and be unable to return to reality. See Jan Goldstein, *Console and Classify: The French Psychiatric Profession in the Nineteenth Century* (Cambridge: Cambridge University Press, 1987), pp. 90–94.

21. "Car il n'est pas donné a l'homme de se faire des idées, il ne peut que les modifier"; "Imagination," in *Encyclopédie*, vol. 8, p. 561.

22. Lacoue-Labarthe, *Typography*, pp. 255–257.

23. Ibid., p. 260. For discussions of imagination see Richard Kearney, *The Wake of Imagination: Toward a Postmodern Culture* (Minneapolis: University of Minnesota Press, 1988); Mary Warnock, *Imagination* (London: Faber, 1976); Iris Murdoch, "Ethics and Imagination," *Irish Theological Quarterly* 52 (1986); Paul Ricoeur, "L'imagination dans le discours et dans l'action," in *Du texte à l'action: Essais d'herméneutique*, vol. 2 (Paris: Seuil, 1986); and Marie-Hélène Huet, *Monstrous Imagination* (Cambridge, Mass.: Harvard University Press, 1993).

24. Cited in Lacoue-Labarthe, *Typography*, p. 47.

25. While for Rousseau the lost state of reverie was desirable, Voltaire treated the loss of bearings as a permanent loss of self. Rousseau celebrates the sense of loss in the first promenade of *Les rêveries du promeneur solitaire* thus: "Tiré, je ne sais comment de l'ordre des choses, je me suis précipité dans un chaos incompréhensible où je n'apperçois rien du tous, et plus je pense à ma situation présente et moins je puis comprendre où je suis": "Pulled, I don't know how, from the order of things, I threw myself into an incomprehensible chaos where I understood

nothing at all, and the more I think about my situation the less I can comprehend where I am." Jean-Jacques Rousseau, *Les rêveries du promeneur solitaire* (1776), in *Oeuvres complètes*, ed. Bernard Gagnebin and Marcel Raymond, 4 vols. (Paris: Gallimard, 1959), vol. 1, p. 995.

26. "Toujours dépourvues d'ordre et de bon sens, [elles] ne peuvent être estimées; on les lit par faiblesse, et on les condamne par raison"; "Imagination," in *Encyclopédie*, vol. 8, p. 561.

27. Cited in Goldstein, *Console and Classify*, p. 92.

28. "L'imagination de la veille est une république policée, où la voix du magistrat remet tout en ordre; l'imagination des songes est la même république dans l'état d'anarchie, encore les passions sont-elles de fréquens attentats contre l'autorité du législateur pendant le temps même où ses droits sont en vigueur"; "Songe," in *Encyclopédie*, vol. 15, p. 354. The article is taken from an essay by M. Formey, *Mélanges philosophiques*, 2 vols. (Leiden, 1754). There is also a distinction here between sleep and waking, passion and reason, public and private. On the complicated boundaries between public and private, see Lucien Jaune, "Le public et le privé chez les Jacobins, (1789–1794)," *Revue française de science politique* 37 (April 1987), 230–248; Lynn Hunt, "The Unstable Boundaries of the French Revolution," in Philippe Ariès and Georges Duby, eds., *A History of Private Life*, trans. Arthur Goldhammer, vol. 4 (Cambridge, Mass.: Harvard University Press, 1990), pp. 13–45; and Dena Goodman, "Enlightenment Salons: The Convergence of Female and Philosophic Ambitions," in *Eighteenth-Century Studies* 22, no. 3 (Spring 1989).

29. "Tout est décousu, sans ordre, sans vérité"; "Songe," in *Encyclopédie*, vol. 15, p. 356.

30. "Cette imagination fougueuse, cet esprit qu'on croirait incoercible, un mot suffit pour l'abattre"; Diderot, *Sur les femmes*, pp. 429 and 431.

31. "Une imagination éxaltée mène les hommes à l'héroisme et précipite les femmes dans d'affreux égarements"; *Supplément du dictionnaire . . . par l'abbé Féraud*, p. 175.

32. "Or, s'il est incontestable que des idées suivies se forment en nous, malgré nous, pendant notre sommeil qui nous assurera qu'elles ne sont pas produite de même dans la veille?" "Imagination," in *Encyclopédie*, vol. 8, p. 561.

33. Marcel Raymond, "Introduction," in Rousseau, *Oeuvres complètes*, vol. 1, p. lxxviii.

34. Jean-Jacques Rousseau, *Discourse on the Origin of Inequality*, in *The Social Contract and Discourses*, trans. G. D. H. Cole (New York: E. P. Dutton, 1950), pp. 247, 229, 241.

35. *Emile*, p. 134, cited in Zerilli, *Signifying Woman*, p. 55. See also Joel Schwartz, *The Sexual Politics of Jean-Jacques Rousseau* (Chicago: University of Chicago Press, 1984); Penny A. Weiss, "Rousseau, Antifeminism, and Woman's Nature," *Political Theory* 15, no. 1 (February 1987), 81–98; Gita May, "Rousseau's 'Antifeminism' Reconsidered," in Samia I. Spencer, ed., *French Women and the Age of Enlightenment* (Bloomington: Indiana University Press, 1984) pp. 309–317.

36. Cited in Carol Blum, *Rousseau and the Republic of Virtue: The Language of Politics in the French Revolution* (Ithaca: Cornell University Press, 1986), p. 208.

37. Cited in Dominique Godineau, "'Qu'y a-t-il de commun entre vous et nous?': Enjeux et discours opposés de la différence des sexes pendant la Révolution française (1789–1793)," in Irène Théry et Christian Biet, eds., *La famille, la loi, l'état de la Révolution au Code civil* (Paris: Imprimerie Nationale Editions), p. 75. The dangers that could follow from such a misidentification had been signaled much earlier by Plato, whose *Republic* was read carefully in eighteenth-century France.

> Have you not observed that imitations, if continued from youth far into life, settle down into habits and second nature in the body, the speech, and the thought?
>
> Yes, indeed, said he.
>
> We will not then allow our charges, whom we expect to prove good men, being men, to play the parts of women and imitate a woman young or old wrangling with her husband, defying heaven, loudly boasting, fortunate in her own conceit, or involved in misfortune and possessed by grief and lamentation—still less a woman that is sick, in love, or in labor.
>
> Most certainly not, he replied.
>
> Nor may they imitate slaves, female and male, doing the offices of slaves.
>
> No, not that either.
>
> Nor yet, as it seems, bad men who are cowards . . . And I take it they must not form the habit of likening themselves to madmen either in words nor yet in deeds. For while knowledge they must have both of mad and bad men and women, they must do and imitate nothing of this kind.
>
> Most true, he said.

Plato, *Republic* (III.395d–396b), trans. Paul Shorey, in *The Collected Dialogues,* ed. Edith Hamilton and Huntington Cairns (Princeton: Princeton University Press, 1961). Cited in Lacoue-Labarthe, *Typography,* pp. 43–44.

38. Jonas Barish, *The Antitheatrical Prejudice* (Berkeley: University of California Press, 1981), pp. 256–294; and Patrick Coleman, *Rousseau's Political Imagination: Rule and Representation in the "Lettre à d'Alembert"* (Geneva: Librairie Droz, 1984).

39. Nina Rattner Gelbart, *Feminine and Opposition Journalism in Old Regime France: Le Journal des Dames* (Berkeley: University of California Press, 1987), pp. 212–213.

40. Groult, "Introduction," in *Oeuvres,* p. 27.

41. "Ce n'est point à moi à répondre de tout mon sexe, mais s'il faut en juger par moi-même, je peux mettre trente pièces à l'étude"; de Gouges, *Le bonheur primitif de l'homme,* p. 75.

42. De Gouges, *Lettre au Peuple, ou projet d'une caisse patriotique par une citoyenne* (Paris, 1788), p. 8.

43. Keith Baker, "Defining the Public Sphere in Eighteenth-Century France:

Variations on a Theme by Habermas," in Craig Calhoun, ed., *Habermas and the Public Sphere* (Cambridge, Mass.: MIT Press, 1992), pp. 181–211; Baker, "Politics and Public Opinion under the Old Regime: Some Reflections," in Jack R. Censer and Jeremey D. Popkin, eds., *Press and Politics in Prerevolutionary France* (Berkeley: University of California Press, 1987), pp. 204–246; Mona Ozouf, "Opinion publique," in Keith Michael Baker, ed., *The French Revolution and the Creation of Modern Political Culture*, vol. 1: *The Political Culture of the Old Regime* (Oxford: Pergamon Press, 1987), pp. 419–434; Daniel Gordon, "'Public Opinion' and the Civilizing Process in France: The Example of Morellet," *Eighteenth-Century Studies* 22, no. 3 (Spring 1989); Joan Landes, *Women and the Public Sphere in the Age of the French Revolution* (Ithaca: Cornell University Press, 1988); Roger Chartier, *Cultural Origins of the French Revolution* (Durham: Duke University Press, 1991). Much of the discussion of public opinion alludes to Jürgen Habermas, *The Structural Transformation of the Public Sphere: An Inquiry into a Category of Bourgeois Society*, trans. Thomas Burger and Frederick Lawrence (Cambridge, Mass.: Harvard University Press, 1989).

44. Dena Goodman, "Public Sphere and Private Life: Toward a Synthesis of Current Historiographical Approaches to the Old Regime," *History and Theory* 31, no. 1 (1992), 1–20. See also Goodman, "Enlightenment Salons: The Convergence of Female and Philosophic Ambitions," *Eighteenth-Century Studies* 22, no. 3 (Spring 1989).

45. Gelbart, *Feminine and Opposition Journalism,* especially pp. 29–37.

46. On these debates see Harriet B. Applewhite and Darline G. Levy, eds., *Women and Politics in the Age of the Democratic Revolution* (Ann Arbor: University of Michigan Press, 1990); Marie-France Brive, ed., *Les femmes et la Révolution française: Modes d'action et d'expression nouveaux droits— nouveaux devoirs*, 3 vols. (Toulouse: Presses Universitaires du Mirail, 1989–1991); Paul Fritz and Richard Morton, eds., *Woman in the Eighteenth Century and Other Essays* (Toronto and Sarasota: Hakkert, 1976); Olwen H. Hufton, *Women and the Limits of Citizenship in the French Revolution* (Toronto: University of Toronto Press, 1992); Sara E. Melzer and Leslie W. Rabine, eds., *Rebel Daughters: Women and the French Revolution* (New York: Oxford University Press, 1992); Samia I. Spencer, ed., *French Women and the Age of Enlightenment* (Bloomington: Indiana University Press, 1984).

47. De Gouges, *Le bonheur primitif de l'homme,* p. 104.

48. Ibid., p. 27.

49. Condorcet, "On the Admission of Women to the Rights of Citizenship" (1790), in *Selected Writings,* ed. Keith Michael Baker (Indianapolis: Bobbs-Merrill, 1976), p. 98.

50. Ibid., p. 102.

51. Baker, "Defining the Public Sphere," p. 202.

52. On Condorcet, see Baker, "Defining the Public Sphere" and *Condorcet: From Natural Philosophy to Social Mathematics* (Chicago: University of Chicago Press, 1975).

53. De Gouges, *Le cri du sage: Par une femme* (1789), in *Oeuvres*, p. 91.

54. "C'est une femme, qui ose se montrer si forte, et si courageuse pour son Roi, et pour sa Patrie"; de Gouges, *Remarques patriotiques: Par la citoyenne, auteur de la Lettre au Peuple* (1788) in *Oeuvres*, p. 73.

55. De Gouges, *Lettre au peuple*, pp. 11–12.

56. "Laissons à part mon sexe: L'héroïsme et la générosité sont aussi le partage des femmes et la Révolution en offre plus d'un exemple"; cited in Groult, "Introduction," in *Oeuvres*, p. 48.

57. Lairtullier, *Les femmes célèbres*, p. 93.

58. Abbé de Sièyes, *Préliminaire de la constitution: Reconnaissance et exposition raisonnée des Droits de l'Homme et du Citoyen*, cited in William H. Sewell, Jr., "Le Citoyen/La Citoyenne: Activity, Passivity, and the Revolutionary Concept of Citizenship," in Colin Lucas, ed., *The French Revolution and the Creation of Modern Political Culture*, vol. 2: *The Political Culture of the French Revolution* (Oxford: Pergamon Press, 1988), p. 110.

59. Richard Tuck, *Natural Rights Theories: Their Origin and Development* (Cambridge: Cambridge University Press, 1979), pp. 5–6; see also the discussion in Sewell, "Le Citoyen/La Citoyenne"; Pierre Rosanvallon, *Le sacre du citoyen: Histoire du suffrage universel en France* (Paris: Gallimard, 1922), pp. 41–101; and Florence Gauthier, *Triomphe et mort du droit naturel en Révolution, 1789–1795–1802* (Paris: Presses Universitaires de France, 1992).

60. Cited in M. J. Sydenham, *The French Revolution*, p. 67.

61. On the history of these theories of representation, see Keith Michael Baker, "Representation Redefined," in *Inventing the French Revolution: Essays on French Political Culture in the Eighteenth Century* (Cambridge: Cambridge University Press, 1990), pp. 224–251. See also Rosanvallon, *Le sacre du citoyen.*

62. Cited in Levy, Applewhite, and Johnson, *Women in Revolutionary Paris*, p. 220.

63. Béatrice Slama, "Ecrits de femmes pendant la Révolution," in Brive, *Les femmes et la Révolution française*, vol. 2, pp. 291–306.

64. On these questions see Derrida, *Of Grammatology;* and Jonathan Culler, *On Deconstruction: Theory and Criticism after Structuralism* (Ithaca: Cornell University Press, 1982).

65. "N'est-ce pas mon bien? n'est-ce pas ma propriété?" De Gouges, *Le bonheur primitif de l'homme*, p. 76.

66. "O vérité sublime, qui m'a toujours guidée, qui soutiens mes opinions, ôte-moi les moyens d'écrire si jamais je peux trahir ma conscience éclairée par ta lumière"; de Gouges, *Lettre au peuple*, p. 9.

67. Cited in Slama, "Ecrits de femmes," p. 297.

68. "J'ai eu la manie d'écrire; j'ai eu celle de me faire imprimer"; cited in Chantal Thomas, "Féminisme et Révolution: Les causes perdues d'Olympe de Gouges," in *La Carmagnole des muses: L'homme de lettres et l'artiste dans la Révolution* (Paris: Librairie Armand Colin, 1988), p. 309. On the question of female authorship in the Revolution see Carla Hesse, "Reading Signatures: Female Author-

ship and Revolutionary Law in France, 1750–1850," *Eighteenth-Century Studies* 22, no. 3 (Spring 1989); see also Hesse, *Publishing and Cultural Politics in Revolutionary Paris, 1789–1810* (Berkeley: University of California Press, 1991). I am grateful to Carla Hesse for alerting me to an uncatalogued collection of de Gouges materials at the New York Public Library and for providing me with copies of them.

69. "Mais en politique et en philosophie, vous ne deviez pas vous attendre à me voir traiter une semblable matière; aussi ce n'est qu'en rêve que j'ai pu l'exercer"; de Gouges, *Séance royale. Motion de Monseigneur le Duc d'Orléans, ou Les songes patriotiques* (Paris, 1789), p. 3.

70. "Jean-Jacques avait trop de lumières pour que son génie ne l'emportât pas trop loin . . ."; "qui me ressens de cette première ignorance, et qui suis placée et déplacée en même temps dans ce siècle éclairé, mes opinions peuvent être plus justes que les siennes"; de Gouges, *Le bonheur primitif de l'homme*, p. 6.

71. "Je suis, dans mes écrits, l'élève de la nature; je dois être, comme elle, irrégulière, bizarre même; mais aussi toujours vraie, toujours simple"; de Gouges, *Le cri du sage*, p. 96.

72. "Cherche, fouille et distingue, si tu le peux, les sexes dans l'administration de la nature. Partout tu les trouveras confondus, partout ils coopèrent avec un ensemble harmonieux à ce chef-d'oeuvre immortel"; de Gouges, *Déclaration des droits de la femme, dédiée à la Reine* (1791), in *Oeuvres*, p. 101.

73. "La couleur de l'homme est nuancée, comme dans tous les animaux que la Nature a produits, ainsi que les plantes et les minéraux. Pourquoi le jour ne le dispute-t-il pas à nuit, le soleil à la lune, et les étoiles au firmament? Tout est varié, et c'est là la beauté de la Nature. Pourquoi donc détruire son Ouvrage?" De Gouges, *Réflexions sur les hommes nègres* (1788), in *Oeuvres*, pp. 84–85.

74. *Repentir de Madame de Gouges* (September 1791). In this pamphlet she answers those who have questioned her patriotism because she criticized the constitution. Those criticisms, she explains, came when "my imagination wandered," p. 1.

75. "Eh bien, Sire, une femme, un être ignoré, un esprit visionnaire . . . a le courage d'avertir son Roi du seul moyen qui peut sauver la France"; de Gouges, *Séance royale . . . ou Les songes patriotiques*, pp. 6, 11, 30.

76. "On s'approchera peut-être de la réalité"; ibid., p. 19.

77. See Judith Butler, "Phantasmatic Identification and the Question of Sex," in *Bodies That Matter* (New York: Routledge, 1993), pp. 93–120.

78. In the *Encyclopédie*, vol. 5, p. 601, emulation is defined as that "noble generous passion which admires the merit, the beauty, and the actions of others; which tries to imitate or even surpass them." It had nothing in common with base feelings of jealousy or envy; rather it was seen as a spur to courageous action, providing an idealized model upon which to base one's construction of one's self.

79. De Gouges, *Lettre au peuple*, pp. 30, 23.

80. "Le même vice, le même penchant avoit subjugué sa raison et sa vertu"; de Gouges, *Le bonheur primitif de l'homme*, pp. 18 and 25.

81. Léopold Lacour argued that this proposal was a mistake because it legitimated adultery in the name of morality. He attributed it to aristocratic influences on her thinking; Lacour, *Trois femmes de la Révolution*, pp. 87–88.

82. Cited in Levy, Applewhite, and Johnson, *Women in Revolutionary Paris*, p. 170.

83. Here it is useful to think in terms of Jacques Derrida's notion of the supplement, as a double and contradictory effect. It is both an addition and a replacement, something superfluous, but also necessary for completion. Its presence is at once excessive and revealing of the incompleteness of what has claimed to be complete and fully present. Jacques Derrida, *Positions*, trans. Alan Bass (Chicago: University of Chicago Press, 1981), especially p. 43; and Derrida, *Of Grammatology*, pp. 141–164. For a concise explication of the concept of the supplement, see Barbara Johnson's introduction to her translation of Derrida's *Disseminations* (Chicago: University of Chicago Press, 1981), p. xiii.

84. *Déclaration*, pp. 99–112. For a different reading of this document, see Ute Gerhard, "Droits de l'homme—Droits de la femme en 1789," in Liliane Crips et al., *Nationalismes, féminismes, exclusions. Mélanges en l'honneur de Rita Thalmann* (Frankfurt and Paris: Peter Lang, 1994), pp. 421–435.

85. Francis Ronsin, *Le contrat sentimental: Débats sur le mariage, l'amour, le divorce, de l'Ancien Régime à la Restauration* (Paris: Aubier, 1990); Roderick Phillips, *Family Breakdown in Late Eighteenth-Century France: Divorces in Rouen, 1792–1803* (Oxford: Oxford University Press, 1980); Phillips, *Putting Asunder: A History of Divorce in Western Society* (Cambridge: Cambridge University Press, 1988); James F. Traer, *Marriage and the Family in Eighteenth-Century France* (Ithaca: Cornell University Press, 1980).

86. Another way of saying this would be to use Carole Pateman's notion of the sexual contract. De Gouges is exposing and overturning the sexual contract (the agreement among men about the exchange of women) that underlies the social contract and inevitably prevents women from attaining equality within its terms; Pateman, *The Sexual Contract* (Stanford: Stanford University Press, 1988). See also Gail Rubin, "The Traffic in Women: Notes on the 'Political Economy' of Sex," in Rayna R. Reiter, ed., *Toward an Anthropology of Women* (New York: Monthly Review Press, 1975), pp. 157–210.

87. On women's virtue, which had to do above all with chastity and female fidelity, see Dorinda Outram, *The Body and the French Revolution* (New Haven: Yale University Press, 1989), p. 126; and Outram, "Le Langage mâle de la Vertu: Women and the Discourse of the French Revolution," in Peter Burke and Roy Porter, eds., *The Social History of Language* (Cambridge: Cambridge University Press, 1987), pp. 120–135. On the concept of virtue more generally, see Blum, *Rousseau and the Republic of Virtue*.

88. De Gouges, *Le bonheur primitif de l'homme*, pp. 12, 14.

89. My reading is here influenced by the work of Jacques Lacan and his feminist interpreters. See Drucilla Cornell, *Beyond Accommodation: Ethical Femi-*

nism, Deconstruction, and the Law (New York: Routledge, 1991); Elizabeth Grosz, *Jacques Lacan: A Feminist Introduction* (New York: Routledge, 1990); and Jane Gallop, *Reading Lacan* (Ithaca: Cornell University Press, 1985).

90. The mixture of principle, political commitment, and personal calculation that drove de Gouges is evident in a short piece she wrote in September 1791, *Repentir de Madame de Gouges.* In it she refutes those who question her patriotism on the basis of her criticisms of the constitution.

91. De Gouges's belief that women's rights could be reconciled with monarchy constitutes for some historians an "aristocratic" feminism that blended with newer, more democratic currents. See Louis Devance, "Le féminisme pendant la Révolution française," in *Annales historiques de la Révolution française,* no. 227 (January–March 1977), 352. See also Lacour, *Trois femmes de la Révolution,* pp. 57–58.

92. *Archives parlementaires* 63 (1781–1799), 564.

93. Cited in Levy, Applewhite, and Johnson, *Women in Revolutionary Paris,* p. 215.

94. Ibid., p. 219.

95. Cited in Ludmilla J. Jordanova, "'Guarding the Body Politic': Volney's Catechism of 1793," in Francis Barker et al., eds., *1789: Reading, Writing Revolution. Proceedings of the Essex Conference on the Sociology of Literature, July 1981* (University of Essex, 1982), p. 15.

96. Cited in Londa Schiebinger, "Skeletons in the Closet: The First Illustrations of the Female Skeleton in Eighteenth-Century Anatomy," *Representations* 14 (Spring 1986), 51. See also Thomas Laqueur, "Orgasm, Generation, and the Politics of Reproductive Biology," *Representations* 14 (1986), 3.

97. Cited in Yvonne Knibiehler, "Les médecins et la 'Nature féminine' au temps du Code civil," *Annales E.S.C.* 31 (1976), 835. The original version can be found in Rousseau's *Emile* and is cited in Denise Riley, *"Am I That Name?" Feminism and the Category of "Women" in History* (London: Macmillan, 1988), p. 37, n. 57. See also D. G. Charlton, *New Images of the Natural in France* (Cambridge: Cambridge University Press, 1984); Jean Borie, "Une gynécologie passionée," in J.-P. Aron, ed., *Misérable et glorieuse: La femme du XIXᵉ siècle* (Paris: Fayard, 1980), pp. 153–189; and Michelle Le Doeuff, "Pierre Roussel's Chiasmas: From Imaginary Knowledge to the Learned Imagination," *Ideology and Consciousness* 9 (1981–82), 39–70.

98. Madelyn Gutwirth, *The Twilight of the Goddesses: Women and Representation in the French Revolutionary Era* (New Brunswick, N.J.: Rutgers University Press, 1992). See also Yvonne Knibiehler and Catherine Fouquet, *L'histoire des mères du moyen-âge à nos jours* (Paris: Editions Montalba, 1980). For a comparative English perspective, see Ruth Perry, "Colonizing the Breast: Sexuality and Maternity in Eighteenth-Century England," *Journal of the History of Sexuality* 2 (October 1991), 204–234.

99. Here I am disagreeing with the interpretation of Gutwirth and others who read the breast in these representations as phallic.

100. Gutwirth, *The Twilight of the Goddesses,* p. 364. It is instructive to compare

this festival with the one produced by de Gouges in June 1792 to honor Jacques-Henri Simonneau, the martyred mayor of Etampes. Then hundreds of beflowered women led a huge cortège in his honor, demonstrating (in de Gouges's interpretation of it) their ability to recognize and reward the heroes of the nation. Led by a woman dressed as Liberty, followed by the National Guard with its commander at its head and then by a woman in the costume of Justice, the parade would recall, she hoped, the glories of ancient republics and show the enemies of France how unified and determined were its female citizens. For de Gouges this event was a way of rallying women and making the case for their active political participation. If its symbolism can also be read as underscoring women's more passive, supportive role, it nonetheless gives women a political role entirely absent in the fête of 1793.

101. Maximilien Robespierre, "On the Principles of Political Morality," in *History of Western Civilization: Selected Readings* (Chicago: College of the University of Chicago, 1964), pp. 79–80.

102. *Oeuvres de la citoyenne de Gouges* (n.d.), p. 15.

103. "À réprimer en moi ces mouvemens d'exaltation dont une ame sensible devroit toujours se défier, et dont les factieux seuls savent si bien tirer parti"; de Gouges, *Réponse à la justification de Robespierre*, p. 1.

104. Ibid., p. 15.

105. The charges and evidence are recorded in "Procès d'Olympe de Gouges," in Tuetey, *Répertoire général*, 156–164.

106. Ibid., p. 159.

107. Outram, *The Body in the French Revolution;* and François Furet, "The Logic of the Terror," in *Interpreting the French Revolution*, trans. Elborg Forster (Cambridge: Cambridge University Press, 1981).

108. "Olympe de Gouges, née avec une imagination exaltée, prit son délire pour une inspiration de la nature. Elle voulut être *homme d'état.* Elle adopta les projets des perfides qui voulaient diviser la France. Il semble que la loi ait puni cette conspiratrice d'avoir oublié les vertus qui conviennent à son sexe"; cited in Lairtullier, *Les femmes célèbres*, p. 140. Note the similarity to Chaumette's comments a few days later: "Remember that virago, that woman-man [*cette femme-homme*], the impudent Olympe de Gouges, who abandoned all the cares of her household because she wanted to engage in politics and commit crimes . . . This forgetfulness of the virtues of her sex led her to the scaffold" (cited in Levy, Applewhite, and Johnson, *Women in Revolutionary Paris*, p. 220). Chaumette's condemnation was offered in the voice of the reasonable, if venomous, magistrate who had detected and disarmed a dangerous misidentification, who was protecting the reality not only of femininity as ordained by nature, but of masculinity as well. Like those doctors and magistrates cited by Diderot, "one word" from Chaumette was meant to dispel the symptoms of other women who might be afflicted by de Gouges's contagious malady.

109. De Gouges, *Réponse à la justification de Robespierre*, p. 8; and de Gouges, *Compte moral rendu et dernier mot à mes chers amis* (Paris, n.d.), p. 5.

110. De Gouges, *Le bonheur primitif de l'homme*, p. 1. Thanks to Sylvia Schafer for this point.

111. *Bulletin du Tribunal criminel révolutionnaire*, (1793), cited in Levy, Applewhite, and Johnson, *Women in Revolutionary Paris*, p. 255.

112. "Procès d'Olympe de Gouges," in Tuetey, *Répertoire général*, pp. 163–164.

113. "Imagination," in Pierre Claude Victoire Boiste, *Dictionnaire universel de la langue française . . .*, 6th ed. (Paris: Verdiere, 1823), p. 354.

114. "Plus d'une fois elle surprit les hommes les plus éloquens de l'époque par la richesse de son imagination et la fécondité de ses idées; et ce fut, à vrai dire, le côté brillant de la célébrité qu'elle ne tarda pas à conquerir"; Lairtullier, *Les femmes célèbres*, pp. 51, 68.

115. Cited in Devance, "Le féminisme pendant la Révolution française," p. 345.

116. Jules Michelet, *Les femmes de la Révolution* (1854), in *Oeuvres complètes*, vol. 16 (Paris: Flammarion, 1980), pp. 400, 401.

117. Cited in Levy, Applewhite, and Johnson, *Women in Revolutionary Paris*, p. 259.

118. Cited in Devance, "Le féminisme pendant la Révolution française," p. 346.

119. Ibid., p. 347.

120. Lacour found her imagination a positive trait and compared her favorably on this score with the Girondist Mme. Roland: "Mais, à son imagination fertile et brulante, à son coeur d'apôtre, donnez des moyens d'expression patiemment acquis, elle apparait supérieure même à Mme Roland par l'étendue et la nouveauté des vues"; *Trois femmes de la Révolution*, p. 5.

121. "Plusieurs ont du, à l'exemple d'Olympe de Gouges, payer de leur vie même leur dévouement à la Justice et à la Verité"; Jeanne Deroin, *Almanach des femmes*, 1853, p. 15.

3. The Duties of the Citizen

1. For biographical and historical details see Léon Abensour, *Le féminisme sous le regne de Louis-Philippe et en 1848* (Paris: Plon-Nourrit, 1913); Laure Adler, *A l'aube du féminisme: Les premières journalistes (1830–1850)* (Paris: Payot, 1979); Adler, "Flora, Pauline et les autres," in Jean-Paul Aron, ed., *Misérable et glorieuse: La femme du XIXᵉ siècle* (Paris: Fayard, 1980); Maïté Albistur and Daniel Armogathe, *Histoire du féminisme français*, vol. 2 (Paris: Editions des Femmes, 1977); dossier "J. Deroin," Bibliothèque Marguerite Durand, Paris; Adrien Ranvier, "Une féministe de 1848: Jeanne Deroin," *La révolution de 1848* 4 (1907–08), 317–355, 421–430, 480–498; Michèle Riot-Sarcey, *La démocratie à l'épreuve des femmes: Trois figures critiques du pouvoir, 1830–1848* (Paris: Editions Albin Michel, 1994); Riot-Sarcey, "La conscience féministe des femmes en 1848: Jeanne Deroin et Désirée Gay," in Stephane Michaud, ed., *Un fabuleux destin: Flora Tristan* (Dijon: Presses Universitaires de Dijon, 1985); Riot-Sarcey, "Histoire et autobiographie: Le 'Vrai livre des femmes' d'Eugénie Niboyet," *Romantisme* 56 (1987); Riot-Sarcey, "Une

vie publique privée d'histoire: Jeanne Deroin ou l'oubli de soi," Université de Paris VIII *Cahiers du CEDREF* 1 (1989), special issue: "Silence: Emancipation des femmes entre privée d'histoire"; Michèle Serrière, "Jeanne Deroin," in *Femmes et travail* (Paris: Editions Martinsart, 1981); Marguerite Thibert, *Le féminisme dans le socialisme français de 1830 à 1850* (Paris: Marcel Giard, 1926); Edith Thomas, *Les femmes de 1848* (Paris: Presses Universitaires de France, 1948); Linda Zerilli, "Motionless Idols and Virtuous Mothers: Women, Art, and Politics in France: 1789–1848," *Berkeley Journal of Sociology* 27 (1982).

2. For the history of the Revolution of 1848, see Maurice Agulhon, *La république au village* (Paris: Mouton, 1970), *Une ville ouvrière au temps du socialisme utopique: Toulon de 1815 à 1851* (Paris and The Hague: Mouton, 1970), and *1848 ou l'apprentissage de la république* (Paris: Seuil, 1973); Peter Amann, *Revolution and Mass Democracy: The Paris Club Movement in 1848* (Princeton: Princeton University Press, 1975); Robert Balland, "De l'organisation à la restriction du suffrage universel en France (1848–1850)," in Jacques Droz, ed., *Réaction et suffrage universel en France et en Allemagne (1848–1850)* (Paris: Rivière, 1963); Louis Blanc, *Pages d'histoire de la révolution de février 1848* (Paris: Au Bureau du Nouveau Monde, 1850); Fredrick de Luna, *The French Republic under Cavaignac, 1848* (Princeton: Princeton University Press, 1969); Rémi Gossez, *Les ouvriers de Paris*, vol. 1: *L'organisation, 1848–1851*, Bibliothèque de la Révolution de 1848, vol. 24 (La Roche-sur-Yon: Imprimerie Centrale de l'Ouest, 1967); Karl Marx, *The Class Struggles in France (1848–1850)* (New York: International Publishers, n.d.); John M. Merriman, *The Agony of the Republic: The Repression of the Left in Revolutionary France, 1848–1851* (New Haven: Yale University Press, 1978); Bernard H. Moss, *The Origins of the French Labor Movement: The Socialism of Skilled Workers, 1830–1914* (Berkeley: University of California Press, 1976); Roger Price, *The French Second Republic: A Social History* (Ithaca: Cornell University Press, 1972); William H. Sewell, Jr., *Work and Revolution in France: The Language of Labor from the Old Regime to 1848* (Cambridge: Cambridge University Press, 1980); Charles Tilly and Lynn Lees, "Le peuple de juin 1848," *Annales E.S.C.* 29 (September–October 1974), 1061–91.

3. "Le droit au travail a son origine et sa légitimité dans les clauses fondamentales et implicites du pacte social et son justificatif dans l'obligation naturelle de travailler"; cited in Félix Ponteil, *Les institutions de la France de 1848 a 1870* (Paris: Presses Universitaires de France, 1966), p. 271.

4. "Le droit au travail est celui qu'a tout homme de vivre en travaillant. La société doit, par les moyens productifs et généraux dont elle dispose et qui seront organisés ultérieurement, fournir du travail aux hommes valides qui ne peuvent s'en procurer autrement"; ibid.

5. "Il n'y a pas un citoyen qui puisse dire à l'autre, 'tu es plus souverain que moi!'" "A dater de cette loi, il n'y a plus de prolétaires en France"; "Proclamation du Gouvernement provisoire à la nation, au sujet des élections prochaines," (Paris, March 16, 1848), in *Recueil complet des actes du Gouvernement provisoire (février,*

mars, avril, mai 1848) (Paris: Librairie August Durand, 1848), pp. 148–149. See also Ponteil, *Les institutions,* pp. 269–352; and Comité National du Centenaire de 1848, *Procès-verbaux du Gouvernement provisoire et de la Commission du pouvoir exécutif (24 février–22 juin 1848)* (Paris: Imprimerie Nationale, 1950).

6. Cited in Joseph Garnier, ed., *Le droit au travail à l'Assemblée nationale: Recueil complet de tous les discours prononcés dans cette mémorable discussion* (Paris, 1848), p. 112.

7. Etienne Balibar, *Masses, Classes, Ideas: Studies on Politics and Philosophy before and after Marx,* trans. James Swenson (New York and London: Routledge, 1994), chaps. 2 and 9. See also Pierre Rosanvallon, *Le sacre du citoyen: Histoire du suffrage universel en France* (Paris: Gallimard, 1992), pp. 280–281; and Jacques Rancière's introduction to Geneviève Fraisse, *La raison des femmes* (Paris: Plon, 1992), pp. 12–13.

8. "La loi electorale provisoire que nous avons faite est la plus large qui, chez aucun peuple de la terre, ait jamais convoqué le peuple à l'éxercice du suprême droit de l'homme, sa propre souveraineté"; "Proclamation . . . au sujet des élections," in *Receuil complet,* p. 149.

9. On feminism in 1848, see Claire Goldberg Moses, *French Feminism in the Nineteenth Century* (Albany: State University of New York Press, 1984) and "Saint-Simonian Men/Saint-Simonian Women: The Transformation of Feminist Thought in 1830s France," *Journal of Modern History* 54 (June 1982), 240–267; C. G. Moses and Leslie Wahl Rabine, *Feminism, Socialism, and French Romanticism* (Bloomington: Indiana University Press, 1993); Laure Adler, *A l'aube du féminisme;* Louis Devance, "Femme, famille, travail et morale sexuelle dans l'idéologie de 1848," *Romantisme,* nos. 13–14 (1976), 79–103; Marguerite Thibert, "Une apôtre socialiste de 1848: Pauline Roland," *La révolution de 1848* 22 (1925–26), 478–502, 524–540; and Edith Thomas, *Pauline Roland: Socialisme et féminisme au XIXe siècle* (Paris: Marcel Rivière, 1956). For English comparisons, see Sally Alexander, "Women, Class, and Sexual Difference in the 1830s and 1840s: Some Reflections on the Writing of a Feminist History," *History Workshop,* no. 17 (Spring 1984), 125–149; and Barbara Taylor, *Eve and the New Jerusalem: Socialism and Feminism in the Nineteenth Century* (New York: Pantheon, 1983).

10. "Nous venons vous demander si les femmes sont comprises dans cette grande généralité aussi bien qu'elles le sont dans le droit concernant les travailleurs; nous sommes d'autant plus fondées à vous faire cette demande que vous ne les avez pas désignées dans les catégories d'exclusion"; cited in Jules Tixerant, *Le féminisme à l'époque de 1848 dans l'ordre politique et dans l'ordre économique* (Paris: V. Girard et E. Brière, 1908), p. 40. For the decrees itemizing exclusions see "Décret du Gouvernement provisoire qui convoque les assemblées électorales, décide le mode d'élection et fixe le nombre des députés" (Paris, March 5, 1848) and "Instruction du Gouvernement provisoire pour l'exécution du décret du 5 mars 1848, relatif aux élections générales" (Paris, March 8, 1948), both in *Recueil complet,* pp. 54–55, 79–81.

11. A certain legalism characterized all the actions of the revolutionary Provisional Government. See Claude Nicolet, *L'idée républicaine en France (1789–1924): Essai d'histoire critique* (Paris: Gallimard, 1982); Geneviève Fraisse, "L'usage du droit naturel dans les écrits feministes (1830–50)," in Stéphane Michaud, ed., *Un fabuleux destin: Flora Tristan* (Dijon: Editions Universitaires de Dijon, 1985); and Roger Soltau, *French Political Thought in the Nineteenth Century* (London: Bouverie House, 1931).

12. Jacques Donzelot, *L'invention du social: Essai sur le déclin des passions politiques* (Paris: Fayard, 1984). See also Sewell, *Work and Revolution*, pp. 143–144, 219–242.

13. On the June Days, see the works listed in note 2 and Alexis de Tocqueville, *Recollections*, trans. Alexander Teixeira de Mattos (Westport, Conn.: Greenwood Press, 1979). On the National Workshops see Donald C. McKay, *The National Workshops: A Study in the French Revolution of 1848* (Cambridge, Mass.: Harvard University Press, 1965). On women's protests about these workshops see Joan W. Scott, "Work Identities for Men and Women: The Politics of Work and Family in the Parisian Garment Trades in 1848," in *Gender and the Politics of History* (New York: Columbia University Press, 1988), pp. 93–112.

14. Alexandre Ledru-Rollin, *Journées illustrées de la révolution de 1848* (Paris: Plon, n.d.), p. 291. See also accounts in Paul Bastid, *Doctrines et institutions politiques de la seconde république*, 2 vols. (Paris: Librairie Hachette, 1945). For the entire discussion see Garnier, *Le droit au travail*.

15. "Du point de vue de la justice, le droit au travail est parallèle au droit de propriété. L'homme qui ne possède pas est l'esclave de celui qui possède. Le droit au travail est la seule réponse à faire au communisme, puisque le travail permet de devenir propriétaire"; Bastid, *Doctrines et institutions*, vol. 2, p. 79.

16. Article 13 read: "La Constitution guarantit aux citoyens la liberté du travail et de l'industrie. La société favorise et encourage le développement du travail par l'enseignement primaire gratuit, l'éducation professionnelle, l'égalité de rapports entre le patron et l'ouvrier, les institutions de prévoyance et de crédit, les institutions agricoles, les associations volontaires, et l'établissement, par l'Etat, les départements et les communes, de travaux publics propres à employer les bras inoccupés; elle fournit l'assistance aux enfants abandonnés, aux infirmes et aux vieillards sans ressources, et que leurs familles ne peuvent secourir"; ibid., p. 326.

17. "Le droit au travail implique le droit de propriété dans la personne de l'ouvrier, qui veut y parvenir comme et par les mêmes moyens que nous y sommes parvenus; car sans notre travail personnel ou sans celui de nos pères comment y serions-nous parvenus?" ibid., p. 55.

18. "Que [l'homme] travaille pour lui-même ou pour vous, vous sentez encore qu'il est homme comme vous . . . politiquement, y reconnaissez-vous un homme, votre égal, un citoyen"; Ledru-Rollin, *Journées illustrées de la révolution de 1848*, p. 291. On the right to work in 1848, see Bastid, *Doctrines et institutions*, vol. 1, pp. 242–246; vol. 2, pp. 36–58, 79–81; Charles Seignobos, "Le Comité de Consti-

tution de 1848," *Bulletin de la Société d'histoire moderne* 2 (1913–14), 277–279; Henry Michel, "Note sur la Constitution de 1848," *La révolution de 1848* 1 (1904), 41–56; *Recueil complet,* pp. 148–149; Ledru-Rollin, *Journées illustrées de la révolution de 1848,* pp. 287–291; Ponteil, *Les institutions,* p. 271. Some of the discussion of the right to work referred back to the Declaration of Rights of the Constitution of June 1793, article 16: "Le droit de propriété est celui qui appartient à tout citoyen de jouir et de disposer à son gré de ses biens, de ses revenus, du fruit de son travail et de son industrie"; cited in Lucien Jaume, *Le discours jacobin et la démocratie* (Paris: Fayard, 1984), p. 412.

19. Cited in Garnier, *Le droit au travail,* pp. 48–49.

20. Bastid, *Doctrines et institutions,* vol. 2, p. 325.

21. There is work to be done in this connection on feminist debates about paternity suits. On this see Françoise Picq, "Par-delà la loi du pére: Le débat sur la recherche de la paternité au Congrès féministe de 1900," *Les temps modernes* 34, no. 391 (February 1979), 1199–1212.

22. Meeting of July 25, 1848, *Compte rendu des séances de l'Assemblée nationale,* vol. 2 (Paris 1849), p. 646.

23. "La place convenable et légitime de la femme est la vie privée et non la vie publique; elle perd toujours à quitter l'une pour l'autre et les souvenirs historiques de la présence des femmes dans les assemblées politiques suffisent pour les en exclure"; ibid. See also Tixerant, *Le féminisme à l'époque de 1848,* p. 26.

24. *Compte rendu des séances de l'Assemblée nationale,* p. 652.

25. Ibid., p. 646.

26. Jeanne Deroin, "Lettre d'une femme à M. Athanase Coquerel" (1848), wall poster, Bibliothèque Nationale Lb54 925.

27. "Une assemblée législative entièrement composée d'hommes est aussi incompétente pour faire des lois qui régissent une société composée d'hommes et de femmes que le serait une assemblée entièrement composée de privilégiés pour discuter les intérêts des travailleurs ou une assemblée des capitalistes pour soutenir l'honneur du pays"; *L'opinion des femmes* 4 (May 1849). The newspaper *L'opinion des femmes* was published irregularly. A first issue appeared in August 1848; in January 1849 more regular publication began, and the January issue was given the number 1. Number 2 appeared on March 10, no. 3 on April 10, no. 4 in May. A no. 5 seems to have come out in June or July, but I have found no copy of it. Number 6, the final issue, appeared in August.

28. The first of the new constitution's declaration of principles stated: "Le travail intellectuel et corporel est la condition fondamentale de l'existence morale et physique des individus, des sociétés, du genre humain." This statement was cited in "La constitution," *L'opinion des femmes,* August 21, 1848, to justify women's claims to suffrage.

29. On this issue in the first revolution, see Florence Gauthier, *Triomphe et mort du droit naturel en révolution, 1789–1795–1802* (Paris: Presses Universitaires de France, 1992).

30. "Les citoyens doivent aimer la Patrie, servir la République, la défendre au prix de leur vie, participer aux charges de l'Etat en proportion de leur fortune; ils doivent s'assurer, par le travail, des moyens d'existence, et, par la prévoyance, des ressources pour l'avenir: ils doivent concourir au bien-être commun en s'entraidant fraternellement les uns les autres, et à l'ordre général en observant les lois morales et les lois écrites qui régissent la société, la famille et l'individu"; Préambule, sec. VII, in Bastid, *Doctrines et institutions,* vol. 2, p. 325.

31. Giovanna Procacci, "Sociology and Its Poor," *Politics and Society* 17 (1989), p. 183. See also Procacci, *Gouverner la misère: La question sociale en France, 1789–1848* (Paris: Seuil, 1993).

32. Procacci, "Sociology and Its Poor," p. 183. See also Donzelot, *L'invention du social;* and Michel Foucault, "Omnes et Singulatim: Towards a Criticism of 'Political Reason,'" in *The Tanner Lectures on Human Values* (Salt Lake City: University of Utah Press, 1981), pp. 223–254.

33. Auguste Comte, *A General View of Positivism,* cited in Denise Riley, *"Am I That Name?" Feminism and the Category of "Women" in History* (London: Macmillan, 1988), p. 48.

34. "La moralité d'une nation tient surtout à la moralité des femmes . . . Pas de dévouement public sans vertus privées, pas de vertus privées sans respect pour la famille, ce temple où la mère se dévoue avec une si complète abnégation"; *La voix des femmes,* March 20, 1848.

35. "En posant mon candidature à l'Assemblée legislative, j'accomplis ma devoir: c'est au nom de la moral publique et au nom de la justice que je demande que le dogme de l'égalité ne soit plus un mensonge"; *L'opinion des femmes,* no. 4 (May 1849).

36. "Le fruit doit porter le nom de l'arbre qui lui donna la vie, non celui du jardinier qu'y greffa le bourgeon"; E. Casaubon, *La femme est la famille* (Paris: Gauthier, 1834), p. 8. See also Susan K. Grogan, *French Socialism and Sexual Difference: Women and the New Society, 1803–44* (London: Macmillan, 1992).

37. Gautier, "De l'affranchissement des femmes," *Le peuple,* January 15, 1849.

38. *L'opinion des femmes,* no. 4 (May 1849). On the question of duties invoked by feminists in this period, see Geneviève Fraisse, "Les femmes libres de 1848. Moralisme et féminisme," *Les révoltes logiques,* no. 1 (December 1975), 23–50.

39. "Le devoir et le droit sont corrélatifs. Mais pour exercer le droit et accomplir le devoir il faut le pouvoir"; Jeanne Deroin, "Les tours," one of a series of letters on "La réscherche de la paternité" written to Léon Richer's newspaper, *Le droit des femmes,* October 7, 1883.

40. "Mais c'est surtout cette sainte fonction de mère, qu'on oppose comme incompatible avec l'exercice des droits de citoyenne, qui impose à la femme le devoir de veiller sur l'avenir de ses enfants et lui donne le droit d'intervenir non seulement dans tous les actes de la vie civile, mais aussi dans tous les actes de la vie politique"; *L'opinion des femmes,* no. 2 (March 10, 1849).

41. Scott, "Work Identities for Men and Women."

42. For another interpretation of this appeal to motherhood, see Moses, *French Feminism*, pp. 132–136.

43. *Almanach des femmes*, 1853, p. 73.

44. Flora Tristan put it this way: "The Jewish people were dead and debased and Jesus raised them up. The Christian people are dead and debased today and Flora Tristan, the first strong woman, will raise them up. Oh! I feel a new world within me and I will give this new world to the old world which is crumbling and dying"; Flora Tristan, *Le tour de France*, 2 vols. (Paris: François Maspero, 1980), vol. 2, p. 231. See also Egérie Casaubon, *Le nouveau contrat social ou la place à la femme* (Paris, 1834), p. 21. On the Virgin Mary see Marina Warner, *Alone of All Her Sex* (New York: Alfred A. Knopf, 1976). For a more general discussion, see Thomas Kselman, *Miracles and Prophecies in Nineteenth-Century France* (New Brunswick, N.J.: Rutgers University Press, 1983); Stéphane Michaud, "Science, droit, religion: Trois contes sur les deux natures," *Romantisme*, no. 13–14 (1976); Michael Marrus, "Cultures on the Move: Pilgrims and Pilgrimages in Nineteenth-Century France," *Stanford French Review* 1 (1977), 205–220; Barbara Corrado Pope, "Immaculate and Powerful: The Marian Revival in the Nineteenth Century," in Clarissa Atkinson, Constance Buchanan, and Margaret R. Miles, eds., *Immaculate and Powerful: The Female in Sacred Image and Social Reality* (Boston: Beacon Press, 1985), pp. 173–200; Sandra Zimdars-Swartz, *Encountering Mary from La Salette to Medjugorje* (Princeton: Princeton University Press, 1991).

45. *La voix des femmes*, March 28, 1848.

46. Jeanne Deroin, "Profession de foi," p. 40. Deroin's "Profession de foi" was transcribed by the editors of *Le Globe* for the St. Simon Archives in 1831–1834. It is available as a handwritten document at the Bibliothèque de l'Arsenal, Fonds Enfantin, 7608, no. 39. I am grateful to Claire Goldberg Moses for sharing her copy of this document with me.

47. *La voix des femmes*, March 20, 1848. For a theoretical discussion see Jacques Lacan: "It is the name-of-the-father that we must recognize as the support of the symbolic function, which, from the dawn of history, has identitifed his person with the figure of the law"; Lacan, *Ecrits: A Selection*, trans. Alan Sheridan (New York: Norton, 1977), p. 67. See also Elizabeth Grosz, *Jacques Lacan: A Feminist Introduction* (New York: Routledge, 1990); and Mary O'Brien, *The Politics of Reproduction* (Boston and London: Routledge and Kegan Paul, 1981).

48. On the practice among St. Simonian women of dropping surnames, see Moses, *French Feminism*, pp. 132–136; Claire Démar, *L'affranchissement des femmes* (Paris: Payot, 1976); Lydia Elhadad, "Femmes prénommées: Les proletaires saint-simoniennes redactrices de 'La femme libre,' 1832–34," *Les révoltes logiques*, nos. 4 and 5 (1977); Elhadad, "Textes sur l'affranchissement des femmes, 1832–33," *Les révoltes logiques*, no. 2 (1976); S. Joan Moon, "The Saint-Simonian Association of the Working-Class Women, 1830–1850," in *Proceedings of the Fifth Annual Meeting of the Western Society for French History*, ed. Joyce Duncan Falk (Santa Barbara,

Calif., 1978); Leslie W. Rabine, "'Ecriture Féminine' as Metaphor," *Cultural Critique* 8 (Winter 1987–88), 19–44; and Suzanne Voilquin, *Souvenirs d'une fille du peuple, ou La Saint-simonienne en Egypte* (Paris: François Maspero, 1978).

49. "De tous les noms dont on marque la femme soit du père, ou du mari, je n'aime que le petit nom qui lui est propre"; letter to Pierre Leroux, *L'Espérance*, June 1858, cited by Michèle Riot-Sarcey, "Une vie publique prové d'histoire," p. 3.

50. Many of those arrested with Deroin were mocked by the prosecutor for their refusal to marry. It became additional evidence of their guilt and subversion. The prosecutor sarcastically described Pauline Roland as "a mother who is not married . . . an enemy of marriage [because it] sanctifies inequality . . . Needless to add, that, according to her, no one has the right to private ownership"; Thomas, *Les femmes de 1848*, pp. 75–77.

51. "L'on ne peut trouver étrange que la femme se réfugie dans le sentiment chrétien et que, voyant la dignité humaine outragée en elle, elle veuille dépouiller la nature humaine et se revêtir de la nature angélique pour s'affranchir de la brutale domination de l'homme et d'une humiliante servitude"; Jeanne Deroin, *Du célibat* (Paris, 1851), p. 13.

52. On the history of women in the St. Simonian movement, see Moses, *French Feminism*, pp. 41–116, and her "Saint-Simonian Men/Saint-Simonian Women."

53. Jeanne Deroin, "La mission des femmes," *L'opinion des femmes*, no. 2 (March 10, 1849).

54. Deroin, *Du célibat*, p. 14.

55. "L'égalité politique des deux sexes, c'est-à-dire l'assimilation de la femme à l'homme dans les fonctions politiques, est un de ces sophismes que repoussent non point seulement le logique, mais encore la conscience humaine et la nature des choses"; Proudhon, *Le Peuple*, April 12, 1849.

56. "C'est parce que la femme est l'égale de l'homme et qu'elle ne lui est pas semblable, qu'elle doit prendre part à l'oeuvre de la réforme sociale"; Jeanne Deroin, "Unité sociale, religieuse et politique," *La démocratie pacifique*, April 13, 1849.

57. *La voix des femmes*, March 26, 1848.

58. "Que Dieu a joint ainsi, que l'homme ne le sépare point"; "Les femmes au gouvernement et au peuple français," petition of March 16, 1848, reprinted in *L'opinion des femmes*, no. 4 (May 1849).

59. Pierre Leroux, *De l'humanité, de son principe et de son avenir; où se trouve exposée la vrai définition de la religion et où l'on explique le sens, la suite et l'enchaînement du mosaïsme et du christianisme*, 2nd ed., 2 vols. (Paris: Perrotin, 1845), p. 532. Leroux argued that there was biblical evidence against the notion that God created woman from man's rib while he slept. Instead, he cited rabbinical texts to insist that the rib story was really about the separation of the androgyne into two equal parts.

60. Naomi Schor, "Feminism and George Sand: *Lettres à Marcie*," in Judith

Butler and Joan Scott, eds., *Feminists Theorize the Political* (New York: Routledge, 1992), pp. 41–53. See also Schor, *George Sand and Idealism* (New York: Columbia University Press, 1993).

61. "C'est le type un et une, être mâle par la virilité(!), femme par l'intuition divine, la poésie. Elle s'est faite homme par l'esprit; elle est restée femme par le côte maternel, la tendresse infinie"; cited in Adler, *A l'aube du féminisme*, p. 138.

62. On St. Simonianism, see Robert B. Carlisle, *The Proffered Crown: St. Simonianism and the Doctrine of Hope* (Baltimore: Johns Hopkins University Press, 1987); David Owen Evans, *Social Romanticism in France, 1830–1848* (Oxford: Clarendon Press, 1951); Moses, "Saint-Simonian Men/Saint-Simonian Women"; Kari Weil, "Feminocentric Utopia and Male Desire: The New Paris of the Saint-Simonians," in Libby Falls Jones and Sarah Webster Goodwin, eds., *Feminism, Utopia, and Narrative*, Tennessee Studies in Literature, vol. 32 (Knoxville: University of Tennessee Press, 1990); Weil, "From General Will to Masculine Desire: Sexual Politics in the 'Paris of the Saint Simonians'" (unpublished paper, 1987); Weil, "'A Spectacle of Faith': Saint-Simonianism and Gender at the Dawn of the Industrial Revolution" (unpublished paper, 1987); Henry Rome d'Allemagne, *Les Saint-Simoniens, 1827–1837* (Paris: Grand, 1930); George Iggers, *The Doctrine of Saint-Simon: An Exposition, First Year, 1828–29* (Boston: Beacon Press, 1958); Frank Manuel and Fritzie Manuel, *Utopian Thought in the Western World* (Cambridge, Mass.: The Belknap Press of Harvard University Press, 1980).

63. Leroux, *De l'humanité*, pp. 530–531; and Leroux, *De l'égalité* (Paris: Boussac, 1848), p. 44. See also Armelle Le Bras-Chopard, *De l'égalité dans la différence: Le socialisme de Pierre Leroux* (Paris: Presses de la Fondation Nationale des Sciences Politiques, 1986); Paul Bénichou, *Le temps des prophètes: Doctrines de l'âge romantique* (Paris: Gallimard, 1977); A. J. L. Busst, "The Image of the Androgyne in the Nineteenth Century," in Ian Fletcher, ed., *Romantic Mythologies* (New York: Barnes and Noble, 1967), pp. 1–96; and Kari Weil, *Androgyny and the Denial of Sexual Difference* (Charlottesville: University Press of Virginia, 1992).

64. "Dieu a crée l'être humain à son image. Il l'a crée mâle et femelle; il l'a animé du souffle divin et des deux moitiés d'un même être il a formé l'individu social, l'homme et la femme pour s'animer, se compléter et marcher ensemble vers un même but. Il a fondé la société humaine"; Deroin, *Cours de droit social pour les femmes* (Paris, 1848), p. 2. Published first as a series of articles in *La politique des femmes*, it was later republished as a brochure.

65. *La politique des femmes* 1 (June 18–24, 1848).

66. Barbara Johnson, *A World of Difference* (Baltimore: Johns Hopkins University Press, 1987), p. 191.

67. "A l'oeuvre hommes de l'avenir! républicains, socialistes de toutes les écoles, à l'oeuvre! Appelez enfin, franchement à vous, la femme, cette moitié de votre âme, de votre coeur, de votre intelligence trop longtemps méconnue et délaissée; travaillez ensemble à fonder l'ère nouvelle, la loi de l'avenir, loi toute de

solidarité, d'indulgence et d'amour"; Jeanne-Marie, "De la femme," *L'opinion des femmes*, no. 1 (January 1, 1849). Jeanne-Marie was one of Deroin's pen-names. See Evelyne Sullerot, *Histoire de la presse féminine en France, des origines à 1848* (Paris: Librairie Armand Colin, 1966), pp. 151–152.

68. *L'opinion des femmes*, no. 4 (May 1849).

69. Cited in Ranvier, "Une féministe de 1848," pp. 334–335.

70. "En politique, l'opinion des femmes quelles que soient leurs tendances républicaines ou aristocratiques, peut encore se résumer en une pensée d'amour et de paix . . . Elles s'accordent toutes à vouloir que la politique de la paix et du travail vienne remplacer cette politique égoiste et cruelle qui excite les hommes à s'entre-détruire . . . Dans toutes les théories sociales, ce que les femmes ont le mieux compris c'est le principe de l'association"; "Qu'est-ce que l'opinion des femmes?" *L'opinion des femmes*, August 21, 1848.

71. *L'opinion des femmes*, no. 4 (May 1849).

72. "La vie privée convient seule à la femme; elle n'est pas faite pour la vie publique"; Athanase Coquerel, cited in Deroin's "Lettre d'une femme à M. Coquerel."

73. "Or, dans l'humanité, la femme a une nature tout à fait distincte de celle de l'homme. L'homme est apprenti, producteur et magistrat; la femme est élève, ménagère et mère de famille. Il faut à la femme des conditions sociales toutes différentes"; cited in Tixerant, *Le féminisme à l'époque de 1848*, p. 86.

74. "Le rôle de la femme n'est point la vie extérieure, la vie de relation et d'agitation, mais bien la vie intime, celle du sentiment et de la tranquillité du foyer domestique. Le socialisme n'est pas venu seulement pour restaurer le travail; il est venu aussi pour réhabiliter le ménage, sanctuaire de la famille, symbole de l'union matrimoniale . . . nous invitons nos soeurs à méditer ce que nous venons de dire et à bien se pénétrer de cette verité, que la pureté et la moralité gagnent plus dans les fêtes patriarcales de la famille que dans le manifestations bruyantes de la vie politique"; *Le Peuple*, December 27, 1848, p. 2.

75. Cited in Tixerant, *Le féminisme à l'époque de 1848*, p. 86.

76. Deroin, "Profession de foi," p. 12.

77. Deroin, *Almanach des femmes*, 1853, p. 11.

78. "A la triple face: materielle, intellectuelle et morale dans le travail"; petition of March 16, 1848, *L'opinion des femmes*, no. 4 (May 1849).

79. Jeanne Deroin, "Unité sociale, réligieuse et politique," *La démocratie pacifique*, April 13, 1849.

80. Gautier, "De l'affranchissement des femmes," *Le Peuple*, January 15, 1849.

81. Ernest Legouvé, *Histoire morale des femmes* (Paris, 1849). Deroin was so enthusiastic about Legouvé's calls for improvement of women's status that she promised to reprint sections of the book. See *L'opinion des femmes*, no. 2 (March 10, 1849). Legouvé's comment is cited in Marc de Villiers du Terrage, *Histoire des clubs de femmes et des légions d'amazones 1793—1848—1871* (Paris: Plon-Nourrits,

1910), p. 334. See also Karen Offen, "Ernest Legouvé and the Doctrine of 'Equality in Difference' for Women: A Case Study of Male Feminism in Nineteenth-Century French Thought," *Journal of Modern History* 58, no. 2 (June 1986), 452–484.

82. The preamble of the constitution was attributed to Deroin; Edouard Dolléans, "Féminisme et syndicalisme," in Charles Moulin, ed., *1848: Le livre du centenaire* (Paris: Editions Atlas, 1948), pp. 245–246. See also de Villiers, *Histoire des clubs de femmes;* and Thibert, *Le féminisme dans le socialisme,* p. 320.

83. "Travailler insensiblement a faire effacer les différences qui existent entre le costume masculin et le costume féminin; sans pour cela dépasser les limites de la pudeur et du ridicule, ni même sans s'éloigner des formes gracieuses et de bon goût. Ce sera, du reste, un changement dont les hommes, à voir leur tenue de croque-mort, n'auront guère sujet de plaindre"; *Les Vésuviennes, ou la Constitution politique des femmes* (Paris, 1848), p. 26.

84. Cited in Theodore Stanton, ed., *The Woman Question in Europe* (New York: G. Putnam's Sons, 1884), p. 243.

85. When a meeting of the Club des Femmes was disrupted by hostile male onlookers, the president responded by recalling the experience of "the first revolutionary": "Eh, lui aussi, le Christ . . . a été hué et bafoué sur la croix!" Frank Paul Bowman, *Le Christ romantique* (Geneva: Librarie Droz, 1973), p. 105.

86. In addition to cartoons, there were written reports that caricatured Deroin. See, for example, *L'Illustration,* April 21, 1849, pp. 123–125.

87. On universal suffrage and individual rights, see Tixerant, *Le feminisme à l'époque de 1848,* pp. 31–32; "L'histoire des femmes," *Annales E.S.C.* 41 (March–April 1986), 288–289.

88. *La voix des femmes,* March 20, 1848.

89. "Inspirées et dirigées par le sentiment du droit et de la justice, nous avons accompli un devoir en reclamant le droit de prendre part aux travaux de l'Assemblée législative"; *L'opinion des femmes,* no. 4 (May 1849).

90. "Fortifiées par le sentiment intime de la grandeur de notre mission, de la sainteté de notre apostolat et profondément convaincue de l'importance et de l'opportunité de notre oeuvre, si éminemment si radicalement révolutionnaire et sociale, nous avons accompli notre devoir en refusant de quitter la tribune"; ibid.

91. Deroin, "Profession de foi."

92. "Vous me fermez les voies du monde, vous me déclarez subalterne et mineure; mais il me reste dans ma conscience un sanctuaire où s'arrête la force de votre bras comme le despotime de votre esprit. Là nul signe d'infériorité ne flétrit mon existence, nul asservissement n'enchaîne ma volonté et ne l'empêche de se tourner vers la sagesse"; *Almanach des femmes,* 1853, p. 95. This article, though signed by "Marie" and probably not written by Deroin, eloquently expresses views she also held.

93. "Quand M. Eugène Pelletan me dit un jour que j'agissais comme si je tirais un coup de pistolet dans la rue pour attirer l'attention, il avait raison, mais ce

n'était pas pour attirer l'attention sur moi, mais sur la cause à laquelle je me dévouais"; letter from Deroin to Léon Richer, Fonds Bouglé, Bibliothèque Historique de la Ville de Paris, cited in Serrière, "Jeanne Deroin," p. 26.

94. Cited in Ranvier, "Une feministe de 1848," pp. 341–343. See also J. Deroin, *L'Association fraternelle des démocrates socialistes des deux sexes pour l'affranchissement politique et social des femmes* (Paris 1849); Deroin, *Lettre aux Associations sur l'organisation du crèdit* (Paris, 1851); and Henri Desroches, *Solidarités ouvrières: Sociétaires et compagnons dans les associations coopératives (1831–1900)* (Paris, 1981), pp. 59–73.

95. Cited in Moses, *French Feminism*, p. 148.

96. Ibid.

97. No one has been able to locate the text of Morris' address.

98. "Comme tous les initiateurs d'une idée nouvelle . . . [elle] a frayé la route sans atteindre le but: elle est montée à l'échafaud sans obtenir le droit de monter à la tribune." "En 1849, une femme vient encore frapper à la porte de la cité, réclamer pour les femmes le droit de participer aux travaux de l'Assemblée législative. Ce n'est pas au vieux monde qu'elle s'addresse . . . Le moment est venu pour la femme de prendre part au mouvement social, à l'oeuvre de régénération qui se prépare"; cited in Alexandre Zévaès, "Une candidature féministe en 1849," in *La révolution de 1848* (Paris: Bibliothèque Nationale, 1948), p. 129.

99. On history in this period see Linda Orr, *Headless History: Nineteenth-Century French Historiography of the Revolution* (Ithaca: Cornell University Press, 1990) and *Jules Michelet: Nature, History, and Language* (Ithaca: Cornell University Press, 1976); Stephen Bann, *The Clothing of Clio: A Study of the Representation of History in Nineteenth-Century Britain and France* (Cambridge: Cambridge University Press, 1984); Roland Barthes, "Historical Discourse," in Michael Lane, ed., *Structuralism: A Reader* (London: Jonathan Cape, 1970), pp. 145–155; Christina Crosby, *The Ends of History: Victorians and "The Woman Question"* (New York and London: Routledge, 1991); and Thérèse Moreau, *Le sang de l'histoire: Michelet, l'histoire, et l'idée de la femme au XIXe siècle* (Paris: Flammarion, 1982).

100. A typed copy of the letter is in the dossier "J. Deroin," Bibliothèque Marguerite Durand, Paris.

101. "Maintenant il ne faut plus de pionniers impulsifs et téméraires, il faut joindre le talent au dévouement, orner la vérité par la beauté du style, c'est pourquoi je ne puis vous offrir mon inutile concours"; cited in Adler, *A L'aube du féminisme*, p. 211.

102. Madeleine Pelletier, *La femme vierge* (Paris, 1933), p. 95.

4. The Rights of "the Social"

1. On socialists' familial rhetoric, see Joan W. Scott, "Mayors versus Police Chiefs: Socialist Municipalities Confront the French State," in John Merriman, ed., *French Cities in the Nineteenth Century* (London: Hutchinson, 1988), pp. 230–245.

2. On the history of socialism, see Claude Willard, *Le mouvement socialiste en France (1893–1905): Les Guesdistes* (Paris: Editions Sociales, 1965).

3. "The Republic was founded by a Monarchist assembly with a Right-wing President and Government in power, on the motion of a Catholic lawyer who insisted that he was not asking for the Republic—and it was passed by a majority of one vote"; David Thomson, *Democracy in France: The Third and Fourth Republics* (London: Oxford University Press, 1958), p. 90.

4. Pierre Rosanvallon, *Le sacre du citoyen: Histoire du suffrage universel in France* (Paris: Gallimard, 1992), pp. 307–338. See also Jean Rivero, "The Jacobin and Liberal Traditions," in Joseph Klaits and Michael H. Haltzel, eds., *Liberty/Liberté: The American and French Experiences* (Washington, D.C.: Woodrow Wilson Center Press; and Baltimore: Johns Hopkins University Press, 1991), p. 128.

5. Cited in Rogers Brubaker, *Citizenship and Nationhood in France and Germany* (Cambridge, Mass.: Harvard University Press, 1992), p. 107. See also Eugen Weber, *Peasants into Frenchmen: The Modernization of Rural France, 1870–1914* (Stanford: Stanford University Press, 1976); and Antoine Prost, *L'histoire de l'enseignement en France, 1800–1967* (Paris: Librairie Armand Colin, 1968).

6. This kind of education is an example of what Althusser refers to as the "interpellation" of a subject. See Louis Althusser, "Ideology and Ideological State Apparatuses," in *Lenin and Philosophy*, trans. Ben Brewster (New York: Monthly Review Press, 1974), pp. 127–186.

7. "Il se dit, par opposition à politique, des conditions qui, laissant en dehors la forme des gouvernements se rapportent au développement intellectuel, moral, et matériel des masses populaires. La question sociale"; E. Littré, ed., *Dictionnaire de la langue française* (Paris, 1877), p. 1957.

8. For a discussion of "the social," see Denise Riley, *"Am I That Name?" Feminism and the Category of "Women" in History* (London: Macmillan, 1988), pp. 44–66. On the social in France, see Jacques Donzelot, *L'invention du social: Essai sur le déclin des passions politiques* (Paris: Fayard, 1984).

9. George D. Sussman, *Selling Mothers' Milk: The Wet-Nursing Business in France, 1715–1914* (Urbana: University of Illinois Press, 1982); Sylvia Schafer, "Children in 'Moral Danger' and the Politics of Parenthood in Third Republic France, 1870–1914" (Ph.D. diss., University of California, Berkeley, 1992); Andrew Aisenberg, "Contagious Disease and the Government of Paris in the Age of Pasteur" (Ph.D. diss., Yale University, 1993); Mary Lynn Stewart, *Women, Work, and the French State: Labour Protection and Social Patriarchy, 1879–1919* (Kingston, Ont.: McGill–Queen's University Press, 1989); and Esther Kanipe, "The Family, Private Property, and the State in France, 1870–1914" (Ph.D. diss., University of Wisconsin, Madison, 1976).

10. François Ewald, "A Concept of Social Law," in Gunther Teubner, ed., *Dilemmas of Law in the Welfare State* (Berlin and New York: W. de Gruyter, 1986), pp. 40–75; and Donzelot, *L'invention du social*. For some of the texts elaborating solidarism, see Eugène d'Eichtal, ed., *La solidarité sociale* (Paris: Institut de France,

Académie des Sciences Morales et Politiques, 1903). For a compelling interpretation of the emergence of the welfare state in France, see François Ewald, *L'état providence* (Paris: Bernard Grasset, 1986).

11. Alain Corbin, "Backstage," in Philippe Ariès and Georges Duby, eds., *A History of Private Life*, trans. Arthur Goldhammer, vol. 4 (Cambridge, Mass.: Harvard University Press, 1990), pp. 451–668; see especially "The Secret of the Individual," pp. 457–548. See also Roxanne Panchasi, "Characteristically 'Modern': Handwriting, Identity, and Psychology in France" (seminar paper, Rutgers University, January 1995).

12. Charles Brunot, "Etude sur la solidarité sociale comme principe des lois," in d'Eichtal, *La solidarité sociale*, pp. 25–84, especially 58–59. See also Ewald, *L'état providence;* Schafer, "Children in 'Moral Danger'"; Aisenberg, "Contagious Disease"; Joshua Hamilton Cole, "The Power of Large Numbers: Population and Politics in Nineteenth-Century France" (Ph.D. diss., University of California, Berkeley, 1991).

13. Emile Durkheim, "Sociology in France," in Robert Bellah, ed., *Emile Durkheim on Morality and Society: Selected Writings* (Chicago: University of Chicago Press, 1973), p. 13.

14. Emile Durkheim, *The Division of Labor in Society*, trans. George Simpson (New York: Free Press, 1964), p. 62.

15. Cited in Ewald, "A Concept of Social Law," p. 52, n. 30.

16. Cited in ibid., p. 53.

17. Michelle Perrot, "Le discours de la Grève," in *Les ouvriers en Grève: France 1871–90*, vol. 2 (Paris: Mouton, 1974), pp. 607–644.

18. Durkheim, *The Division of Labor*, citing the English psychologist Alexander Bain's *The Emotions and the Will* (1859), p. 55.

19. Léon Bourgeois, *La solidarité* (1895), cited in Stephen Lukes, *Emile Durkheim: His Life and Works* (New York: Harper and Row, 1972), p. 352; Brunot, "La solidarité sociale," p. 70: "Le droit individuel de chacun est égal au droit individuel des autres; c'est que tous ces droits sont réellement des unitées de même espèce, comparables les unes aux autres, interchangeables, et égales entre elles." See also Theodore Zeldin, *France: 1848–1945*, vol. 1: *Ambition, Love and Politics* (Oxford: Oxford University Press, 1973), pp. 640–682; and J. E. S. Hayward, "The Official Social Philosophy of the French Third Republic: Léon Bourgeois and Solidarism," *International Review of Social History* 6 (1961), 19–48.

20. "Tout le monde ne peut pas remplir le même rôle: la diversité est au contraire indispensable à la bonne harmonie de la société . . . Le devoir imposé à tous est différent pour chacun. Le droit inhérent à l'individu est égal pour tous"; "Une objection banale," *La Citoyenne*, March 6, 1881, in Edith Taïeb, ed., *Hubertine Auclert: La Citoyenne. Articles de 1881 à 1891* (Paris: Syros, 1982), p. 95.

21. Michelle Perrot, "L'éloge de la ménagère dans le discours des ouvriers français au XIXe siècle," in *Mythes et répresentations de la femme XIXe siècle* (Paris: Champion, 1977), pp. 105–121; and Perrot, "Le syndicalisme français et les

femmes: Histoire d'un malentendu," *Aujourd'hui* 66 (March 1984), 41–49. See also Charles Sowerwine, *Les femmes et le socialisme* (Paris: Presses de la Fondation Nationale des Sciences Politiques, 1978).

22. Durkheim, *The Division of Labor,* p. 60.

23. Ibid. On Le Bon, see Susanna Barrows, *Distorting Mirrors: Visions of the Crowd in Late Nineteenth-Century France* (New Haven: Yale University Press, 1981); Ruth Harris, *Murders and Madness: Medicine, Law, and Society in the Fin de Siècle* (Oxford: Clarendon Press, 1989); and Robert A. Nye, *The Origins of Crowd Psychology: Gustave Le Bon and the Crisis of Mass Democracy in the Third Republic* (Beverly Hills: Sage, 1975).

24. Durkheim, *The Division of Labor,* p. 58.

25. "L'idée de subordonner l'exercice du droit à une question de rôle, avant d'été invoquée par les adversaires du votes des femmes, a servir d'objection au suffrage universel pour les hommes"; "Une objection banale," *La Citoyenne,* March 6, 1881, in Taïeb, *Auclert,* p. 94.

26. "Une République qui maintiendra les femmes dans une condition d'infériorité, ne pourra pas faire les hommes égaux"; "Rapport de Hubertine Auclert au 3ᵉ Congrès national ouvrier," in Madeleine Reberioux, Christiane Dufrancatel, and Béatrice Slama, "Hubertine Auclert et la question des femmes à 'l'immortel congrès' (1879)," *Romantisme* 13–14 (1976), 123.

27. "Le suffrage des femmes," *La Citoyenne,* February 5–March 4, 1883, in Taïeb, *Auclert,* p. 132.

28. Richer's group was later called the Association pour l'Avenir des Femmes, then the Société pour l'Amélioration du Sort de la Femme, and then the Société pour l'Amélioration du Sort de la Femme et la Revindication de Ses Droits. See Steven C. Hause, *Hubertine Auclert: The French Suffragette* (New Haven: Yale University Press, 1987), p. 31.

29. For biographical details see Hause, *Hubertine Auclert;* Taïeb, "Preface," in *Auclert,* pp. 7–53.

30. Hause, *Hubertine Auclert,* p. 78.

31. "Pour la femme, la possession de son nom et la possession de son revenu ou de son salaire: voilà le fondement de la liberté dans le mariage"; "Le nom et l'argent," *La Citoyenne,* August 1889, in Taïeb, *Auclert,* p. 73.

32. "Alors, désespérée de ne point voir aboutir mes efforts légaux, j'ai songé que les hommes avaient fait des barricades pour pouvoir voter . . ."; cited in Taïeb, "Preface," in *Auclert,* p. 43. (Unpersuaded by this defense, the judges fined her and ordered her jail sentence suspended pending five years of good conduct.)

33. Cited in Hause, *Hubertine Auclert,* p. 79.

34. "Jamais on n'a essayé de prendre un nombre déterminé d'enfants des deux sexes, de les soumettre à la même méthode d'éducation, aux mêmes conditions d'existence"; "Rapport de Hubertine Auclert," *Romantisme,* 13–14 (1976), 124. The text was also published as a separate pamphlet: H. Auclert, *Egalité sociale et politique de la Femme et de l'Homme (Discours prononcé au Congrès ouvrier socialiste de Marseille)* (Marseilles, 1879).

35. "L'objection qu'on fait aux femmes de leur ignorance de la vie publique est nulle puisque c'est seulement par la pratique qu'on peut s'initier à la vie publique"; "Malheur aux absentes!" *La Citoyenne,* May 8, 1881, in Taïeb, *Auclert,* p. 112.

36. Neil Hertz, "Medusa's Head: Male Hysteria under Political Pressure," *Representations* 4 (Fall 1983), 27–54; Gay Gullickson, "La Pétroleuse: Representing Revolution," *Feminist Studies* 17 (Summer 1991), 240–265; Edith Thomas, *Les "pétroleuses"* (Paris: Gallimard, 1963).

37. Edwin Child, cited in Gullickson, "La Pétroleuse," p. 250.

38. Cited in Christiane Dufrancatel, "L'oratrice," in Reberioux, Dufrancatel, and Slama, "Hubertine Auclert et la question des femmes," p. 134.

39. Jules Michelet, *Du prêtre, la femme et la famille* (Paris, 1845). This went through numerous editions after its publication. The 1900 edition was edited with comments by solidarist philosopher Alfred Fouillée.

40. Cited in Hause, *Hubertine Auclert,* p. 41.

41. "Il y a déjà tant d'incompétences qui s'occupent de politique, que je ne verrais pas sans inquiétudes les femmes se jeter dans la mêlée des partis. Dans les pays catholiques, le vote de la plupart des femmes serait celui de leurs confesseurs, qui recevraient eux-mêmes le mot d'ordre de Rome. Au lieu de contribuer au progrès, il amènerait, je crois, un recul. Attendons; la question me semble prématurée"; cited in Rosanvallon, *Le sacre,* p. 394.

42. Cited in Steven C. Hause with Anne R. Kenney, *Women's Suffrage and Social Politics in the French Third Republic* (Princeton: Princeton University Press, 1984), p. 16.

43. The great socialist histories of the French Revolution perpetuate this idea of women's religious loyalties by their references to women's role in the counter revolution. See Jules Michelet, *Les femmes de la Révolution* (Paris, 1854); Alphonse Aulard, *Le culte de la raison et de l'Etre suprême, 1793–94* (Paris, 1892); idem, *Paris pendant la réaction thermidorienne et sous le Directoire* (Paris, 1898–1902); Jean Jaurès, *Histoire socialiste de la Révolution française,* 8 vols. (Paris, 1922–1924).

44. "Le nom et l'argent," *La Citoyenne,* August 1889, in Taïeb, *Auclert,* pp. 71, 76.

45. "Une objection banale," *La Citoyenne,* March 6, 1881, in Taïeb, *Auclert,* p. 92.

46. *La Citoyenne,* February 13, 1881.

47. "Les chiffres sont éloquents, ils prouveront mieux que des mots que nous avons raison de nous méfier"; "Pourquoi les femmes veulent contrôler les budgets," *La Citoyenne,* June 5, 1887, in Taïeb, *Auclert,* p. 104.

48. On these surveys or *enquêtes,* see Aisenberg, "Contagious Disease," chap. 5.

49. "Rapport de Hubertine Auclert," p. 128.

50. Jacques Alary, *Le travail de la femme dans l'imprimerie typographique: Ses conséquences physiques et morales* (Paris, 1883), pp. 15, 18: "elle se déforme, prend le regard, la voix, et l'allure grossière des hommes qu'elle fréquente dans l'atelier; elle retombe enfin à l'état de nature ou de simple femelle"; "Quelle est la negresse

de la Havane ou la circassienne de Constantinople qui consentirait à échanger la maison turque ou l'hacienda espagnole contre une place dans l'imprimerie?"

51. H. Auclert, "La femme imprimeur," *La Citoyenne*, December 3, 1883–January 6, 1884, in Taïeb, *Auclert*, pp. 80–84.

52. "Les hypocrites," *La Citoyenne*, March 27, 1881: "L'homme a fait ces lois et même à notre époque d'athéisme et de libre examen, il les conserve religieusement."

53. "Pour contrebalancer l'influence fâcheuse des femmes réactionnaires, il faudrait l'influence bienfaisant des femmes républicaines"; *Le droit politique des femmes* (Paris, 1878), p. 10.

54. "Montrons que nous ne sommes pas avec eux. Levons-nous, et que, d'un bout à l'autre de la France, notre cri de protestation soit entendu. Disons bien haut au monde que nous voulons la lumière, la liberté"; letter signed by Auclert, *Le petit parisien*, June 1, 1877, in Taïeb, *Auclert*, p. 10.

55. "Le suffrage des femmes," *La Citoyenne*, February 5–March 4, 1883, ibid., p. 132.

56. "On ne peut exiger de la nature humaine plus de perfection qu'elle n'en comporte; pendant que les hommes feront seul les lois, ils les feront pour eux contre nous;" ibid., p. 133.

57. See Michelle Perrot, *Les ouvriers en grève: France 1871–1890*, 2 vols. (Paris: Mouton, 1974); and Harvey Goldberg, *Jean Jaurès* (Madison: University of Wisconsin Press, 1963).

58. On the limits of persuasion, see Ellen Rooney, *Seductive Reasoning: Pluralism as the Problematic of Contemporary Literary Theory* (Ithaca: Cornell University Press, 1989).

59. Auclert, "L'académie et la langue," *Le Radical*, April 18, 1898, in Taïeb, *Auclert*, pp. 15–17: "N'est-ce pas à force de prononcer certains mots, qu'on finit par en accepter le sens qui tout d'abord heurtait?" "La féminisation initiale est celle de la langue, car le féminin non distinctement établi sera toujours absorbé par le masculin." See also Mary Poovey, "Figures of Arithmetic, Figures of Speech: The Discourse of Statistics in the 1830s," *Critical Inquiry* 19 (Winter 1993), 256–276.

60. E. Littré, ed., *Dictionnaire de la langue française* (Paris, 1877), p. 1078.

61. *Le Temps*, May 17, 1880; *Gil Blas*, March 12, 1880.

62. On this history see Hause with Kenney, *Women's Suffrage*, pp. 212–247; Laurence Klejman and Florence Rochefort, *L'égalité en marche: Le féminisme sous la Troisième République* (Paris: Editions des Femmes, 1989), pp. 262–302; and Patrick K. Bidelman, *Pariahs Stand Up! The Founding of the Liberal Feminist Movement in France, 1858–1889* (Westport, Conn.: Greenwood Press, 1982). On concessions to women's interests in civil law (including the right of divorce granted in 1884) and on the family legislations of the Third Republic more generally, see Schafer, "Children in 'Moral Danger'"; Esther Kanipe, "The Family, Private Property, and the State"; Claudia S. Kselman, "The Modernization of Family Law: The

Politics and Ideology of Family Reform in Third Republic France" (Ph.D. diss., University of Michigan, 1980).

63. "On s'est aperçu qu'il est, dans la vie publique, un grand nombre d'intérêts que la femme est aussi apte, plus apte que l'homme à surveiller et à servir"; Ferdinand Buisson, *Le vote des femmes* (Paris, 1911), p. 2.

64. Ibid., p. 208.

65. "Intérêt," in Littré, *Dictionnaire de la langue française*, pp. 131–132. On the analysis of the notion of "interest," see Gareth Stedman Jones, *Languages of Class: Studies in English Working Class History, 1832–1982* (Cambridge: Cambridge University Press, 1983), p. xx: "We cannot . . . decode political language to reach a primal and material expression of interest since it is the discursive structure of political language which conceives and defines interest in the first place. What we must therefore do is to study the production of interest, identification, grievance and aspiration within political languages themselves."

66. "A ceux qui nous accuseront d'être exclusifs, de faire de la question des femmes une question particulière, nous répondons que nous serons obligés de faire une question des femmes aussi longtemps qu'il y aura une situation particulière faite aux femmes, et qu'avant que cette situation ait cessé d'exister, avant que la femme ait le pouvoir d'intervenir partout où ses intérêts sont en jeu pour les défendre, un changement dans la condition économique ou politique de la société ne remédierait pas au sort de la femme"; *La Citoyenne*, February 13, 1881.

67. "La femme ménagère nationale mettra bien plus d'humanité que de gloire dans sa fonction"; "Pourquoi les femmes veulent contrôler les budgets," *La Citoyenne*, June 5, 1887; and "La politique n'intéresse pas les femmes," *La Citoyenne*, July 3, 1881, both in Taïeb, *Auclert*, pp. 111 and 106.

68. "Rapport de Hubertine Auclert," p. 123.

69. Ibid.: "Je viens, toute pénétrée d'estime pour cette grande assemblée, le premier des corps libres élus en France depuis tant de siècles, qui permette à une femme, non parce qu'elle est ouvrière, mais parce qu'elle est femme—c'est-à-dire exploitée—esclave déléguée de neuf millions d'esclaves, de faire entendre les réclamations de la moitié déshéritée du genre humain."

70. Ibid., p. 129: "Nous nous adressons à vous, prolétaires, comme à nos compagnons d'infortune, pour appuyer notre droit à sortir de la servitude." "Vous êtes électeurs, vous avez la puissance du nombre, tous vous êtes femmes par le coeur, vous êtes nos frères. Aidez-nous à nous affranchir."

71. Beatrice Slama, "Le discours," in Rebérioux, Dufrancatel, and Slama, "Hubertine Auclert et la question des femmes," p. 137.

72. "Il n'est pas possible, en effet, d'être à la fois homme et femme, on troverait étrange qu'un homme cumulât dans la famille le rôle de père et de mère et l'on admet que les hommes cumulent dans la commune ce double rôle"; Auclert, *Le vote des femmes* (Paris, 1908), p. 13.

73. Ibid., pp. 106, 20.

74. Ibid., pp. 23, 57, 217.

75. Ibid., p. 215.

76. "Les législateurs libres-penseurs mutilent le corps social, rentrachant la moitié de ses membres, pour s'épargner l'impur contact féminin"; ibid., p. 57.

77. "Les Françaises ont le sens de l'utilitarianisme démocratique. Quand elles seront électeurs et éligibles, elles forceront les assemblées administratives et législatives à se pénétrer des besoins humains et à les satisfaire"; ibid., p. 20.

78. H. Auclert, *Les femmes Arabes en Algérie* (Paris, 1900), p. 63.

79. "C'est en voyant le préjugé de race dominer tout en Algérie, que l'on comprend bien l'absurdité du préjugé de sexe. Ainsi la race arabe, si belle et si bien douée, est absolument méprisée par les européens qui, rarement cependant sont aussi beaux et possèdent autant d'aptitudes naturelles que les arabes. Et voyez cette contradiction. Le Français vainqueur dit au musulman: 'Je méprise ta race, mais j'abaisse ma loi devant la tienne; je donne au Koran le pas sur le Code'"; ibid.

80. Edward Said, *Orientalism* (New York: Vintage, 1979).

81. H. Auclert, *Le vote des femmes*, pp. 196–197.

82. "Quand les femmes qui ont dans l'Etat les mêmes intérêts que les hommes, seront comme ceux-ci, armeés des droits nécessaires pour se protéger, pour se défendre, pour ascensionner; la France, en possession de l'intégralité de sa force cérébrale, prendra dans le monde un rôle prépondérant"; ibid., p. 217.

83. Ibid., pp. 15–17, 23, 71–195.

84. Alary, *Le travail de la femme*, p. 57.

85. Ibid., p. 9: "Il est inadmissible que l'homme puisse vivre à l'état de frelon et rester à la maison pour soigner le ménage."

86. "Les femmes à l'assaut des urnes," *L'Eclair*, May 4, 1908, cited in Hause, *Hubertine Auclert*, p. xvii. (I am grateful to Steven Hause for this information and for lending me his copy of Auclert's diary.)

87. Sigmund Freud, *The Standard Edition of the Complete Psychological Works*, trans. and ed. James Strachey (London, 1955). References to castration: vol. 19, p. 144, n. 3; vol. 22, p. 24; "Medusa's Head," vol. 18, pp. 273–274.

88. Freud, "Medusa's Head," p. 273.

89. Ibid., p. 274.

90. Ibid., p. 273.

91. I am indebted to Neil Hertz's analysis in "Medusa's Head: Male Hysteria under Political Pressure," *Representations* 4 (Fall 1983), 27–54. See also Christina Crosby, *The Ends of History: Victorians and "The Woman Question"* (New York and London: Routledge, Chapman, and Hall, 1991), p. 41; and Freud's "Fetishism," in *Standard Edition*, vol. 21, pp. 152–157.

92. "Est-ce que notre démission d'hommes que dame Hubertine nous demande? Qu'elle le dise franchement"; Emile Villemot, *Le Gaulois*, June 7, 1877.

93. "Etre homme ou être femme n'importe pas plus dans la distribution des fonctions sociales, qu'être grand ou petit, brun ou blond, gras ou maigre"; "La sphère des femmes," *La Citoyenne*, February 19, 1882.

94. "En devenant citoyenne, la Française remplira encore mieux le devoir, puisque son rôle d'éducatrice s'étendra de l'unité à la collectivité humaine et que sa sollicitude maternelle embrassera la nation entière"; Auclert, *Le vote des femmes*, p. 10.

95. Ibid., p. 60. The terms of debate about women's vote at the moment may also have been affected by the debates on citizenship for immigrants from 1882 until a law was finally passed in 1889. See Brubaker, *Citizenship and Nationhood.*

96. Auclert, *Le vote des femmes*, p. 49 and p. 46: "Il serait infiniment moins facile aux hommes d'être mères qui aux femmes d'être soldats."

97. H. Auclert, "Programme électoral des femmes," *La Citoyenne*, August 1885, p. 42, in Taïeb, *Auclert*, p. 43.

98. Ibid., p. 41.

99. "Le suffrage des femmes," *La Citoyenne*, February 5–March 4, 1883, ibid., p. 132.

100. "Le 89 des femmes," *La Citoyenne*, June 1889, ibid., p. 126.

101. Cited in Hause, *Hubertine Auclert*, p. 206.

102. Ibid., pp. 216–218.

103. "Nécrologie, Mme. Hubertine Auclert," *La femme de demain*, May 1914; article in the Fonds Auclert, Bibliothèque Marguerite Durand.

104. Hause, *Hubertine Auclert*, p. 218.

105. "Le suffrage est une machine à progrès . . . De même que beaucoup d'inventions modernes, qui ne deviennent utilisables qu'à l'aide de certaines combinaisons, le suffrage a besoin de toutes les énergies féminines et masculines de la nation, pour devenir l'instrument d'évolution capable de transformer l'état social"; Auclert, *Le vote des femmes*, p. 5.

106. Ibid., especially pp. 15–19, 50–52, and 65–195.

5. The Radical Individualism of Madeleine Pelletier

1. "N'être femme comme la société suppose"; Doctoresse Pelletier, "Mémoire d'une féministe," unpublished memoir, dossier "M. Pelletier," Fonds Marie-Louise Bouglé, Bibliothèque Historique de la Ville de Paris, p. 1.

2. M. Pelletier, *La femme en lutte pour ses droits* (Paris, 1908), p. 48.

3. For this formulation, see Denise Riley, *"Am I That Name?" Feminism and the Category of "Women" in History* (London: Macmillan, 1988), p. 51.

4. "Le seul devoir de la société est de n'entraver personne dans l'exercice de son activité; que chacun s'oriente dans la vie comme il lui plaît et à ses risques et perils"; Pelletier, *La femme en lutte*, p. 41.

5. The phrase is Tania Modleski's. Modleski misunderstands the various attempts of those she criticizes to historicize the category of "women," as they have historicized gender, all in an attempt to de-essentialize sexual difference. See *Feminism without Women: Culture and Criticism in a "Postfeminist" Age* (New York and London: Routledge, 1991).

6. "Elle sera un individu avant d'être un sexe"; M. Pelletier, "Les femmes et le féminisme," *La revue socialiste*, January 1906, p. 44.

7. "Suppression de l'heritage, instruction gratuite à tous les degrès, large assistance aux enfants, vieillards et malades, plus de distinctions de classes, plus d'adoration de l'argent. L'intelligence et le travail seuls moyens de parvenir"; Pelletier, "Mémoire," p. 30.

8. For biographical details see Felicia Gordon, *The Integral Feminist: Madeleine Pelletier, 1874–1939* (Minneapolis: University of Minnesota Press, 1990); Charles Sowerwine and Claude Maignien, *Madeleine Pelletier: Une féministe dans l'arène politique* (Paris: Les Editions Ouvrières, 1992); Charles Sowerwine, "Madeleine Pelletier (1874–1939): Femme, médecin, militante," *L'information psychiatrique* 9 (November 1988), 1183–93; Sowerwine, "Madeleine Pelletier (1874–1939): Socialism, Feminism and Psychiatry, or Making It in a Man's World," lecture, University of Bath, November 2, 1987; Sowerwine, "Socialism, Feminism, and Violence: The Analysis of Madeleine Pelletier," *Proceedings of the Annual Meeting of the Western Society for French History* 8 (1980); and Christine Bard, ed., *Madeleine Pelletier (1874–1939): Logique et infortunes d'un combat pour l'égalité* (Paris: Côté-Femmes, 1992). See also Marilyn Boxer, "When Radical and Socialist Feminism Were Joined: The Extraordinary Failure of Madeleine Pelletier," in Jane Slaughter and Robert Kern, eds., *European Women of the Left: Socialism, Feminism, and the Problems Faced by Political Women, 1880 to the Present* (Westport, Conn.: Greenwood Press, 1981), pp. 51–74; Marilyn Boxer and Jean Quataert, eds., *Socialist Women: European Socialist Feminism in the Nineteenth and Early Twentieth Centuries* (New York: Elsevier, 1978).

9. On individualism, but without its gender components, see Stephen Lukes, *Individualism* (New York: Harper and Row, 1973). See also George Kateb, *The Inner Ocean: Individualism and Democratic Culture* (Ithaca: Cornell University Press, 1992).

10. On these issues see R. C. Grogin, *The Bergsonian Controversy in France, 1900–1914* (Calgary: University of Calgary Press, 1988); Zeev Sternhell, *Ni droite ni gauche: L'idéologie fasciste en France* (Paris: Seuil, 1983); Eugen Weber, *Action Française: Royalism and Reaction in Twentieth-Century France* (Stanford: Stanford University Press, 1962).

11. The "discovery" of the unconscious in France predated the translation of Freud (in 1922) and differed in marked ways from what is now retrospectively considered early mainstream psychoanalytic thinking. The French psychologists writing from the 1880s and 1890s on did not consider sex or sexuality to be a primary factor in the structure of psychic life, nor did they make the unconscious the starting point for an analysis of subjectivity. Rather they most often took the unconscious to be one of the ingredients of the psyche: the cause of pathological behavior, or the intuitive "élan vital" posited by Henri Bergson, or the "invisible cause" or "latent force" that Gustave Le Bon thought could account for collective phenomena such as the behavior of crowds, the "soul" of the nation, or the "genius

of the race." See Elizabeth Roudinesco, *Histoire de la psychanalyse en France,* vol. 1: *1885–1939* (Paris: Seuil, 1986); Rosi Braidotti, *Patterns of Dissonance* (New York: Routledge, 1991); and Henri F. Ellenberger, *The Discovery of the Unconscious: The History and Evolution of Dynamic Psychiatry* (New York: Basic Books, 1970). See also Jan Goldstein, *Console and Classify: The French Psychiatric Profession in the Nineteenth Century* (Cambridge: Cambridge University Press, 1987).

12. Gustave Le Bon, *The Crowd: A Study of the Popular Mind* (New York: Viking Press, 1960), pp. 6–7.

13. The microbe analogy is used often by Le Bon. See ibid., pp. 18, 28, 126.

14. "Certains ensembles de conditions déterminant les actes de la conscience sans être nécessairement connus de celle-ci"; Henri Bergson, "L'inconscient" (1909), in Bergson, *Mélanges* (Paris: Presses Universitaires de France, 1972), p. 807. On Bergson see also Gilles Deleuze, *Bergsonism,* trans. Hugh Tomlinson and Barbara Habberjam (New York: Zone Books, 1991); and Martin Jay, *Downcast Eyes: The Denigration of Vision in Twentieth-Century French Thought* (Berkeley: University of California Press, 1993).

15. "Tout ce qui peut apparaître dans un état conscient quand intervient cet instrument groississant qu'on appelle l'attention, pourvu qu'on étende beaucoup le sens de ce dernier mot et qu'il s'agisse d'une attention élargie, intensifiée, qu'aucun de nous ne possède jamais tout entière"; Bergson, "L'inconscient," p. 809.

16. Le Bon, *The Crowd,* p. 42.

17. Ibid., pp. 102–103.

18. See, for example, Robert A. Nye, *The Origins of Crowd Psychology: Gustave Le Bon and the Crisis of Mass Democracy in the Third Republic* (Beverly Hills: Sage, 1975); and Susanna Barrows, *Distorting Mirrors: Visions of the Crowd in Late Nineteenth-Century France* (New Haven: Yale University Press, 1981). See also Ruth Harris, *Murders and Madness: Medicine, Law, and Society in the Fin de Siècle* (Oxford: Clarendon Press, 1989); and Robert Nye, *Crime, Madness, and Politics in Modern France: The Medical Concept of National Decline* (Princeton: Princeton University Press, 1984).

19. Le Bon, *The Crowd,* p. 6. Le Bon thought that language was so volatile that "the absolute translation of a language, especially of a dead language, is totally impossible . . . We merely put the images and ideas with which modern life has endowed our intelligence in the place of absolutely distinct notions and images which ancient life had brought into being in the mind of races submitted to conditions of existence having no analogy with our own"; ibid., p. 104.

20. Ibid., pp. 106–107.

21. Ibid., pp. 36–37.

22. Ibid., p. 50.

23. Ibid., p. 39. On the misogyny of the turn of the century, see Annelise Maugue, *L'identité masculine en crise: Au tournant du siècle, 1871–1914* (Paris: Editions Rivages, 1987).

24. Le Bon, *The Crowd,* p. 185.

25. Grogin, *The Bergsonian Controversy,* pp. 175–176.

26. On this see ibid., p. 30. There is a Nietzschean quality to all this: "My idea is, as you see, that consciousness does not really belong to man's individual existence but rather to his social or herd nature . . . Fundamentally, all our actions are altogether incomparably personal, unique, and infinitely individual; there is no doubt of that. But as soon as we translate them into consciousness, *they no longer seem to be*"; Friedrich Nietzsche, *The Gay Science,* as cited in Kateb, *The Inner Ocean,* p. 235.

27. "Nous allons voir que les contradictions inhérentes aux problèmes de la causalité, de la liberté, de la personnalité en un mot, n'ont pas d'autre origine, et qu'il suffit, pour les écarter, de substituer le moi réel, le moi concret, à sa représentation symbolique"; Henri Bergson, "Essai sur les données immédiates de la conscience" (1888), in *Oeuvres* (Paris: Presses Universitaires de France, 1970), p. 92.

28. "Une psychologie qui fait une place si large et si belle à la sensibilité"; Bergson, "Les deux sources de la morale" (1932), in *Oeuvres,* p. 1012.

29. "Moins capable d'émotion . . . Il s'agit, bien entendu, de la sensibilité profonde, et non pas de l'agitation en surface"; ibid. The attacks from Maurras and Benda are cited in Grogin, *The Bergsonian Controversy,* pp. 181, 187. Benda argued that Bergson was no philosopher but a literary scholar. His style was feminine inasmuch as it glorified life and exalted feelings over ideas, the feminine over the virile, the musical over the plastic. Maurras associated Bergson's femininity with the fact that he was Jewish, with his romanticism, and with his "metaphysics of instinct."

30. Bergson, "Essai sur les donnés immédiates," in *Oeuvres,* p. 109.

31. Le Bon, *The Crowd,* p. 106.

32. Madeleine Pelletier, *L'éducation féministe des filles* (Paris, 1914), p. 11.

33. On the problem of sexual difference for democracy see Etienne Balibar, "'Rights of Man' and 'Rights of Citizens,'" in *Masses, Classes, Ideas: Studies on Politics and Philosophy before and after Marx,* trans. James Swenson (New York and London: Routledge, 1994), p. 55.

34. Madeleine Pelletier, *Philosophie sociale: Les opinions, les parties, les classes* (Paris, 1912), pp. 1–3.

35. Pelletier, "Mémoire," p. 46.

36. "Il faut être des hommes socialement"; ibid., p. 18.

37. "Une loi mystérieuse; un arrangement particulier du tissus osseux qui aurait avec le sexe des rapports aussi étranges qu'inconnus . . . Si la femme a un crâne plus lourd que son fémur ce n'est pas en tant que femme; mais en tant qu'être plus grêle et dont le tissu musculaire et osseux est moins développé que celui de l'homme"; Madeleine Pelletier, "Recherches sur les indices pondéraux du crâne et des principaux os longs d'une série de squelettes japonais," *Bulletins et mémoires de la Société d'anthropologie de Paris,* 5th ser., 1, no. 1 (1900), 519.

38. Ibid., p. 523.

39. "Cette sorte de chimie mentale dont les réactions sont encore inconnues"; ibid., p. 524.

40. Pelletier, *L'éducation féministe*, p. 64; and *La femme en lutte*, p. 41.

41. "Le fossé profond qui sépare psychologiquement les sexes est avant tout l'oeuvre de la société"; Madeleine Pelletier, *L'amour et la maternité* (Paris, 1923), p. 9.

42. "L'observation des petits enfants dans leurs jeux, montre qu'au début de la vie, la mentalité est la même dans l'un et l'autre sexe; c'est la mère qui commence à créer le sexe psychologique et le sexe psychologique féminin est inférieur"; Pelletier, *L'éducation féministe*, p. 11.

43. Pelletier, "Les femmes et le féminisme," p. 44; *La femme en lutte*, p. 32. For a recent discussion of these issues, see also Judith Butler, *Bodies That Matter* (New York and London: Routledge, 1993), pp. 1–2.

44. "A la longue, et sous l'influence des individualités d'élite, des évolutions sociales s'effectuent"; Pelletier, *L'éducation féministe*, p. 64.

45. "Outre les services qu'il peut prendre en cas de danger, le revolver a un pouvoir psychodynamogène, ce fait seul de le sentir sur soi rend plus hardi"; Madeleine Pelletier, *L'émancipation sexuelle de la femme* (Paris, 1926), p. 9.

46. Shari Benstock, *Women of the Left Bank, Paris 1900–1940* (Austin: University of Texas Press, 1986), p. 48.

47. Pelletier, *La femme en lutte*, p. 38.

48. Letter from Pelletier to Arria Ly, November 2, 1911, cited in Gordon, *The Integral Feminist*, p. 173. Pelletier signed this letter "Salut féministe, Dr. Pelletier, vierge incorruptible."

49. Pelletier, "Mémoire," p. 35.

50. Pelletier to Arria Ly, November 2, 1911, cited in Gordon, *The Integral Feminist*, p. 18. In her 1933 novel, *La femme vierge*, Pelletier also condemned veils as a symbol of women's subservience to men. On veils in French history, see Marni Kessler, "Women's Surveillance: Strategies of Effacement in Late Nineteenth-Century French Avant-Garde Painting" (Ph.D. diss. in progress, Yale University).

51. Jacques Lacan, "The Meaning of the Phallus," in Juliet Mitchell and Jacqueline Rose, *Feminine Sexuality: Jacques Lacan and the école freudienne* (New York: Pantheon Books, 1982), p. 82.

52. Lacan, cited in ibid., p. 84. See also Drucilla Cornell, *Beyond Accommodation: Ethical Feminism, Deconstruction, and the Law* (New York and London: Routledge, 1991), especially p. 53; Elizabeth Grosz, *Jacques Lacan: A Feminist Introduction* (London and New York: Routledge, 1990); Jane Gallop, "Reading the Phallus," in her *Reading Lacan* (Ithaca: Cornell University Press, 1985), pp. 133–156; and Rose and Mitchell's introduction to *Feminine Sexuality*.

53. Pelletier, *L'éducation féministe*, p. 10; *La femme en lutte*, p. 31; "Mémoire," pp. 9, 35, 38. See also Benstock, *Women of the Left Bank*, p. 48; and Mary Louise Roberts, "Sampson and Delilah Revisited: The Politics of Women's Fashion in 1920s France," *American Historical Review* 98, no. 3 (June 1993), 657–684.

54. "Ce sont les porteurs de cheveux courts and de faux cols qui ont toute les libertés, tous les pouvoirs, eh bien! Je porte moi aussi cheveux courts et faux cols à la face des sots et des méchants, bravant les injustices du voyou de la rue, et de la femme esclave en tablier de cuisine"; Pelletier, "Les demi-émancipées," *La Suffragiste*, January 1912, cited in Christine Bard, "La virilisation des femmes et l'égalité des sexes," in Bard, *Madeleine Pelletier*, p. 92. The equation of equality and masculine costume was noted in Laure-Paul Flobert, *La femme et le costume masculin* (Lille, 1911), p. 3: Breeches "réprésentait l'autorité, la culotte étant le privilège de l'homme, c'est-à-dire du maître."

The issue of clothing clearly preoccupied Pelletier. When discussing the pressure society placed on individuals to conform she cited this example: "La moindre originalité de couleur, de formes dans nos vêtements, la façon de nos cheveux, nos gestes, notre allure générale arme les mille bras de la société. Qu'est-ce que le mois de prison infligé au voleur en comparaison des injures, des sarcasmes que devrait endurer l'homme qui par exemple aurait la fantaisie de s'habiller d'une robe de soie jaune et de se promener ainsi sur les boulevards parisiens, que dis-je les sarcasmes, la force armée interviendrait pour l'emprisonner pendant un temps indéterminée dans un asile d'aliénés?" A.-M. Pelletier, *L'individualisme* (Paris, 1919), p. 82.

55. "Les demi-émancipées," cited in Gordon, *The Integral Feminist*, p. 155.

56. Madeleine Pelletier, "Du costume," *La Suffragiste*, July 1919.

57. Bard, "La virilisation," pp. 96–97. See also Sowerwine and Maignien, *Madeleine Pelletier*, p. 122.

58. M. Pelletier, "War Diary," cited in Gordon, *The Integral Feminist*, p. 142.

59. Gordon, *The Integral Feminist*, pp. 154–155; Claude Maignien, "L'expérience communiste ou la foi en l'avenir radicaux," in Bard, *Madeleine Pelletier*, p. 160; and Sowerwine and Maignien, *Madeleine Pelletier*, pp. 156–157.

60. On "passing" see Butler, *Bodies That Matter*, pp. 167–186.

61. "A force de jouer le personnage que l'on veut paraître, on finit par l'être un peu en réalité"; Pelletier, *Philosophie sociale*, p. 112.

62. Letter from Pelletier to Arria Ly, November 2, 1911, cited in Sowerwine, "Madeleine Pelletier: Making It in a Man's World," p. 25.

63. Cited in Gordon, *The Integral Feminist*, p. 122.

64. Pelletier, "Mémoire," p. 38.

65. Jane Gallop, *The Daughter's Seduction: Feminism and Psychoanalysis* (Ithaca: Cornell University Press, 1982), p. 120.

66. Pelletier, "Mémoire," p. 38.

67. Letter from Pelletier to Arria Ly, October 22, 1911, cited in Sowerwine, "Madeleine Pelletier: Making It in a Man's World," p. 25.

68. The police reports of 1916 are cited in Gordon, *The Integral Feminist*, p. 122. On Paris as "the capital of Lesbos," see Benstock, *Women of the Left Bank*.

69. "Je n'ai pas voulu faire l'éducation de mon sens génital; un tel choix n'est que la conséquence de la situation injuste faite à la femme"; cited in Marie-Victoire Louis, "Sexualité et prostitution," in Bard, *Madeleine Pelletier*, p. 117.

70. "Certes, je considère que la femme est libre de son corps, mais ces affaires de bas ventres me dégoutent profondément: moi, aussi, je suis vierge"; cited in ibid., p. 113.

71. Monique Wittig, "One Is Not Born a Woman," *Feminist Issues* 1, no. 2 (Winter 1981), 53.

72. See Benstock, *Women of the Left Bank.*

73. Madeleine Pelletier, *Une vie nouvelle* (Paris, 1932), p. 206. For her views on homosexuality see her comments in P. Vigné d'Octon, *La vie et l'amour: Les doctrines freudiennes et la psychoanalyse* (Paris: Editions de l'Idée Libre, 1934), pp. 71–72. For the history of attitudes about homosexuality in this period, see Anthony Copley, *Sexual Moralities in France, 1780–1980: New Ideas on the Family, Divorce, and Homosexuality* (London and New York: Routledge, 1989).

74. Pelletier, *L'émancipation sexuelle*, pp. 20–22.

75. Pelletier, *Une vie nouvelle*, p. 60.

76. "La femme désire; l'instinct sexuel parle aussi en elle"; Pelletier, *L'émancipation sexuelle*, p. 39. In *L'amour et la maternité*, Pelletier wrote (p. 11): "Dans un roman récent, 'La Garçonne,' Victor Margueritte a présenté une femme qui fait ce que fait un garçon et prétend être quand même honnête; le livre, bien que timide, a fait scandale. Le public, qui admet la prostitution, ne reconnaît pas à la femme le droit de se conduire comme se conduisent tous les hommes." On *La garçonne*, see Mary Louise Roberts, *Civilization without Sexes: Reconstructing Gender in Postwar France, 1917–1927* (Chicago: University of Chicago Press, 1994), pp. 46–62. See also Ann Marie Sohn, "*La garçonne* face à l'opinion publique: Type littéraire ou type social des années 20?" *Le mouvement social* 80 (1972).

77. Madeleine Pelletier, *Le droit au travail pour la femme* (1931), in Claude Maignien, ed., *Madeleine Pelletier: l'éducation féministe des filles* (Paris: Editions Syros, 1978), p. 161.

78. "La femme affranchie ne se sent pas diminuée par une initiation sexuelle qu'elle a voulue . . . L'acte sexuel n'est pas le don de la personne. C'est la réunion éphémère de deux êtres de sexe différent; son but est le plaisir"; Pelletier, *L'amour et la maternité*, p. 11. See also Pelletier, *Le célibat: Etat supérieur*, (n.d.; probably 1908), p. 6.

79. "Plus de cohabitation et c'en sera fini des haines familiales si bien décrites par Freud"; Pelletier, *Le célibat*, p. 6.

80. "L'individualisme aura fait comprendre que chacun n'étant qu'à lui ne se donne à personne"; Pelletier, *L'individualisme*, p. 74.

81. Pelletier, *La femme en lutte*, p. 37.

82. "Avant tout, c'est l'individu qui est sacré . . . il a le droit absolu de vivre à sa guise, de procréer ou de ne pas procréer. En voulant, dans un intérêt national, mettre un frein aux libertés individuelles, on fait toujours plus de mal que de bien"; Pelletier, *L'émancipation sexuelle*, p. 59.

83. "L'enfant qui est né est un individu, mais le foetus au sein de l'utérus n'en est pas un; il fait partie du corps de la mère"; Madeleine Pelletier, *Le droit à l'avortement*, in Maignien, *Madeleine Pelletier*, p. 137.

84. Pelletier, *L'émancipation sexuelle*, p. 57.

85. "La sexualité est une fonction naturelle, mais ce n'est pas une fonction noble"; Pelletier, *L'amour et la maternité*, p. 13. See her contribution to Vigné d'Octon, *La vie et l'amour* (p. 70): sex "est l'expression d'un besoin . . . comme le besoin de manger et de respirer."

86. "La gamme des joies animales est vite parcourue . . . Mais la vie de l'intellectuel est infiniment plus variée"; Pelletier, *L'individualisme*, p. 104.

87. "Au lieu d'être la femelle penchée sur sa couvée, comme une mère poule, la femme sera un être pensant, artisan independant de son bonheur"; Madeleine Pelletier, *La rationalisation sexuelle* (Paris, 1935), p. 72.

88. Pelletier, *L'éducation féministe*, p. 114. See also Pelletier, *L'amour et la maternité*, p. 10.

89. Madeleine Pelletier, *La femme vierge: Roman* (Paris, 1933), p. 16.

90. "Certes, elle n'était pas sans sexe; elle aussi éprouvait des désirs, mais elle avait du les refouler pour être libre, elle ne le regrettait pas . . . Elle, Marie, avait remplacé l'amour par la vie cérébrale, mais combien peu sont capables de le faire. Plus tard la femme pourra s'affranchir sans renoncer à l'amour. Il ne sera plus pour elle une chose vile . . . La femme pourra, sans être diminuée, vivre sa vie sexuelle"; ibid., p. 241.

91. "La dépopulation, loin d'être un mal, est un bien essentiel, corollaire de l'évolution générale des êtres, elle est l'expression de la victoire de l'individu sur l'espèce"; Pelletier, *L'émancipation sexuelle*, p. 60.

92. "Tous les individus étaient semblables et il n'y avait pas de sexe. La reproduction se faisait par des oeufs que les individus allaient prendre dans un établissement special maintenu à une température élevée"; Pelletier, *Une vie nouvelle*, p. 188.

93. Pelletier, *L'amour et la maternité*, p. 21.

94. "Je suis et je suis seul . . . Avant la réflexion, je me croyais rattaché aux hommes et aux choses par toutes sortes de fils . . . A la réflexion, j'ai compris que tous ces liens sont illusoires et que je suis bien seul, la seule réalité"; Pelletier, *L'individualisme*, pp. 94–95.

95. "Je suis seul et tout m'est extérieur"; ibid., p. 95.

96. "L'individualisme est en contradiction avec la démocratie telle que le vulgaire la comprend"; ibid., p. 116.

97. "Devoir, dévouement, sacrifice, je ne vous connais pas, vous êtes des mots et je sais qu'avec ces mots on ne veut que me tromper"; ibid., p. 94.

98. Pelletier, "Les femmes et le féminisme," p. 41; *Philosophie sociale*, pp. 143 and 146; *L'éducation féministe*, p. 64; *Mon voyage aventureux en Russie communiste* (1922), cited in Gordon, *The Integral Feminist*, p. 163.

99. "La nuit les bandes d'hommes ivres parcouraient les rues en exhibant leurs organes et en hurlant des propos obscènes"; Pelletier, *Une vie nouvelle*, p. 37.

100. Ibid., p. 201.

101. "La masse se désinteressait des affaires publiques"; ibid., p. 178.

102. Pelletier, "Mémoire," p. 6. For a discussion of her connection to anarchists, see Gordon, *The Integral Feminist,* p. 21.

103. Pelletier, "Mémoire," p. 43.

104. "Ma conception de la maçonnerie serait ainsi celle d'une oligarchie éclairée assez forte pour obliger le gouvernement à compter avec elle, et qui n'aurait pas les défauts des autres oligarchies puisque ses rangs seraient ouverts à toutes les intelligences"; M. Pelletier, "L'idéal maçonique" (1904), cited in Sowerwine and Maignien, *Madeleine Pelletier,* pp. 56–57.

105. "Dans un groupement politique qui ne parle pas n'existe pas"; Pelletier, *La femme en lutte,* pp. 65–66.

106. Ibid., p. 72.

107. Ibid., p. 156.

108. Ibid., p. 152. "Je suis taillée pour la lutte politique," she wrote to Arria Ly in 1913; "on me refuse parce que femme"; cited in Sowerwine and Maignien, *Madeleine Pelletier,* p. 91.

109. Pelletier, "Mémoire," p. 43.

110. M. Pelletier, "Ma candidature à la députation" (1910), cited in Gordon, *The Integral Feminist,* p. 126.

111. Maignien, "L'expérience communiste," p. 164.

112. On the history of neo-Malthusians in France, see Francis Ronsin, *La grève des ventres: Propagande neo-Malthusienne et baisse de la natalité française XIX–XXe siècles* (Paris: Aubier Montagne, 1980); Angus McLaren, "Abortion in France: Women and the Regulation of Family Size 1800–1914," *French Historical Studies* 10 (Spring 1978), 461–485. On the pronatalism of the early twentieth century, see Roberts, *Civilization without Sexes,* pp. 93–147; and Joshua H. Cole, "'There Are Only Good Mothers': The Ideological Work of Women's Fertility in Late Nineteenth-Century France," *French Historical Studies* 20 (Spring 1996).

113. Angus McLaren, "Sex and Socialism: The Opposition of the French Left to Birth Control in the Nineteenth Century," *Journal of the History of Ideas* 27 (1976), 475–492; André Armengaud, "Mouvement ouvrier et néomalthusianisme au début de XXe siècle," *Annales de démographie historique,* 1966, pp. 7–19; Léon Gani, "Jules Guesde, Paul Lafargue et les problèmes de la population," *Population* 34, nos. 4–5 (July–October 1979), 1023–43; Alfred Sauvy, "Les Marxistes et le malthusianisme," *Cahiers internationaux de sociologie* 41 (July–December 1966), 1–14. Pelletier commented on this: "I have often wondered why the PSU [Parti Socialiste Unifié] showed itself hostile to neo-Malthusian propaganda . . . Paul Robin in effect made neo-Malthusianism into a genuine social system . . . A reformer of a sort, he mainly wanted to improve the workers' lot by limiting the demand for work through a wise limitation of proletarian fertility . . . understood in this way, neo-Malthusianism was in some sense a separate party from socialism . . . But voluntary birth control is not necessarily linked to a social theory. However

one envisages a future society, it remains true that at the present time it is easier for a working-class family to feed two children than six"; cited in Gordon, *The Integral Feminist,* p. 137.

114. Cornell, *Beyond Accommodation,* pp. 9, 13.

115. Pelletier, *L'amour et la maternité,* p. 6.

116. Gordon has a convincing discussion of the evidence in *The Integral Feminist,* p. 261, n. 8. See also Léonor Penalva, "Madeleine Pelletier: Une approche psychanalytique," in Bard, *Madeleine Pelletier,* pp. 141–144.

117. Cited in Gordon, *The Integral Feminist,* p. 48.

118. Ibid., p. 219.

119. Ibid., p. 228.

120. Ibid., p. 230.

121. "Tout le groupe est là . . . et même une partie des groupes de H. Auclert et de Mme Oddo. On me félicite. C'est la première fois que le féminisme comparait devant les tribunaux. On me souhaite bon courage"; Pelletier, *Mémoire,* pp. 25–26.

122. Pelletier talked of the importance of the vote in the final pages of her "Mémoire," inscribed by hand in a bound red-leather book with her portrait at the front and titled "Doctoresse Pelletier: Mémoires d'une féministe." Disavowing charges that she was a "patriot" because she suggested that when men were mobilized for war, women should be allowed (as in 1914) to take their jobs, she noted that "comme femme je ne puis aimer la patrie qui m'entrave et me contraint à une vie peu intéressante et précaire par surcroît." France was hypocritical by comparison with other countries: "Maintenant les femmes votent à peu près partout; il n'y a guère que la France qui en depit de ses pretentions apparait en réalité comme un pays très conservateur"; p. 47.

123. Pelletier, *La femme vierge,* p. 95.

124. "Je puis dire que j'ai toujours été féministe; du moins depuis que j'eu l'âge de comprendre"; Pelletier, "Mémoire," p. 1.

125. "D'ailleurs je reste féministe. Je le resterai jusqu'à ma mort"; ibid., p. 46.

126. "La valeur sociale de la mère et de la menagère, vertus feminins et vices masculins"; ibid., p. 16.

127. "Nous voulons d'égalité, voilà tout—le droit de vote"; ibid.

128. "Une jeune avocate me dit 'conduisez-nous à la victoire!' Je sens mon coeur qui bat très fort. Pendant une minute, ma parole, j'ai cru que c'était arrivé! Mais cela n'arrivera pas si tôt"; ibid., p. 16.

129. "Evidemment, la présidente était sympathique, mais le féminisme, au travers de l'esprit un peu confus de la vieille militante, lui appraissent comme quelque chose de très faible, et elle l'aurait voulu si fort!" Pelletier, *La femme vierge,* p. 99.

130. Pelletier often used Jeanne d'Arc—the woman whose virginity allowed her to rise above her sex—for such purposes herself. She signed a 1911 letter to Ly "Docteur Pelletier, capable de délivrer Orléans," and it was not the only time she so designated herself; Louis, "Sexualité et prostitution," p. 118.

131. "On pouvait rouler Paris, on ne trouverait pas une autre Marie"; Pelletier, *La femme vierge*, p. 110.

132. Ibid., pp. 126, 151.

133. "C'est Marie, je ne suis pas morte, personne ne meurt. Je vois le monde nouveau qui s'avance. Travaillez, travaillez, marchez vers la lumière par dessus les tombeaux, le monde nouveau s'avance"; ibid., p. 253.

6. Citizens but Not Individuals

1. Maurice Durverger, *Manuel de droit constitutionnel et de science politique* (Paris: Presses Universitaires de France, 1948), p. 304.

2. Steven C. Hause with Anne R. Kenney, *Women's Suffrage and Social Politics in the French Third Republic* (Princeton: Princeton University Press, 1984); Pierre Rosanvallon, *Le sacre du citoyen: Histoire du suffrage universel en France* (Paris: Gallimard, 1992), pp. 393–412; Laurence Klejman and Florence Rochefort, *L'égalité en marche: Le féminisme sous la Troisième République* (Paris: Editions des Femmes, 1989), pp. 261–301.

3. The text of the Constitution of the Fourth Republic is translated in David Thomson, *Democracy in France: The Third and Fourth Republics,* 3rd ed. (London and New York: Oxford University Press, 1958), pp. 273–291. See also Peter Campbell, *French Electoral Systems and Elections since 1789* (London: Faber and Faber, 1958), pp. 102–113.

4. Cited in Hause with Kenney, *Women's Suffrage in the Third Republic,* p. 251. On the role of de Gaulle and on the deliberations leading to the vote, see Albert du Roy and Nicole du Roy, *Citoyennes! Il y a cinquante ans, le vote des femmes* (Paris: Flammarion, 1994).

5. "L'accession mondiale des femmes à un statu civil identique à celui des hommes est sans doute le plus grand phénomène collectif de la première moitié de ce siècle. Nous n'en connaissons pas encore toutes les conséquences, mais il me plaît d'y avoir eu ma part"; Louise Weiss, *Mémoires d'une Européene,* vol. 3: *Combats pour les femmes, 1934–39* (Paris: Albin Michel, 1980), p. 268.

6. Thomson, *Democracy in France,* p. 232.

7. Durverger, *Manuel de droit,* p. 304. In fact there does not seem to have been such a decisive "gender gap" in the voting after 1944; and in any case there was no clear way to measure it. Sociologist Duverger's suggestion that ballots be collected in two separate boxes—one for men and one for women—was never taken up. It would have been ironic if it had been, since separate ballot boxes were placed outside polling places in Paris during the 1930s to collect women's illegal votes as a feminist protest against disenfranchisment. On the way women voted see Maurice Duverger, *La participation des femmes à la vie politique* (Paris: UNESCO, 1955); and Janine Mossuz-Lavan, "Le vote des femmes en France (1945–1993)," *Revue française de science politique* 43, no. 4 (August 1993), 673–689.

8. Félix de Grand' Combe (Felix Francois Boillot), *The Three Years of Fighting France, June 1940–June 1943* (London: Wells, Gardner, & Darton, 1943), p. 83.

9. "Les Français n'ont qu'une seule patrie . . . La France est et restera une et indivisible"; Charles de Gaulle, *Discours et messages du Général de Gaulle (18 juin 1940–31 décembre 1941),* 2 vols. (London: Oxford University Press, 1942), vol. 2, p. 83. On the story of the Provisional Government, see Gordon Wright, *The Reshaping of French Democracy* (New York: Fertig, 1970); and Grand' Combe, *The Three Years of Fighting France.*

10. There were also attempts to extend the rhetorical gestures of unity to inhabitants of the colonies. De Gaulle's speeches make a point of including them in the nation (see *Discours et messages,* passim). The Constitution of 1946 stated that "France forms with the people of its overseas territories a Union based upon equality of rights and duties without distinction of race or religion"; Thomson, *Democracy in France,* p. 275. This aspect of the Fourth Republic's attempt at universalism deserves separate study, as does the relationship of colonial enfranchisement to women's suffrage. On the issue of citizenship for colonial subjects see Rogers Brubaker, *Citizenship and Nationhood in France and Germany* (Cambridge, Mass.: Harvard University Press, 1992); and Etienne Balibar, "Propositions sur la citoyenneté," in Catherine Wihtol de Wenden, ed., *La citoyenneté et les changements de structures sociales et nationales de la population française* (Paris: Fondation Diderot, 1988), pp. 221–234.

11. For biographical studies of Weiss, see all six volumes of her *Mémoires d'une Européene.* See also Michael Bess, *Realism, Utopia, and the Mushroom Cloud: Four Activist Intellectuals and Their Strategies for Peace, 1945–89* (Chicago: University of Chicago Press, 1993); and Nicole Zand, "La mort de Louise Weiss," *Le Monde,* May 28, 1983, pp. 1 and 9.

12. "Sans le dur combat que j'avais mené, les Françaises auraient-elles, à ce moment-là, obtenu leurs droits politiques? Oui, incontestablement, grâce à la conjoncture internationale"; Weiss, *Combats pour les femmes,* p. 268.

13. "Sans ce combat, la décision du général de Gaulle eut été le fait du Prince au lieu de répondre à une aspiration. Une comparaison s'impose. Imaginons le débarquement des Anglo-Américains en Normandie sans maquisards pour se porter à leur rencontre. La France eut été libérée quand même, toutefois l'événement au lieu de demeurer une victorie stratégique, prit immédiatement figure exemplaire"; ibid.

14. The notion of struggle to obtain or defend the republic dates back to the first French Revolution and continues as a theme in subsequent republican discourse. It is that association of struggle to achieve a virtuous cause which Weiss evokes here.

15. Pelletier and Weiss crossed paths more than once: both were in Russia in 1921, and in June 1936 both appeared on the same program at the Club du Faubourg to discuss the implications for the vote of the fact that three women had been named to Léon Blum's Popular Front cabinet as undersecretaries of

education, health, and scientific research. Charles Sowerwine and Claude Maignien, *Madeleine Pelletier: Une féministe dans l'arène politique* (Paris: Les Editions Ouvrières, 1992), p. 201. On the women undersecretaries, see Julian Jackson, *The Popular Front in France: Defending Democracy, 1934–38* (Cambridge: Cambridge University Press, 1988), p. 151. Weiss says she turned down one of the undersecretaryships because she thought it was an attempt to buy off feminist demands, and she was dismayed by the timidity displayed by the women (especially former feminist Cécile Brunschweig) who did take the posts. She titled the section of her memoir in which she recounted this development "Three Swallows Do Not Make a Summer"; Weiss, *Combats pour les femmes*, pp. 123–126.

16. "Avoir quitté l'influente *Europe Nouvelle* pour me consacrer à des malheureuses priveés de tous droits et donc de toute importance, leur semblait une étrange folie"; Weiss, *Combats pour les femmes*, p. 26.

17. The expression is Luce Irigaray's; see Margaret Whitford, ed., *The Irigaray Reader* (Oxford: Blackwell, 1991), p. 126.

18. Weiss, *Combats pour les femmes*, p. 18.

19. On the question of assuming "the feminine role deliberately" and subversively, see Luce Irigaray, "The Power of Discourse and the Subordination of the Feminine," in Whitford, *The Irigaray Reader*, p. 124.

20. "Revendiquer nos droits en une période si dramatique semblerait inopportun, insolent, dangereux à des gens de métier qui commençaient à trembler pour leur avenir"; Weiss, *Combats pour les femmes*, p. 90.

21. Ibid., p. 114.

22. On the Conseil d'Etat see Thomson, *Democracy in France*, pp. 59–60.

23. Cited in Weiss, *Combats pour les femmes*, p. 92.

24. "Le droit de vote supprime le droit de l'insurrection, Madame . . . Vous n'aviez donc pas lu Victor Hugo?" "Si, mon cher ministre. Mais, dites-moi, jouissons nous de ce droit de vote?" Cited ibid., p. 32.

25. Ibid., p. 268.

26. Pierre Rosanvallon too quickly and too optimistically associates the vote for women with their attainment of autonomous individuality. In this, as throughout his book, he neglects to treat the contradictions within the concept of the individual itself, preferring to oppose sociological reality to legal right and ignoring the historical changes in the concept of the individual. See the section of *Le sacre du citoyen* called "L'avènement de la femme-individu," pp. 393–412.

27. Simone de Beauvoir, *The Second Sex*, trans. and ed. H. M. Parshley (New York: Vintage Books, 1974), p. 150.

28. Ibid., pp. xxxiii and 486.

29. Ibid., p. 758.

30. Ibid., p. 813.

31. On de Beauvoir and her place in contemporary feminism, see Deirdre Bair, *Simone de Beauvoir* (New York: Simon and Schuster, 1990); Judith Butler, "Variations on Sex and Gender: Beauvoir, Wittig and Foucault," in Seyla Benhabib and

Drucilla Cornell, eds., *Feminism as Critique* (Minneapolis: University of Minnesota Press, 1987), pp. 128–142; Naomi Schor, "This Essentialism Which Is Not One: Coming to Grips with Irigaray," *differences* 1 (Summer 1989), 38–56; Margaret Whitford, "Introduction," in *The Irigaray Reader*, pp. 23–25; and Claire Duchen, *Feminism in France: From May '68 to Mitterrand* (London: Routledge and Kegan Paul, 1986).

32. Beauvoir, *The Second Sex*, p. 799.

33. Ibid., pp. 806, 809–810.

34. Elisabeth Badinter, *L'un est l'autre* (Paris: Editions O. Jacob, 1986); Badinter, *X Y, de l'identité masculine* (Paris: Editions O. Jacob, 1992); Badinter, *L'amour en plus* (Paris: Flammarion, 1980).

35. Luce Irigaray, "Equal to Whom?" trans. Robert L. Mazzola, *differences* 1 (Summer 1989), 70.

36. On these questions, see Schor, "This Essentialism Which Is Not One;" Duchen, *Feminism in France*; Rosi Braidotti, *Patterns of Dissonance* (New York: Routledge, 1991); and Sandrine Garcia, "Un cas de dispute: Egalité ou différence" (Etude annexe au Diplome d'Etudes Approfondies de Sociologie, Ecole des Hautes Etudes en Science Sociales, n.d.). I am grateful to Luc Boltanski, in whose seminar the Garcia paper was presented, for passing it on to me. It is especially useful for its transcription of a remarkable radio debate (in what seems to be 1990), on the program France Culture, between Badinter and Irigaray and moderated by political philosopher Alain Finkielkraut.

37. Theodore Zeldin, *France 1848–1945*, vol. 1: *Ambition, Love and Politics* (Oxford: Oxford University Press, 1973), p. 350, n. 4.

38. A brief list includes Michel Foucault, *The Archaeology of Knowledge*, trans. A. M. Sheridan Smith (New York: Harper Colophon Books, 1976) and *The History of Sexuality*, vol. 1: *An Introduction*, trans. Robert Hurley (New York: Vintage Books, 1980); the special issue of *Cahiers Confrontation* 20 (Winter 1989), "Après le sujet, qui vient?"; Louis Althusser, "Ideology and Ideological State Apparatuses," in *Lenin and Philosophy*, trans. Ben Brewster (New York: Monthly Review Press, 1974); Luce Irigaray, *Speculum of the Other Woman*, trans. Gillian C. Gill (Ithaca: Cornell University Press, 1974); and Irigaray, *This Sex Which Is Not One*, trans. Catherine Porter (Ithaca: Cornell University Press, 1975).

Index